# Learn, Teach...

# Succeed...

With **REA's MTEL® Communication &
Literacy Skills Test (Field 01)** test prep,
you'll be in a class all your own.

## WE'D LIKE TO HEAR FROM YOU!
Visit **www.rea.com** to send us your comments

# MTEL

MASSACHUSETTS TESTS FOR EDUCATOR LICENSURE®

## COMMUNICATION & LITERACY SKILLS TEST
### (FIELD 01)

**Gail Rae, M.A.**
Department of English
McKee Technical High School
Staten Island, NY

**Ann Jenson-Wilson**
Department of English
Southern Methodist University
Dallas, TX

**Bernadette Brick**
Department of English
University of Rochester
Rochester, NY

**Brian Walsh**
Department of English
Rutgers University
New Brunswick, NJ

*Free!*
*Diagnostic Exam*
www.rea.com/mtel

**Research & Education Association**

***Research & Education Association***
61 Ethel Road West
Piscataway, New Jersey 08854
E-mail: info@rea.com

**MTEL®: Massachusetts Tests for Educator Licensure®
Communication and Literacy Skills Test [Field 01], 8th Edition**

**Published 2016**

Copyright © 2012 by Research & Education Association, Inc.
Previous editions copyright © 2010, 2007, 2006, 2005, 2004,
2003, 2001 by Research & Education Association, Inc. All
rights reserved. No part of this book may be reproduced in
any form without permission of the publisher.

Printed in the United States of America

Library of Congress Control Number 2011929891

ISBN-13: 978-0-7386-0954-6
ISBN-10: 0-7386-0954-4

Cover image: Comstock/Getty Images

REA® is a registered trademark of
Research & Education Association, Inc.

## About REA

Founded in 1959, Research & Education Association (REA) is dedicated to publishing the finest and most effective educational materials—including study guides and test preps—for students in middle school, high school, college, graduate school, and beyond.

Today, REA's wide-ranging catalog is a leading resource for students, teachers, and other professionals. Visit *www.rea.com* to see a complete listing of all our titles.

## REA Acknowledgments

We would like to thank REA's Larry B. Kling, Vice President, Editorial, for supervising development; Pam Weston, Publisher and Senior Vice President, for setting the quality standards for production integrity and managing the publication to completion; Kathleen Casey, Senior Editor, for project management; Alice Leonard, Senior Editor, and Diane Goldschmidt, Managing Editor, for preflight editorial review; Barbara McGowran and Marjorie Roueche for copyediting the manuscript; and Christine Saul, Senior Graphic Artist, for cover design.

We also gratefully acknowledge Caragraphics for typesetting the manuscript.

# Contents

# CONTENTS

# MTEL Communication and Literacy Skills

## CHAPTER 1:
## Passing the Communication and Literacy Skills Test

# Passing the Communication and Literacy Skills Test

If you're a teacher candidate in the Commonwealth of Massachusetts, this REA test preparation book is designed expressly with you and your needs in mind. This book will help you pass the latest computer-based MTEL Communication and Literacy Skills Test (Field 01). The test is composed of two subtests: reading and writing. Our book provides targeted review material for both subtests, a full-length diagnostic exam, and three full-length practice tests. These practice tests contain the very types of questions you can expect to encounter on the actual MTEL exam. Following each of our model tests, you will find an answer key with detailed explanations designed to help you master the test material.

## ABOUT THE TEST

### Who takes the test and what is it used for?

The Massachusetts Tests for Educator Licensure must be taken by individuals seeking certification to teach in Massachusetts. Prospective teachers are required to take and pass two tests: a two-part test in communication and literacy skills and an additional test in the subject of the candidate's chosen area of certification.

### Who administers the test?

The Massachusetts Tests for Educator Licensure are administered by the Massachusetts Department of Elementary and Secondary Education and Pearson Education, Inc. A comprehensive test development process was designed and implemented specifically to ensure that the content and difficulty level of the exam is appropriate.

## When and where is the test given?

The MTEL Communication and Literacy Skills Test is administered Monday through Saturday (excluding some holidays) by appointment, year-round throughout the U.S. at Pearson Professional Centers.

The MTEL Communication and Literacy Skills Test is offered only on computer. Check the MTEL website at *www.mtel.nesinc.com* for the latest information and updates.

## Is there a registration fee?

To take the Communication and Literacy Skills Test, you must pay a fee. A complete summary of the registration fees is included in your registration bulletin.

## When will I receive my score report?

Your score report will be available for you on the MTEL website for 45 days, beginning at 10:00 P.M. Eastern Time on your score report date. Your score report also has information about your passing status and how to interpret the score report.

You may request that your score report be sent to you by e-mail on the score report day. If you request this service, your score report will be sent to the e-mail address that you provide at registration. To change that address, you will need to log into your account on the MTEL website and update your contact information.

## Format of the Communication and Literacy Skills Test

The Communication and Literacy Skills Test is designed to ensure your ability to effectively convey your subject knowledge to a student and to communicate with a student's family.

|  | Type | Number of Items |
|---|---|---|
| **Reading Subtest** | Multiple-Choice Questions | 42 |
| **Writing Subtest** | Multiple-Choice Questions | 35 |
|  | Short-Answer Questions | 7 |
|  | Open-Response Item Assignments | 2 |

The reading subtest of the Communication and Literacy Skills Test is composed of multiple-choice questions relating to reading passages and open-ended vocabulary questions, while the writing subtest consists of multiple-choice questions on grammar and usage and written mechanics, as well as a written summary, and written composition. The full test is 4 hours long.

## Test Objectives

| READING SUBTEST | |
|---|---|
| **Multiple-Choice** | **Approximate Test Weighting** |
| Meaning of Words and Phrases | 16.7% |
| Main Idea and Supporting Details | 16.7% |
| Writer's Purpose and Point of View | 16.7% |
| Relationships Among Ideas | 16.7% |
| Critical Reasoning | 16.7% |
| Outlining, Summarizing, Graph Interpretation | 16.7% |
|  | **100%** |

| WRITING SUBTEST | |
|---|---|
| **Multiple-Choice/Short-Answer 50%** | |
| Establish and Maintain a Main Idea | 15% |
| Sentence Construction, Grammar, Usage | 10% |
| Spelling, Capitalization, Punctuation | 10% |
| Revise Sentences Containing Errors | 15% |
| **Open-Response 50%** | |
| Summary Exercise | 15% |
| Composition Exercise | 35% |
| | **100%** |

## STUDYING FOR THE COMMUNICATION AND LITERACY SKILLS TEST

There is no one correct way to study for the Communication and Literacy Skills Test. You must find the method that works best for you. Some test-takers prefer to set aside a few hours every morning to study, while others prefer to study at night before going to sleep. Only you can determine when and where your study time will be most effective. To help you budget your time, refer to the study schedule which appears at the end of this chapter.

When taking the practice tests you should try to duplicate the actual testing conditions as closely as possible. Keep in mind that the Communication and Literacy Skills Test is four hours long. It will be helpful to time yourself when you take the practice tests so you will have a better idea of how much time to spend on each section of the actual exam. A quiet, well-lit room, free from such distractions as the television or radio, is preferable. As you complete each practice test, thoroughly review the explanations. Keep track of the number of correct answers you receive on each test so you can gauge your progress accurately, and develop a clear sense of where you need improvement.

# HOW TO USE THIS BOOK

## When should I start studying?

An eight-week study schedule is provided in this text to assist you in preparing for the exam. This schedule can be adjusted to meet your unique needs. If your test date is only four weeks away, you can halve the time allotted to each section; keep in mind, however, that this is not the most effective way to study. If you have several months before your test date, you may wish to extend the time allotted to each section. Remember, the more time you spend studying, the better your chances of achieving your aim—a passing score on the MTEL.

## About the review sections

By using our review material in conjunction with our practice tests, you should be well prepared for the actual Communication and Literacy Skills Test. At some point in your educational experience, you have probably studied all the material that makes up this test. For many candidates, however, this may have been some time ago. REA's targeted reviews will serve to refresh your memory of these topics, and our practice tests will help you gauge which areas need additional study and practice.

# ABOUT THE PRACTICE TESTS

## How Do I Score My Practice Test?

The Massachusetts Tests for Educator Licensure have a score range of 0-100 points for all tests. You must achieve a minimum of 70 to pass the exam. Your total score will derive from a combination of all test sections.

According to administrators of the MTEL, the reading subtest of the Communication and Literacy Skills Test contains approximately 30 multiple-choice items and six open-response items, while the writing subtest contains approximately 14 multiple-choice items and six to nine open-response items. Our practice tests approximate the number of questions you will encounter on the actual exam. Because MTEL test forms vary, we cannot provide score conversions for the practice tests. It is safe to assume, however, that a score of 70 percent on each section equates with a passing score. It may be helpful to have a friend or colleague score your practice test essays, since you will benefit from his or her ability to be more objective in judging the clarity and organization of your written responses.

If you do not achieve a passing score on your first practice test, don't worry. Review those sections with which you have had the most difficulty, and try the second practice test and later, the third test. With each practice test, you will sharpen the skills you need to pass the actual exam.

## COMMUNICATION AND LITERACY SKILLS TEST STUDY SCHEDULE

This study schedule allows for thorough preparation for the Communication and Literacy Skills Test. Although designed for eight weeks, it can be condensed into a four-week course by collapsing each two-week block into a one-week period. Be sure to set aside enough time—at least two or three hours each day—to study. No matter which study schedule works best for you, the more time you spend studying, the more prepared and relaxed you will feel on the day of the exam.

| Week | Activity |
|------|----------|
| 1 | Take the diagnostic test, which can be found at *www.rea.com/mtel*. This will allow you to pinpoint topics where you need the most review. |
| 2 | Study REA's review material and answer the drill questions provided. Highlight key terms and information. Take notes on the important theories and key concepts, since writing will aid in the retention of information. |
| 3 & 4 | Review your references and sources. Use any supplementary material that your education instructors recommend. Take Practice Test 1, which is printed in this book. |
| 5 | Condense your notes and findings. You should have a structured outline with specific facts. You may want to use index cards to help you memorize important information. |
| 6 | Test yourself using the index cards. You may want to have a friend or colleague quiz you on key facts and items. Take Practice Test 2. Review the explanations for the items you answered incorrectly. |
| 7 | Study any areas you consider to be your weaknesses by using your study materials, references, and notes. |
| 8 | Take Practice Test 3. Review the explanations for the items you answered incorrectly. |

# TEST-TAKING TIPS

Although you may have taken standardized tests like the Communication and Literacy Skills Test before, it is crucial that you become familiar with the format and content of each section of this exam. This will help to alleviate any anxiety about your performance. Following are several ways to help you become accustomed to the test.

➤ *Become comfortable with the format of the test.* The Communication and Literacy Skills Test covers a great deal of information, and the more comfortable you are with the format, the more confidence you will have when you take the actual exam. If you familiarize yourself with the requirements of each section individually, the whole test will be much less intimidating.

➤ *Read all of the possible answers.* Even if you believe you have found the correct answer, read all four options. Often answers that look right at first prove to be "magnet responses" meant to distract you from the correct choice.

➤ *Eliminate obviously incorrect answers.* In this way, even if you do not know the correct answer, you can make an educated guess.

➤ *Work quickly and steadily.* Remember, you will have to write a composition for the writing subtest. You need more time to compose a clear, concise, well-constructed essay than you need to answer a multiple-choice question, so don't spend too much time on any one item. Try to pace yourself. If you feel that you are spending too much time on any one question, mark the answer choice that you think is most likely the correct one, circle the item number in your test booklet, and return to it if time allows. Timing yourself while you take the practice tests will help you learn to use your time wisely.

➤ *Be sure that the circle you are marking corresponds to the number of the question in the test booklet.* The multiple-choice sections of the test are graded by a computer, which has no sympathy for clerical errors. One incorrectly placed response can upset your entire score.

# THE DAY OF THE TEST

Try to get a good night's rest, and wake up early on the day of the test. You should have a good breakfast so you will not be distracted by hunger. Dress in layers that can be removed or applied as the conditions of the testing center require. The Communication and Literacy Skills Test has a reporting time of 7:45 a.m., but you should plan to arrive early. This will allow you to become familiar with your surroundings in the testing center, and minimize the possibility of distraction during the test. The testing time is four hours. You may register for one subtest or both for the one test session.

Before you leave for the testing center, make sure you have any admissions material you may need, two pieces of identification, one must be a current government issued photo identification and sharpened No. 2 pencils. Pencils will not be supplied at the test site. For the Communication and Literacy Skills subtests, a calculator is neither necessary nor permitted. No eating, drinking, or smoking will be permitted during the test, but if you are scheduled for both the morning and afternoon test sessions, you may want to bring food to eat in the interim.

As part of the identification process, your thumbprint will be taken. If you refuse to do so, you will not be allowed to take the test and will lose any fees paid.

# MTEL Communication and Literacy Skills

## CHAPTER 2:
## Reading Subtest Review

# Reading Subtest Review

## 2

I. Vocabulary Review

II. Reading Review

## I. Vocabulary Review

It is important to understand the meanings of all words—not just the ones you are asked to define. Possession of a good vocabulary is a strength that can help you perform well on all sections of this test. The following information will build your skills for determining the meanings of words.

### SIMILAR FORMS AND SOUNDS

The complex nature of language sometimes makes reading difficult. Words often become confusing when they have similar forms and sounds. In fact, the author may have a correct meaning in mind, but an incorrect word choice (or spelling) can dramatically alter the meaning of the sentence or even make it totally illogical.

> NO: Martha was always part of that *cliché.*
> YES: Martha was always part of that *clique.*

(A *cliché* is a trite or hackneyed expression; a *clique* is an exclusive group of people.)

> NO: The minister spoke of the soul's *immorality.*
> YES: The minister spoke of the soul's *immortality.*

(*Immorality* means wickedness; *immortality* means imperishable or unending life.)

> NO: Where is the nearest *stationary* store?
> YES: Where is the nearest *stationery* store?

(*Stationary* means immovable; *stationery* is paper used for writing.)

Below are groups of words that are often confused because of their similar forms and sounds.

1. **accent**—*v.*—to stress or emphasize (You must *accent* the last syllable.)

   **ascent**—*n.*—a climb or rise (John's *ascent* of the mountain was dangerous.)

   **assent**—*n.*—consent; compliance (We need your *assent* before we can go ahead with the plans.)

2. **accept**—*v.*—to take something offered (She *accepted* the gift.)

   **except**—*prep.*—other than; but (Everyone was included in the plans *except* him.)

3. **advice**—*n.*—opinion given as to what to do or how to handle a situation (Her sister gave her *advice* on what to say at the interview.)

   **advise**—*v.*—to counsel (John's guidance counselor will *advise* him on where he should apply to college.)

4. **affect**—*v.*—to influence (Mary's suggestion did not *affect* me.)

   **effect**—1. *v.*—to cause to happen (The plan was *effected* with great success.); 2. *n.*–result (The *effect* of the medicine is excellent.)

5. **allusion**—*n.*—indirect reference (In the poem, there are many biblical *allusions*.)

   **illusion**—*n.*—false idea or conception; belief or opinion not in accord with the facts (Greg was under the *illusion* that he could win the race after missing three weeks of practice.)

6. **all ready**—*adv. + adj.*—prepared (The family was *all ready* to leave on vacation.)

   **already**—*adv.*—previously (I had *already* read that novel.)

7. **altar**—*n.*—table or stand used in religious rites (The priest stood at the *altar.*)

   **alter**—*v*—to change (Their plans were *altered* during the strike.)

8. **capital**—*n.*—1. a city where the government meets (The senators had a meeting in Boston, the *capital* of Massachusetts.); 2. money used in business (They had enough *capital* to develop the industry.)

   **capitol**—*n.*—building in which the legislature meets (Senator Brown gave a speech at the *Capitol* in Washington.)

9. **choose**—*v.*—to select (Which camera did you *choose*?)

   **chose**—past tense of *choose* (Susan *chose* to stay home.)

10. **cite**—*v.*—to quote (The student *cited* evidence from the text.)

    **site**—*n.*—location (They chose the *site* where the house would be built.)

11. **clothes**—*n.*—garments (Because she got caught in the rain, her *clothes* were wet.)

    **cloths**—*n.*—pieces of material (The *cloths* were used to wash the windows.)

12. **coarse**—*adj.*—rough; unrefined (Sandpaper is *coarse*.)

    **course**—*n.*—1. path of action (She did not know what *course* would solve the problem.); 2. passage (We took the long *course* to the lake.); 3. series of studies (We both enrolled in the physics *course*.); 4. part of a meal (She served a five-*course* meal.)

13. **consul**—*n.*—a person appointed by the government to live in a foreign city and represent the citizenry and business interests of his or her native country there (The *consul* was appointed to Naples, Italy.)

    **council**—*n.*—a group used for discussion, advisement (The *council* decided to accept his letter of resignation.)

    **counsel**—*v.*—to advise (Tom *counsels* Jerry on tax matters.)

14. **decent**—*adj.*—proper; respectable (He was very *decent* about the entire matter.)

    **descent**—*n.*—1. moving down (In Dante's *Inferno*, the *descent* into Hell was depicted graphically.); 2. ancestry (He is of Irish *descent*.)

15. **device**—*n.*—1. plan; scheme (The *device* helped her win the race.); 2. invention (We bought a *device* that opens the garage door automatically.)

    **devise**—*v.*—to contrive (He *devised* a plan so John could not win.)

16. **emigrate**—*v.*—to go away from a country (Many Japanese *emigrated* from Japan in the late 1800s.)

    **immigrate**—*v.*—to come into a country (Her relatives *immigrated* to the United States after World War I.)

17. **eminent**—*n.*—prominent (He is an *eminent* member of the community.)

    **imminent**—*adj.*—impending (The decision is *imminent.*)

    **immanent**—*adj.*—existing within (Maggie believed that religious spirit is *immanent* in human beings.)

18. **fair**—*adj.*—1. beautiful (She was a *fair* maiden.); 2. just (She tried to be *fair.*); 3. *n.*—festival (There were many games at the *fair.*)

    **fare**—*n.*—amount of money paid for transportation (The city proposed that the subway *fare* be raised.)

19. **forth**—*adv.*—onward (The soldiers moved *forth* in the blinding snow.)

    **fourth**—*n., adj.*—4th (She was the *fourth* runner-up in the beauty contest.)

20. **its**—possessive form of *it* (Our town must improve *its* roads.)

    **it's**—contraction of *it is* (*It's* time to leave the party.)

21. **later**—*adj., adv.*—at a subsequent date (We will take a vacation *later* this year.)

    **latter**—*n.*—second of the two (Susan can visit Monday or Tuesday. The *latter,* however, is preferable.)

22. **lead**—1. *n.*—[led] a metal (The handgun was made of *lead.*); 2. *v.*—[leed] to show the way (The camp counselor *leads* the way to the picnic grounds.)

    **led**—past tense of *lead* (#2 above) (The dog *led* the way.)

23. **loose**—*adj.*—free; unrestricted (The dog was let *loose* by accident.)

    **lose**—*v.*—to suffer the loss of (He was afraid he would *lose* the race.)

24. **moral**—1. *n.*—lesson taught by a story, incident, etc. (Most fables end with a *moral.*); 2. *adj.*—virtuous (She is a *moral* woman with high ethical standards.)

    **morale**—*n.*—mental condition (After the team lost the game, their *morale* was low.)

25. **of**—*prep.*—from (She is *of* French descent.)

    **off**—*adj.*—away; at a distance (The television fell *off* the table.)

26. **passed**—*v.*—having satisfied some requirement (He *passed* the test.)

    **past**—1. *adj.*—gone by or elapsed in time (His *past* deeds got him in trouble.); 2. *n.*—a period of time gone by (His *past* was shady.); 3. *prep.*—beyond (She ran *past* the house.)

27. **personal**—*adj.*—private (Jack was unwilling to discuss his childhood; it was too *personal.*)

    **personnel**—*n.*—staff (The *personnel* at the department store was primarily young adults.)

28. **principal**—1. *adj.*—first or highest in rank or value (Her *principal* reason for leaving was boredom.); 2. *n.*—head of a school (The *principal* addressed the graduating class.)

    **principle**—n.—the ultimate source, origin, or cause of something; a law, truth (The *principles* of physics were reviewed in class today.)

29. **prophecy**—*n.*—prediction of the future (His *prophecy* that he would become a doctor came true.)

    **prophesy**—*v.*—to declare or predict (He *prophesied* that we would win the lottery.)

30. **quiet**—*adj.*—still; calm (At night all is *quiet.*)

    **quite**—*adv.*—really; truly (She is *quite* a good singer.)

    **quit**—*v.*—to free oneself (Peter had little time to spare so he *quit* the chorus.)

31. **respectfully**—*adv.*—with respect, honor, esteem (He declined the offer *respectfully.*)

    **respectively**—*adv.*—in the order mentioned (Jack, Susan, and Jim, who are members of the club, were elected president, vice president, and secretary, *respectively.*)

32. **straight**—*adj.*—not curved (The road was *straight.*)

    **strait**—1. *adj.*—restricted; narrow; confined (The patient was put in a *strait* jacket.); 2. *n.*—narrow waterway (He sailed through the *Strait* of Magellan.)

33. **than**—*conj.*—used most commonly in comparisons (Maggie is older *than* I.)

    **then**—*adv.*—soon afterward (We lived in Boston; *then* we moved to New York.)

34. **their**—possessive form of *they* (That is *their* house on Tenafly Drive.)

    **there**—*adv.*—at that place (Who is standing *there* under the tree?)

    **they're**—contraction of *they are* (*They're* leaving for California next week.)

35. **to**—*prep.*—in the direction of; toward; as (She made a turn *to* the right on Norman Street.)

    **too**—*adv.*—1. more than enough (She served *too* much for dinner.); 2. also (He is going to Maine, *too.*)

    **two**—1. *n.*—the number 2; one plus one (The total number of guests is *two.*); 2. *adj.*—amounting to more than one (We have *two* pet rabbits.)

36. **weather**—*n.*—the general condition of the atmosphere (The *weather* is expected to be clear on Sunday.)

    **whether**—*conj.*—if it be a case or fact (We don't know *whether* the trains are late.)

37. **who's**—contraction of *who is* or *who has* (*Who's* willing to volunteer for the night shift?)

    **whose**—possessive form of *who* (*Whose* book is this?)

38. **your**—possessive form of *you* (Is this *your* seat?)

    **you're**—contraction of *you are* (I know *you're* going to do well on the test.)

# MULTIPLE MEANINGS

In addition to words that sound alike, you must be careful when dealing with words that have multiple meanings. For example:

> **The boy was thrilled that his mother gave him a piece of chewing *gum*.**

> **Dentists advise people to floss their teeth to help prevent *gum* disease.**

As you can see, one word can have different meanings depending on the context in which it is used. For more examples of multiple meaning words, refer to *capital, course,* and *fair* on pages 14–16.

# CONNOTATION AND DENOTATION

The English language can become even more complicated. Not only can a single word have numerous definitions and subtle meanings, but it may also take on added meanings through implication. The *connotation* is the idea suggested by its place near, or association with, other words or phrases. The *denotation* of a word is the direct, explicit meaning.

## Connotation

Sometimes you will be asked to tell the meaning of a word in the context of the paragraph. You may not have seen the word before, but from your understanding of the writer's intent you should be able to interpret the meaning. For example, read the following paragraph:

> **Paris is a beautiful city, perhaps the most beautiful on Earth. Long, broad avenues are lined with seventeenth- and eighteenth-century apartments, office buildings, and cafés. Flowers give the city a rich and varied look. The bridges and the river lend an air of lightness and grace to the whole urban landscape.**

1. In this paragraph, "rich" most nearly means

   (A) wealthy.

   (B) polluted.

   (C) colorful.

   (D) dull.

If you chose "colorful," you would be right. Although "rich" literally means "wealthy" (that is its denotation, or literal meaning), here the writer implies more than the word's literal meaning and seems to be highlighting the variety and color that the flowers add to the avenues. In this context, "richness" is used in a figurative sense.

The writer is using a nonliteral meaning, or connotation, that we associate with the word "rich" to show what he or she means. When we think of something "rich," we usually also think of abundance, variety, and color.

## Denotation

Determining a word's denotation is different from determining its connotation. Read this paragraph:

> Many soporifics are on the market to help people sleep. Take a glass of water and two *Sleepeze* and you get the "zzzzz" you need. *Sominall* supposedly helps you get the sleep you need so you can go on working. With *Morpho,* your head hits the pillow and you're asleep before the light goes out.

1. From this paragraph, a "soporific" is probably a

   (A)  drug that stimulates you to stay awake.

   (B)  kind of sleeping bag.

   (C)  kind of bed.

   (D)  drug that helps you sleep.

What is a soporific? You can figure out what it means by looking at what is said around it. People take these "soporifics" to go to sleep, not to wake up, so it can't be (A). You can't take two beds and a glass of water to go to sleep, so it can't be (C) either. Soporifics must therefore be some sort of pill that you take to sleep. Because pills are usually drugs of some kind, the answer is (D).

# VOCABULARY BUILDER

Although the context in which a word appears can help you determine the meaning of the word, the one surefire way to know a definition is to learn it. By studying the following lists of words and memorizing their definition(s), you will be better equipped to answer Reading Section questions that deal with word meanings.

To get the most from this vocabulary list, study the words and their definitions and then answer all of the drill questions; make sure to check your answers with the answer key that appears at the end of each drill.

## Words for Drill 1

**abstract**—*adj.*—not easy to understand; theoretical

**acclaim**—*n.*—loud approval; applause

**acquiesce**—*v.*—to agree or consent to an opinion

**adamant**—*adj.*—not yielding; firm

**adversary**—*n.*—an enemy; foe

**advocate**—1. *v.*—to plead in favor of; 2. *n.*—supporter; defender

**aesthetic**—*adj.*—showing good taste; artistic

**alleviate**—*v.*—to lessen or make easier

**aloof**—*adj.*—distant in interest; reserved; cool

**altercation**—*n.*—controversy; dispute

**altruistic**—*adj.*—unselfish

**amass**—*v.*—to collect together; to accumulate

**ambiguous**—*adj.*—not clear; uncertain; vague

**ambivalent**—*adj.*—undecided

**ameliorate**—*v.*—to make better; to improve

**amiable**—*adj.*—friendly

**amorphous**—*adj.*—having no determinate form

**anarchist**—*n.*—one who believes that a formal government is unnecessary

**antagonism**—*n.*—hostility; opposition

**apathy**—*n.*—lack of emotion or interest

**appease**—*v.*—to make quiet; to calm

**apprehensive**—*adj.*—fearful; aware; conscious

**arbitrary**—*adj.*—based on one's preference or whim

**arrogant**—*adj.*—acting superior to others; conceited

**articulate**—*v.*—1. to speak distinctly; 2. to hinge; to connect; 3. to convey; to express effectively; *adj.*—4. eloquent; fluent; 5. capable of speech.

# Drill 1

*Directions:* Match each word in the left column with the word in the right column that is most *opposite* in meaning.

| Word | | Match | |
|------|------|------|------|
| 1. __ articulate | 6. __ abstract | A. hostile | F. disperse |
| 2. __ apathy | 7. __ acquiesce | B. concrete | G. enthusiasm |
| 3. __ amiable | 8. __ arbitrary | C. selfish | H. certain |
| 4. __ altruistic | 9. __ amass | D. reasoned | I. resist |
| 5. __ ambivalent | 10. __ adversary | E. ally | J. incoherent |

*Directions:* Match each word in the left column with the word in the right column that is most *similar* in meaning.

| Word | | Match | |
|------|------|------|------|
| 11. __ adamant | 14. __ antagonism | A. afraid | D. insistent |
| 12. __ aesthetic | 15. __ altercation | B. disagreement | E. hostility |
| 13. __ apprehensive | | C. tasteful | |

## Drill 1 Answers

| | | | | | | | |
|------|------|------|------|------|------|------|------|
| 1. | (J) | 5. | (H) | 9. | (F) | 13. | (A) |
| 2. | (G) | 6. | (B) | 10. | (E) | 14. | (E) |
| 3. | (A) | 7. | (I) | 11. | (D) | 15. | (B) |
| 4. | (C) | 8. | (D) | 12. | (C) | | |

## Words for Drill 2

**assess**—*v.*—to estimate the value of

**astute**—*adj.*—cunning; sly; crafty

**atrophy**—*v.*—to waste away through lack of nutrition

**audacious**—*adj.*—fearless; bold

**augment**—*v.*—to increase or add to; to make larger

**austere**—*adj.*—harsh; severe; strict

**authentic**—*adj.*—real; genuine; trustworthy

**authoritarian**—*adj.*—acting as a dictator; demanding obedience

**banal**—*adj.*—common; petty; ordinary

**belittle**—*v.*—to make small; to think lightly of

**benefactor**—*n.*—one who helps others; a donor

**benevolent**—*adj.*—kind; generous

**benign**—*adj.*—mild; harmless

**biased**—*adj.*—prejudiced; influenced; not neutral

**blasphemous**—*adj.*—irreligious; profane; impious; away from acceptable standards

**blithe**—*adj.*—happy; cheery; merry

**brevity**—*n.*—briefness; shortness

**candid**—*adj.*—honest; truthful; sincere

**capricious**—*adj.*—changeable; fickle

**caustic**—*adj.*—burning; sarcastic; harsh

**censor**—*v.*—to examine and delete objectionable material

**censure**—*v.*—to criticize or disapprove of

**charlatan**—*n.*—an imposter; fake

**coalesce**—*v.*—to combine or come together

**collaborate**—*v.*—to work together; to cooperate

# Drill 2

***Directions:*** Match each word in the left column with the word in the right column that is most *opposite* in meaning.

| Word | | Match | |
|------|------|-------|------|
| 1. __ augment | 6. __ authentic | A. permit | F. malicious |
| 2. __ biased | 7. __ candid | B. respectful | G. neutral |
| 3. __ banal | 8. __ belittle | C. praise | H. mournful |
| 4. __ benevolent | 9. __ blasphemous | D. diminish | I. unusual |
| 5. __ censor | 10. __ blithe | E. dishonest | J. fake |

***Directions:*** Match each word in the left column with the word in the right column that is most *similar* in meaning.

| Word | | Match | |
|------|------|-------|------|
| 11. __ collaborate | 14. __ censure | A. harmless | D. cooperate |
| 12. __ benign | 15. __ capricious | B. cunning | E. criticize |
| 13. __ astute | | C. changeable | |

**Drill 2 Answers**

| | | | |
|---|---|---|---|
| 1. (D) | 5. (A) | 9. (B) | 13. (B) |
| 2. (G) | 6. (J) | 10. (H) | 14. (E) |
| 3. (I) | 7. (E) | 11. (D) | 15. (C) |
| 4. (F) | 8. (C) | 12. (A) | |

# Words for Drill 3

**compatible**—*adj.*—in agreement; harmonious

**complacent**—*adj.*—content; self-satisfied; smug

**compliant**—*adj.*—yielding; obedient

**comprehensive**—*adj.*—all-inclusive; complete; thorough

**compromise**—*v.*—to settle by mutual adjustment

**concede**—*v.*—1. to acknowledge; to admit; 2. to surrender; to abandon one's position

**concise**—*adj.*—in few words; brief; condensed

**condescend**—*v.*—to consciously come down from one's position or rank

**condone**—*v.*—to overlook; to forgive

**conspicuous**—*adj.*—easy to see; noticeable

**consternation**—*n.*—amazement or terror that causes confusion

**consummation**—*n.*—the completion; finish

**contemporary**—*adj.*—living or happening at the same time; modern

**contempt**—*n.*—scorn; disrespect

**contrite**—*adj.*—regretful; sorrowful

**conventional**—*adj.*—traditional; common; routine

**cower**—*v.*—to crouch down in fear or shame

**defamation**—*n.*—any harm to a name or reputation; slander

**deference**—*n.*—a yielding to the opinion of another

**deliberate**—1. *v.*—to consider carefully; to weigh in the mind; 2. *adj.*—intentional

**denounce**—*v.*—to speak out against; to condemn

**depict**—*v.*—to portray in words; to present a visual image

**deplete**—*v.*—to reduce; to empty

**depravity**—*n.*—moral corruption; badness

**deride**—*v.*—to ridicule; to laugh at with scorn

---

# Drill 3

*Directions:* Match each word in the left column with the word in the right column that is most *opposite* in meaning.

| Word | | Match | |
|------|------|-------|------|
| 1. ___ deplete | 6. ___ condone | A. unintentional | F. support |
| 2. ___ contemporary | 7. ___ conspicuous | B. disapprove | G. beginning |
| 3. ___ concise | 8. ___ consummation | C. invisible | H. ancient |
| 4. ___ deliberate | 9. ___ denounce | D. respect | I. virtue |
| 5. ___ depravity | 10. ___ contempt | E. fill | J. verbose |

*Directions:* Match each word in the left column with the word in the right column that is most *similar* in meaning.

| Word | | Match | |
|------|------|-------|------|
| 11. __ compatible | 14. __ comprehensive | A. portray | D. thorough |
| 12. __ depict | 15. __ complacent | B. content | E. common |
| 13. __ conventional | | C. harmonious | |

## Drill 3 Answers

| | | | | | | | |
|---|---|---|---|---|---|---|---|
| 1. | (E) | 5. | (I) | 9. | (F) | 13. | (E) |
| 2. | (H) | 6. | (B) | 10. | (D) | 14. | (D) |
| 3. | (J) | 7. | (C) | 11. | (C) | 15. | (B) |
| 4. | (A) | 8. | (G) | 12. | (A) | | |

## Words for Drill 4

**desecrate**—*v.*—to violate a holy place or sanctuary

**detached**—*adj.*—separated; not interested; standing alone

**deter**—*v.*—to prevent; to discourage; to hinder

**didactic**—*adj.*—1. instructive; 2. dogmatic; preachy

**digress**—*v.*—to stray from the subject; to wander from the topic

**diligence**—*n.*—hard work

**discerning**—*adj.*—distinguishing one thing from another

**discord**—*n.*—disagreement; lack of harmony

**discriminate**—*v.*—1. to distinguish one thing from another; 2. to demonstrate bias; 3. *adj.*— able to distinguish

**disdain**—1. *n.*—intense dislike; 2. *v.*—to look down upon; to scorn

**disparage**—*v.*—to belittle; to undervalue

**disparity**—*n.*—difference in form, character, or degree

**dispassionate**—*adj.*—lack of feeling; impartial

**disperse**—*v.*—to scatter; to separate

**disseminate**—*v.*—to circulate; to scatter

**dissent**—*v.*—to disagree; to differ in opinion

**dissonance**—*n.*—harsh contradiction

**diverse**—*adj.*—different; dissimilar

**document**—1. *n.*—official paper containing information; 2. *v.*—to support; to substantiate or verify

**dogmatic**—*adj.*—stubborn; biased; opinionated

**dubious**—*adj.*—doubtful; uncertain; skeptical; suspicious

**eccentric**—*adj.*—odd; peculiar; strange

**efface**—*v.*—to wipe out; to erase

**effervescence**—*n.*—1. liveliness; spirit; enthusiasm; 2. bubbliness

**egocentric**—*adj.*—self-centered

## Drill 4

**Directions:** Match each word in the left column with the word in the right column that is most *opposite* in meaning.

| Word | | Match | |
|---|---|---|---|
| 1. __ detached | 6. __ dubious | A. agree | F. respect |
| 2. __ deter | 7. __ diligence | B. certain | G. compliment |
| 3. __ dissent | 8. __ disdain | C. lethargy | H. sanctify |
| 4. __ discord | 9. __ desecrate | D. connected | I. harmony |
| 5. __ efface | 10. __ disparage | E. assist | J. restore |

**Directions:** Match each word in the left column with the word in the right column that is most *similar* in meaning.

| Word | | Match | |
|---|---|---|---|
| 11. __ effervescence | 14. __ document | A. belittle | D. liveliness |
| 12. __ disparage | 15. __ eccentric | B. distribute | E. odd |
| 13. __ disseminate | | C. substantiate | |

### Drill 4 Answers

| | | | |
|---|---|---|---|
| 1. (D) | 5. (J) | 9. (H) | 13. (B) |
| 2. (E) | 6. (B) | 10. (G) | 14. (C) |
| 3. (A) | 7. (C) | 11. (D) | 15. (E) |
| 4. (I) | 8. (F) | 12. (A) | |

## Words for Drill 5

**elaboration**—*n.*—act of clarifying; adding details

**eloquence**—*n.*—the ability to speak well

**elusive**—*adj.*—hard to catch; difficult to understand

**emulate**—*v.*—to imitate; to copy

**endorse**—*v.*—to support; to approve of; to recommend

**engender**—*v.*—to create; to bring about

**enhance**—*v.*—to improve; to complement; to make more attractive

**enigma**—*n.*—mystery; secret; perplexity

**ephemeral**—*adj.*—temporary; brief; short-lived

**equivocal**—*adj.*—doubtful; uncertain

**erratic**—*adj.*—unpredictable; strange

**erroneous**—*adj.*—untrue; inaccurate; not correct

**esoteric**—*adj.*—incomprehensible; obscure

**euphony**—*n.*—pleasant sound

**execute**—*v.*—1. to put to death; to kill; 2. to carry out or fulfill

**exemplary**—*adj.*—serving as an example; outstanding

**exhaustive**—*adj.*—thorough; complete

**expedient**—*adj.*—helpful; practical; worthwhile

**expedite**—*v.*—to speed up

**explicit**—*adj.*—specific; definite

**extol**—*v.*—to praise; to commend

**extraneous**—*adj.*—irrelevant; not related; not essential

**facilitate**—*v.*—to make easier; to simplify

**fallacious**—*adj.*—misleading

**fanatic**—*n.*—enthusiast; extremist

---

# Drill 5

***Directions:*** Match each word in the left column with the word in the right column that is most *opposite* in meaning.

### Word

1. __ extraneous
2. __ ephemeral
3. __ exhaustive
4. __ expedite
5. __ erroneous

6. __ erratic
7. __ explicit
8. __ euphony
9. __ elusive
10. __ elaborate

### Match

A. incomplete
B. delay
C. dependable
D. comprehensible
E. dissonance

F. eternal
G. abridge
H. relevant
I. indefinite
J. accurate

---

***Directions:*** Match each word in the left column with the word in the right column that is most *similar* in meaning.

### Word

11. __ endorse
12. __ expedient
13. __ facilitate

14. __ fallacious
15. __ engender

### Match

A. enable
B. recommend
C. create

D. worthwhile
E. deceptive

## Drill 5 Answers

|     |     |     |     |     |     |     |     |
| --- | --- | --- | --- | --- | --- | --- | --- |
| 1.  | (H) | 5.  | (J) | 9.  | (D) | 13. | (A) |
| 2.  | (F) | 6.  | (C) | 10. | (G) | 14. | (E) |
| 3.  | (A) | 7.  | (I) | 11. | (B) | 15. | (C) |
| 4.  | (B) | 8.  | (E) | 12. | (D) |     |     |

## Words for Drill 6

**fastidious**—*adj.*—fussy; hard to please

**fervor**—*n.*—passion; intensity

**fickle**—*adj.*—changeable; unpredictable

**fortuitous**—*adj.*—accidental; happening by chance; lucky

**frivolity**—*n.*—giddiness; lack of seriousness

**fundamental**—*adj.*—basic; necessary

**furtive**—*adj.*—secretive; sly

**futile**—*adj.*—worthless; unprofitable

**glutton**—*n.*—overeater

**grandiose**—*adj.*—extravagant; flamboyant

**gravity**—*n.*—seriousness

**guile**—*n.*—slyness; deceit

**gullible**—*adj.*—easily fooled

**hackneyed**—*adj.*—commonplace; trite

**hamper**—*v.*—to interfere with; to hinder

**haphazard**—*adj.*—disorganized; random

**hedonistic**—*adj.*—pleasure seeking

**heed**—*v.*—to obey; to yield to

**heresy**—*n.*—opinion contrary to popular belief

**hindrance**—*n.*—blockage; obstacle

**humility**—*n.*—lack of pride; modesty

**hypocritical**—*adj.*—two-faced; deceptive

**hypothetical**—*adj.*—assumed; uncertain

**illuminate**—*v.*—to make understandable

**illusory**—*adj.*—unreal; false; deceptive

---

## Drill 6

***Directions:*** Match each word in the left column with the word in the right column that is most *opposite* in meaning.

### Word

1. __ heresy
2. __ fickle
3. __ illusory
4. __ frivolity
5. __ grandiose

6. __ fervent
7. __ fundamental
8. __ furtive
9. __ futile
10. __ haphazard

### Match

A. predictable
B. dispassionate
C. simple
D. extraneous
E. real

F. beneficial
G. orthodoxy
H. organized
I. candid
J. seriousness

*Directions:* Match each word in the left column with the word in the right column that is most *similar* in meaning.

**Word**                                    **Match**

11. __ glutton       14. __ hackneyed       A. hinder      D. overeater

12. __ heed          15. __ hindrance       B. obstacle    E. obey

13. __ hamper                               C. trite

---

**Drill 6 Answers**

| 1. | (G) | 5. | (C) | 9. | (F) | 13. | (A) |
|----|-----|----|-----|----|-----|-----|-----|
| 2. | (A) | 6. | (B) | 10. | (H) | 14. | (C) |
| 3. | (E) | 7. | (D) | 11. | (D) | 15. | (B) |
| 4. | (J) | 8. | (I) | 12. | (E) | | |

---

# Words for Drill 7

**immune**—*adj.*—protected; unthreatened by

**immutable**—*adj.*—unchangeable; permanent

**impartial**—*adj.*—unbiased; fair

**impetuous**—*adj.*—1. rash; impulsive; 2. forcible; violent

**implication**—*n.*—suggestion; inference

**inadvertent**—*adj.*—not on purpose; unintentional

**incessant**—*adj.*—constant; continual

**incidental**—*adj.*—extraneous; unexpected

**inclined**—*adj.*—1. apt to; likely to; 2. angled

**incoherent**—*adj.*—illogical; rambling

**incompatible**—*adj.*—disagreeing; disharmonious

**incredulous**—*adj.*—unwilling to believe; skeptical

**indifferent**—*adj.*—unconcerned

**indolent**—*adj.*—lazy; inactive

**indulgent**—*adj.*—lenient; patient

**inevitable**—*adj.*—sure to happen; unavoidable

**infamous**—*adj.*—having a bad reputation; notorious

**infer**—*v.*—to form an opinion; to conclude

**initiate**—1. *v.*—to begin; to admit into a group; 2. *n.*—a person who is in the process of being admitted into a group

**innate**—*adj.*—natural; inborn

**innocuous**—*adj.*—harmless; innocent

**innovate**—*v.*—to introduce a change; to depart from the old

**insipid**—*adj.*—uninteresting; bland

**instigate**—*v.*—to start; to provoke

**intangible**—*adj.*—incapable of being touched; immaterial

# Drill 7

*Directions:* Match each word in the left column with the word in the right column that is most *opposite* in meaning.

Word | Match

1. __ immutable    6. __ innate

2. __ impartial    7. __ incredulous

3. __ inadvertent  8. __ inevitable

4. __ incoherent   9. __ intangible

5. __ incompatible 10. __ indolent

A. intentional    F. changeable

B. articulate     G. avoidable

C. gullible       H. harmonious

D. material       I. learned

E. biased         J. energetic

*Directions:* Match each word in the left column with the word in the right column that is most *similar* in meaning.

Word | Match

11. __ impetuous   14. __ instigate

12. __ incidental  15. __ indulgent

13. __ infer

A. lenient        D. conclude

B. impulsive      E. extraneous

C. provoke

# Drill 7 Answers

| | | | |
|---|---|---|---|
| 1. (F) | 5. (H) | 9. (D) | 13. (D) |
| 2. (E) | 6. (I) | 10. (J) | 14. (C) |
| 3. (A) | 7. (C) | 11. (B) | 15. (A) |
| 4. (B) | 8. (G) | 12. (E) | |

## Words for Drill 8

**ironic**—*adj.*—contradictory; inconsistent; sarcastic

**irrational**—*adj.*—not logical

**jeopardy**—*n.*—danger

**kindle**—*v.*—to ignite; to arouse

**languid**—*adj.*—weak; fatigued

**laud**—*v.*—to praise

**lax**—*adj.*—careless; irresponsible

**lethargic**—*adj.*—lazy; passive

**levity**—*n.*—silliness; lack of seriousness

**lucid**—*adj.*—1. shining; 2. easily understood

**magnanimous**—*adj.*—forgiving; unselfish

**malicious**—*adj.*—spiteful; vindictive

**marred**—*adj.*—damaged

**meander**—*v.*—to wind on a course; to travel or wander aimlessly

**melancholy**—*n.*—depression; gloom

**meticulous**—*adj.*—exacting; precise

**minute**—*adj.*—extremely small; tiny

**miser**—*n.*—penny-pincher; stingy person

**mitigate**—*v.*—to alleviate; to lessen; to soothe

**morose**—*adj.*—moody; despondent

**negligence**—*n.*—carelessness

**neutral**—*adj.*—impartial; unbiased

**nostalgic**—*adj.*—longing for the past; filled with bittersweet memories

**novel**—*adj.*—new and different

## Drill 8

*Directions:* Match each word in the left column with the word in the right column that is most *opposite* in meaning.

| Word | | Match | |
|------|------|-------|------|
| 1. __ irrational | 6. __ magnanimous | A. extinguish | F. ridicule |
| 2. __ kindle | 7. __ levity | B. jovial | G. kindly |
| 3. __ meticulous | 8. __ minute | C. selfish | H. sloppy |
| 4. __ malicious | 9. __ laud | D. logical | I. huge |
| 5. __ morose | 10. __ novel | E. seriousness | J. stale |

*Directions:* Match each word in the left column with the word in the right column that is most *similar* in meaning.

| Word | | Match | |
|------|------|-------|------|
| 11. __ ironic | 14. __ jeopardy | A. lessen | D. carelessness |
| 12. __ marred | 15. __ negligence | B. damaged | E. danger |
| 13. __ mitigate | | C. sarcastic | |

**Drill 8 Answers**

| | | | |
|---|---|---|---|
| 1. (D) | 5. (B) | 9. (F) | 13. (A) |
| 2. (A) | 6. (C) | 10. (J) | 14. (E) |
| 3. (H) | 7. (E) | 11. (C) | 15. (D) |
| 4. (G) | 8. (I) | 12. (B) | |

# Words for Drill 9

**nullify**—*v.*—to cancel; to invalidate

**objective**—1. *adj.*—open-minded; impartial; 2. *n.*—goal

**obscure**—*adj.*—not easily understood; dark

**obsolete**—*adj.*—out of date; passé

**ominous**—*adj.*—threatening

**optimist**—*n.*—person who hopes for the best; sees the good side

**orthodox**—*adj.*—traditional; accepted

**pagan**—1. *n.*—polytheist; 2. *adj.*—polytheistic

**partisan**—1. *n.*—supporter; follower; 2. *adj.*—biased; one-sided

**perceptive**—*adj.*—full of insight; aware

**peripheral**—*adj.*—marginal; outer

**pernicious**—*adj.*—dangerous; harmful

**pessimism**—*n.*—seeing only the gloomy side; hopelessness

**phenomenon**—*n.*—1. miracle; 2. occurrence

**philanthropy**—*n.*—charity; unselfishness

**pious**—*adj.*—religious; devout; dedicated

**placate**—*v.*—to pacify

**plausible**—*adj.*—probable; feasible

**pragmatic**—*adj.*—matter-of-fact; practical

**preclude**—*v.*—to inhibit; to make impossible

**predecessor**—*n.*—one who has occupied an office before another

**prodigal**—*adj.*—wasteful; lavish

**prodigious**—*adj.*—exceptional; tremendous

**profound**—*adj.*—deep; knowledgeable; thorough

**profusion**—*n.*—great amount; abundance

---

## Drill 9

*Directions:* Match each word in the left column with the word in the right column that is most *opposite* in meaning.

| Word | | Match | |
|------|------|-------|------|
| 1. __ objective | 6. __ plausible | A. scarcity | F. minute |
| 2. __ obsolete | 7. __ preclude | B. assist | G. anger |
| 3. __ placate | 8. __ prodigious | C. superficial | H. pessimism |
| 4. __ profusion | 9. __ profound | D. biased | I. modern |
| 5. __ peripheral | 10. __ optimism | E. improbable | J. central |

**Directions:** Match each word in the left column with the word in the right column that is most *similar* in meaning.

|  | Word | | Match | |
|---|---|---|---|---|
| 11. __ nullify | 14. __ pernicious | A. invalidate | D. threatening |
| 12. __ ominous | 15. __ prodigal | B. follower | E. harmful |
| 13. __ partisan | | C. lavish | |

## Drill 9 Answers

| 1. (D) | 5. (J) | 9. (C) | 13. (B) |
|---|---|---|---|
| 2. (I) | 6. (E) | 10. (H) | 14. (E) |
| 3. (G) | 7. (B) | 11. (A) | 15. (C) |
| 4. (A) | 8. (F) | 12. (D) | |

# Words for Drill 10

**prosaic**—*adj.*—tiresome; ordinary

**provincial**—*adj.*—regional; unsophisticated

**provocative**—*adj.*—1. tempting; 2. irritating

**prudent**—*adj.*—wise; careful; prepared

**qualified**—*adj.*—1. experienced; 2. indefinite

**rectify**—*v.*—to correct

**redundant**—*adj.*—1. repetitious; 2. unnecessary

**refute**—*v.*—to challenge; to disprove

**relegate**—*v.*—to banish; to put to a lower position

**relevant**—*adj.*—of concern; significant

**remorse**—*n.*—guilt; sorrow

**reprehensible**—*adj.*—wicked; disgraceful

**repudiate**—*v.*—to reject; to cancel

**rescind**—*v.*—to retract; to discard

**resignation**—*n.*—1. quitting; 2. submission

**resolution**—*n.*—proposal; promise; determination

**respite**—*n.*—recess; rest period

**reticent**—*adj.*—silent; reserved; shy

**reverent**—*adj.*—respectful

**rhetorical**—*adj.*—having to do with verbal communication; concerned with style and effect

**rigor**—*n.*—severity

**sagacious**—*adj.*—wise; cunning

**sanguine**—*adj.*—1. optimistic; cheerful; 2. red

**saturate**—*v.*—to soak thoroughly; to drench

**scanty**—*adj.*—inadequate; sparse

## Drill 10

**Directions:** Match each word in the left column with the word in the right column that is most *opposite* in meaning.

**Word**                          **Match**

1. __ provincial    6. __ remorse       A. inexperienced    F. affirm

2. __ reticent      7. __ repudiate      B. joy               G. extraordinary

3. __ prudent       8. __ sanguine       C. pessimistic       H. sophisticated

4. __ qualified     9. __ relevant       D. unrelated         I. forward

5. __ relegate     10. __ prosaic        E. careless          J. promote

**Directions:** Match each word in the left column with the word in the right column that is most *similar* in meaning.

**Word**                          **Match**

11. __ provocative   14. __ rescind        A. drench        D. severity

12. __ rigor         15. __ reprehensible  B. tempting      E. blameworthy

13. __ saturate                            C. retract

## Drill 10 Answers

| 1. (H) | 5. (J) | 9. (D) | 13. (A) |
|--------|--------|--------|---------|
| 2. (I) | 6. (B) | 10. (G) | 14. (C) |
| 3. (E) | 7. (F) | 11. (B) | 15. (E) |
| 4. (A) | 8. (C) | 12. (D) | |

## Words for Drill 11

**scrupulous**—*adj.*—honorable; exact

**scrutinize**—*v.*—to examine closely; to study

**servile**—*adj.*—slavish; groveling

**skeptic**—*n.*—doubter

**slander**—*v.*—to defame; to maliciously misrepresent

**solemnity**—*n.*—seriousness

**solicit**—*v.*—to ask; to seek

**stagnant**—*adj.*—motionless; uncirculating

**stanza**—*n.*—group of lines in a poem having a definite pattern

**static**—*adj.*—inactive; changeless

**stoic**—*adj.*—detached; unruffled; calm

**subtlety**—*n.*—1. understatement; 2. propensity for understatement; 3. sophistication; 4. cunning

**superficial**—*adj.*—on the surface; narrow-minded; lacking depth

**superfluous**—*adj.*—unnecessary; extra

**surpass**—*v.*—to go beyond; to outdo

**sycophant**—*n.*—flatterer

**symmetry**—*n.*—correspondence of parts; harmony

**taciturn**—*adj.*—reserved; quiet; secretive

**tedious**—*adj.*—time-consuming; burdensome; uninteresting

**temper**—*v.*—to soften; to pacify; to compose

**tentative**—*adj.*—not confirmed; indefinite

**thrifty**—*adj.*—economical; pennywise

**tranquility**—*n.*—peace; stillness; harmony

**trepidation**—*n.*—apprehension; uneasiness

**trivial**—*adj.*—unimportant; small; worthless

---

# Drill 11

**Directions:** Match each word in the left column with the word in the right column that is most *opposite* in meaning.

### Word                                        ### Match

1. __ scrutinize      6. __ tentative        A. frivolity        F. skim

2. __ skeptic         7. __ thrifty          B. enjoyable        G. turbulent

3. __ solemnity       8. __ tranquility      C. prodigal         H. active

4. __ static          9. __ solicit          D. chaos            I. believer

5. __ tedious         10. __ stagnant        E. give             J. confirmed

---

**Directions:** Match each word in the left column with the word in the right column that is most *similar* in meaning.

### Word                                        ### Match

11. __ symmetry       14. __ subtle          A. understated      D. fear

12. __ superfluous    15. __ trepidation     B. unnecessary      E. flatterer

13. __ sycophant                             C. balance

**Drill 11 Answers**

| | | | |
|---|---|---|---|
| 1. (F) | 5. (B) | 9. (E) | 13. (E) |
| 2. (I) | 6. (J) | 10. (G) | 14. (A) |
| 3. (A) | 7. (C) | 11. (C) | 15. (D) |
| 4. (H) | 8. (D) | 12. (B) | |

## Words for Drill 12

**tumid**—*adj.*—swollen; inflated

**undermine**—*v.*—to weaken; to ruin

**uniform**—*adj.*—consistent; unvaried; unchanging

**universal**—*adj.*—concerning everyone; existing everywhere

**unobtrusive**—*adj.*—inconspicuous; reserved

**unprecedented**—*adj.*—unheard of; exceptional

**unpretentious**—*adj.*—simple; plain; modest

**vacillation**—*n.*—fluctuation

**valid**—*adj.*—acceptable; legal

**vehement**—*adj.*—intense; excited; enthusiastic

**venerate**—*v.*—to revere

**verbose**—*adj.*—wordy; talkative

**viable**—*adj.*—1. capable of maintaining life; 2. possible; attainable

**vigor**—*n.*—energy; forcefulness

**vilify**—*v.*—to slander

**virtuoso**—*n.*—highly skilled artist

**virulent**—*adj.*—deadly; harmful; malicious

**vital**—*adj.*—important; spirited

**volatile**—*adj.*—changeable; undependable

**vulnerable**—*adj.*—open to attack; unprotected

**wane**—*v.*—to grow gradually smaller

**whimsical**—*adj.*—fanciful; amusing

**wither**—*v.*—to wilt or shrivel; to humiliate

**zealot**—*n.*—believer; enthusiast; fan

**zenith**—*n.*—point directly overhead in the sky

## Drill 12

**Directions:** Match each word in the left column with the word in the right column that is most *opposite* in meaning.

| Word | | Match | |
|------|------|-------|------|
| 1. __ uniform | 6. __ vigorous | A. amateur | F. support |
| 2. __ virtuoso | 7. __ volatile | B. trivial | G. constancy |
| 3. __ vital | 8. __ vacillation | C. visible | H. lethargic |
| 4. __ wane | 9. __ undermine | D. placid | I. wax |
| 5. __ unobtrusive | 10. __ valid | E. unacceptable | J. varied |

---

*Directions:* Match each word in the left column with the word in the right column that is most *similar* in meaning.

|  Word |  |  | Match |  |
|---|---|---|---|---|
| 11. __ wither | 14. __ vehement | A. intense | D. possible |
| 12. __ whimsical | 15. __ virulent | B. deadly | E. shrivel |
| 13. __ viable |  | C. amusing |  |

---

**Drill 12 Answers**

| 1. (J) | 5. (C) | 9. (F) | 13. (D) |
|---|---|---|---|
| 2. (A) | 6. (H) | 10. (E) | 14. (A) |
| 3. (B) | 7. (D) | 11. (E) | 15. (B) |
| 4. (I) | 8. (G) | 12. (C) |  |

# II. Reading Review

## UNDERSTANDING THE MEANINGS OF WORDS AND PHRASES THROUGH CONTEXT CLUES

Many times a reader will come across unfamiliar words but seldom take the time to look up the definitions. The reading passage often will provide the necessary information to let the reader determine the definition. The following techniques can assist the reader in defining unfamiliar words.

### Context Definition

The context of a passage may give the definition of the new word, using other wording to explain it. The definition may come as an appositive, a word or group of words that follow a word and restate its meaning.

> **Where can I find a specialist in *graphology,* the study of handwriting to reveal character?**

> **Harry hoped to *appease* his grandmother by taking her some flowers for missing her birthday. (definition: make happy)**

## Contrasting Words

Certain words or phrases indicate that the unknown word is opposite in meaning to other wording in the passage. Some words or phrases that indicate contrast are the following: *however, but, although, nevertheless, despite, not, even though,* and *on the other hand.*

> **Although the voters *impugn* the idea of a tax increase, they accept all other legislative changes. (definition: reject or criticize)**

## Words of Comparison

Words or phrases, like *also, moreover, in addition to, likewise, like,* and *as,* are signals that the new word is similar in meaning to the words in the comparison phrase.

> **The coach often started arguments or challenged rulings of the referee; moreover, his *bellicose* outbursts embarrassed his team members. (definition: eager to fight)**

## Use of Examples

An example of the unfamiliar word may reveal its meaning.

> **The list of *errata* included grammatical problems, misspellings, and capitalization errors. (definition: errors and corrections)**

## Cause and Effect

Signal words or phrases for a cause-and-effect relationship between a new word and other wording in the passage include the following: *because, therefore, thus, since,* and *for that reason.*

> **Because the *megaliths* had been standing for several thousand years, the local people thought little of the giant rocks. (definition: large stones, often used in ancient constructions)**

## Tone of the Passage

The general tone of the passage can indicate something about the unfamiliar word. For instance, whether the word is positive or negative can often be deduced by tone clues.

> Rocco was *ostracized* from the study group after others found his sarcastic, mordant, and rude comments disturbing. (definition: to exclude by common agreement. The reader cannot miss the heavy negative tone of the words in the passage.)

# Drill 1

*Directions:* Determine a working meaning for the underlined word in each of the following passages.

1. Romeyn de Hooghe, the first <u>limner</u> to limit his work to narrative strips, used his talent to create pictorial criticism of the persecution of the Huguenots under Louis XIV.

2. The somber clouds and the dreary rain caused the child to <u>mope</u> about the house.

3. The <u>veracity</u> of the witness's testimony, revealed through his eye-to-eye contact with the jury and lack of stumbling over words, was not doubted.

4. Why isn't the evening sun described as <u>moribund</u>, not setting; after all, it is coming to the day's end?

5. As president, state warden, and security chief, the leader described in Gilbert and Sullivan's "The Mikado" is a <u>poohbah</u>.

6. Robin Hood's <u>audacious</u> actions included conducting dangerous rescues of Maid Marian and visiting enemy territory disguised as a local.

7. Among common household health products are <u>St. John's Wort</u> and <u>Echinacea</u>, herbs from the garden.

8. My father is a <u>numismatist</u>; he spends several hours each week studying his coins from other countries and time periods.

**Drill 1 Answers**

1. artist; line drawer

2. unhappily move about

3. truthfulness

4. dying or dead

5. leader who holds several offices

6. daring

7. herbs used for good health

8. coin collector

# PURPOSE, AUDIENCE, AND POINT OF VIEW

## Purpose and Audience

With any writing assignment, the author must first select a subject. Next the writer must decide the following:

1. Why am I writing about this subject? What do I want to achieve with what I write; that is, what is my purpose?

2. For whom or to whom am I writing? Who will be reading my words?

The writer's intended meaning, or purpose, can be any of the following:

| | |
|---|---|
| to entertain | to classify |
| to explain | to compare or contrast |
| to describe | to prove |
| to inform | to negate |

to persuade                    to contradict

to define                      to restate

Often two or more of these purposes will control the writer's choice of wording and method of organizing thoughts. For instance, the writer may wish to explain his or her fear of high places and, at the same time, entertain his or her readers; the writer may wish, at another time, to explain the fear of high places and to compare this feeling to another's fear of open areas.

After establishing the purpose of writing, the author must then determine the audience–to whom he or she is addressing his or her comments. For example, in writing for his or her grandparents, the writer will probably be writing for a sympathetic reader. However, if the audience is a group of strangers the tone of the writing may be more effective if the writer chooses to explain the reason for this fear.

These two major considerations—purpose and audience—control other aspects of tone, persona, voice, and word choice.

## Point of View

The point of view refers to the person. With the first-person point of view, the viewpoint is that of the speaker or writer. The pronouns *I, me, my, mine, myself, we, us, our, ours,* and *ourselves* will be used, referring to the "speaker"—the persona or voice of the piece of writing. This type of writing is subjective, strongly influenced by the speaker's personal feelings and beliefs. With the second-person point of view, the writer uses the pronoun *you.* Some sentences may have the word *you* understood. (An example of this is *Read the passage carefully.*)

Third-person point of view is identified by the lack of first person or second person pronouns, unless such pronouns are used in conversation. The pronoun forms identifying the third person are *he, she, him, her, his, hers, himself, herself, they, them, their, theirs,* and *themselves.* The third-person point of view is objective and makes no direct reference to the writer.

## Drill 2

*Directions:* Read the passages and answer the questions that follow.

### Passage 1

I have just spent another four hours in the yard. Creating an English garden à la Arkansas is neither an easy nor fast endeavor. My fourth pickax is now attacking the granite mountainside, more successfully than the previous three. (Slinging my sledge, I often feel like John Henry!) Beneath the scant ground cover—a true trail mix of acorn shells, gravel, natural compost from leaf decay, and small gravel—surprises await each hefty swing. Most common are the small, hairlike roots of nonexistent plants; equally common are the small rocks that sometimes include a tiny piece of crystal. The giant relatives of these two finds create the greatest problem I encounter. Big rocks are often heavier than I can maneuver out of the hole I've started. Real trouble occurs when the boulder begins widening as I dig down around its edges. Wisdom tells me to cover it back up and set a potted plant atop. The equally troublesome roots call for a Paul Bunyan remedy. Chop!

Nevertheless, every day I spend time pursuing my dream of a mountainside covered with perennial loveliness. Signs of possible success, after two years of never failing effort (and ever flailing pickaxes), are showing. Next spring, a blaze of blooms will encourage another season of palm blisters and a sun-burnt neck.

### Passage 2

Creating an English garden on a mountainside in the Ouachita Mountains in central Arkansas may sound like an impossible endeavor, but after two years the dream is becoming reality. Digging up the rocks and replacing them with bags of top soil, humus, and peat, the persistent gardener now has sprouts that are not all weeds. Gravel paths meander through the beds of shasta daisies, marigolds, lavender, valerian, iris, day lilies, Mexican heather, and other flowers. Ornamental grasses, dogwood trees, and shrubs back up the flowers. Along the periodic waterway created by an underground spring, swamp hibiscus, helenium, hosta, and umbrella plants display their colorful and seasonal blooms. The flower beds are outlined by large rocks dug up by a pickax. Blistered hands are worth the effort when people stop by to view the mountainside beauty.

1. The author probably wrote Passage 1 with the following audience in mind:

   (A) a reader of a gardening magazine.

   (B) a young child.

   (C) a close, literate friend or relative.

   (D) a neighbor gardener.

2. The author probably wrote Passage 2 with the following audience in mind:

   (A) a young child.                  (C) a close friend.

   (B) an experienced gardener.        (D) a relative.

3. Passage 1 is written in the point of view known as

   (A) first person.                   (C) third person.

   (B) second person.                  (D) fourth person.

4. Not appearing in Passage 1 is/are the following:

   (A) a humorous tone.                (C) step-by-step directions.

   (B) literary allusions.             (D) word play examples.

5. The writer of Passage 2 is

   (A) unfamiliar with gardening.

   (B) a lazy gardener.

   (C) interested in changing the natural mountainside.

   (D) using only native plants to create a natural setting.

6. The point of view of Passage 2 is

   (A) first person.                   (C) third person.

   (B) second person.                  (D) first and third person.

7. Not found in both passages is/are

   (A) a reference to the rocky ground of the gardens.

   (B) literary allusions.

   (C) the use of a pickax to dig.

   (D) a feeling of success in gardening.

Passage 3

My daughter Marie has two cats. The older cat is named Annie. She is white with large black spots. Annie has long hair and sheds constantly in warm weather. Cinnamon is a two-year-old male tabby. He loves to chase squirrels in the backyard, but he probably would be very surprised to catch one. Cinnamon prefers to stay outside all night unless it is extremely cold. In the morning, Cinnamon wants to come into the house and sleep. Annie seldom goes outside. She prefers to sit on the table or a chair where she can look outside through the windows. Marie has cared for both of the cats since they were kittens. She is very fond of both of them.

8. The audience intended for this passage is

   (A) the daughter Marie.

   (B) a relative.

   (C) an unspecified person, probably somewhat young.

   (D) Marie's father.

9. A major purpose of this passage is to

   (A) explain Marie's sense of responsibility.

   (B) contrast the two cats.

   (C) explain how cats are good pets.

   (D) persuade the reader to get a cat as a pet.

10. The point of view used in this passage is

(A) first person.

(C) third person.

(B) second person.

(D) first and third person.

Passage 4

House fires result in the deaths of dozens of people every year. Smoke inhalation is the cause of death in most cases. Tragically, most house fires could easily be prevented. Many more house fires occur during cold winter months than during the summer. Unreliable space heaters account for the difference. Woodburning fireplaces, especially those that do not have screens to prevent igniting nearby objects, are another cause of house fires. The third most common cause of house fires is untended pans left cooking on the stove. A pan of food can burn dry in a very short period of time. This situation creates so much heat that the cabinets and surrounding objects can burst into flames.

11. The audience for whom this passage is written is

(A) older people who live alone.

(B) people who have small children.

(C) people who have fireplaces.

(D) All of the above.

12. The author's purpose in writing this passage is to

(A) describe fires in the kitchen.

(B) persuade people to be more careful of fireplaces.

(C) explain the major reasons for house fires.

(D) prove that smoke inhalation is the major cause of deaths with house fires.

13. According to this passage, which of the following is NOT true?

    (A) Smoke causes many deaths in house fires.

    (B) Space heaters cause some house fires.

    (C) Household fires in the kitchen can be avoided if glassware pots are used on the stove.

    (D) More house fires occur in the winter than in the summer.

## Passage 5

Representatives of the world's seven richest and most industrialized nations held a three-day economic summit in London, England, on July 14–16, 1991. On the second day of the summit, Mikhail Gorbachev of Russia appealed for help. The seven leaders offered him support for his economic reforms and his "new thinking" regarding political reforms. Because the allies were split on giving Gorbachev a big financial aid package, the seven leaders decided to provide help in the form of technical assistance in fields such as banking and energy, rather than hard cash.

14. Which one of the following statements best synthesizes the author's purpose in writing?

    (A) To announce that an economic summit was held in London

    (B) To announce that an economic summit of the world's seven richest nations was held in London in July 1991

    (C) To report that Mikhail Gorbachev appealed for financial help and that the seven leaders expressed support for his economic reforms

    (D) To report that the leaders of the world's seven richest and most industrialized nations met July 14–16, 1991, at an economic summit in London and agreed to provide technical support to Gorbachev

15. This passage is written for the following audience:

    (A) financial leaders throughout the world.

    (B) those throughout the world interested in the economic business decisions of the seven richest and most industrialized nations in the world.

    (C) Russian political leaders.

    (D) the citizens of the seven nations represented at the meeting.

16. Of the purposes for writing, which one is most prominent in this passage?

    (A) To entertain            (C) To prove

    (B) To persuade             (D) To inform

## Drill 2 Answers

| | | | | | | |
|---|---|---|---|---|---|---|
| 1. | (C) | 5. | (C) | 9. | (B) | 13. (C) |
| 2. | (B) | 6. | (C) | 10. | (A) | 14. (D) |
| 3. | (A) | 7. | (B) | 11. | (D) | 15. (B) |
| 4. | (C) | 8. | (C) | 12. | (C) | 16. (D) |

## Detailed Explanations of Answers

1. **(C)** Although choice (A) is tempting, the presence of literary allusions such as John Henry and Paul Bunyan make choice (C) the better answer. Choice (B) is inappropriate due to the word choice and content, too advanced for a young child. Choice (D) is possible if the better response is not present; however, logic tells us the neighboring gardener would already be aware of the two years of work.

2. **(B)** The specific references to many plants are subject matter only for an informed reader. Choice (A) is inappropriate because the content and vocabulary are not addressing a young child. Choices (C) and (D) have equal drawing power without more information about the gardening background of the friend or the relative.

3. **(A)** The use of first-person pronouns as well as the sense of humor expressed indicates the correct choice. No fourth person point of view exists.

4. **(C)** Although the writer mentions several details about the gardening process, they are not organized in a step-by-step manner. Thus, choice (C) is best. Choices (A), (B), and (D) add to the writer's creative expression.

5. **(C)** The writer's evident knowledge of gardening and the hard work that created blisters rule out choices (A) and (B). No reference to native plants is made; therefore, choice (D) cannot be correct.

6. **(C)** The third-person point of view is the correct answer. The point of view is objective and makes no direct reference to the writer.

7. **(B)** The literary allusions to John Henry and Paul Bunyan occur only in Passage 1. Both passages use (A), (C), and (D).

8. **(C)** The simple sentence structure, word choice, and subject matter indicate a younger person as the intended audience. There is no reason given to explain why it would have been written to Marie (A). (More personalization should occur between a mother and daughter passage.) Choices (B) and (D) are similar to one another. Without more information, neither could be selected over the other.

9. **(B)** The two cats are contrasted in both physical appearance and behavior. Although choice (A) may be implied, it is not the focus of the passage. Neither choice (C) nor (D) is addressed by the writer.

10. **(A)** The use of first-person pronouns indicates the point of view.

11. **(D)** Choices (A), (B), and (C) could be the audience; therefore, none alone could be the only answer.

12. **(C)** The writer refers to the content of choices (A), (B), and (D); however, none of these is the major purpose of writing. The type of writing in each of these wrong answers—to describe, to persuade, or to prove—is also incorrect.

13. **(C)** No mention of glassware cooking utensils is given in this passage. (It would be faulty information anyway.) Choices (A), (B), and (D) all include information given in the passage.

14. **(D)** Only this response gives a thorough overview of the passage. Choices (A) and (B) are very vague, missing the main point and result of the summit meeting. Choice (C) does not clarify the decision made about the type of support that will be given to Gorbachev.

15. **(B)** Choices (A), (C), and (D) are all equally good answers. The information in choice (B) includes all three of the other answers as well as other interested persons.

16. **(D)** Information about the meeting is given with no attempt to entertain, persuade, or prove.

## EVALUATING AN ARGUMENT IN WRITTEN MATERIAL

In making or evaluating an argument, be aware of the three types of supporting evidence: facts, examples, and opinions. A *fact* is verifiable. However, be aware that the same fact can be interpreted differently. For example, it could be a fact that unemployment decreased by two percent in the last year. One person might interpret this fact as a sign of a strong economy; another person might read the statistic as reflecting how the growing number of low-paying service jobs outweighs the shrinking number of high-paying professional jobs. Facts are also constantly changing with new research; this makes it crucial to use the most recent authoritative texts available to support your argument. In the same vein, you should be suspicious of any current argument that uses only outdated sources for support.

An *example* is a specific instance of the generalized argument. If the argument is that children are better prepared for school when they attend pre-kindergarten, a good example would be to compare two children from the same kindergarten class: one who had attended pre-kindergarten and one who hadn't. If the child who had gone to pre-kindergarten does better in school than the one who hadn't, the example supports the generalized argument.

An *opinion* is an interpretation of a fact. Pay particular attention to how well an opinion is supported in the written material. In your own writing, be sure to support your opinion with the opinions of experts who agree with you. For example, if it is your opinion that a recent rise in traffic accidents in the United States is due to the increasing use of cell phones in the car, it would help your argument if you could find experts who interpret the increase in accidents the same way you do.

**MTEL COMMUNICATION AND LITERACY SKILLS**

Arguments are usually based on appeals to authority, logic, or emotion. To be effective, appeals to authority should use recognized authorities in the field in which the argument is being made. Again, be suspicious of quotations from unknown or outdated sources. Appeals to emotion attempt to convince the reader to place the same importance on the topic that the writer does, and usually try to motivate the reader to do something about the situation.

Arguments based on logic usually follow certain lines of argument, such as generalization, causation, sign, and parallel case. Arguments of generalization depend upon a wide enough sample experience from which a generalization could be drawn. In other words, if every time you buy milk at a certain store it turns out to be sour, you can argue that the store tends to sell sour milk. Arguments of causation have been reviewed in their own section in this book. Arguments of sign depend upon a correlation between two factors, so that if one occurs, the argument can be made that the other is present as well. A well-known example of this type of argument is the saying, "Where there's smoke, there's fire." Parallel case arguments are made about two similar cases: because it worked a certain way for the first case, the second case should work the same way. For this argument to work, the two cases must be closely related.

## SCANNING FOR BASIC FEATURES

If the literature is a textbook, read the *introduction*, scan the *chapter titles*, and quickly review any *subheadings, charts, pictures, appendices,* and *indexes* that the book includes. If it is an article, read the first and last paragraphs. These are the most likely places to find the writer's *main point* or *thesis*.

Note that there is a significant difference between a thesis and a main point. Here is an example of a *main point*:

> **The Rocky Mountains have three important geological features: abundant water, gold- and silver-bearing ore, and oil-bearing shale.**

Notice that this statement is not a matter of the writer's opinion. It is a fact. Now, notice the following *thesis*:

> **The Rocky Mountains are the most important source of geological wealth in the United States.**

What is the difference? The second statement offers an arguable conclusion or informed opinion. It may be an informed opinion on the part of the writer, but it is still an opinion.

A thesis, then, is a statement offered by a writer as true or correct, although it is actually a matter of opinion.

In the first statement, whether the author has an opinion about it or not, these features are an important part of the makeup of the Rocky Mountains. In the second statement, the author may have contrary evidence to offer about Alaska or the Everglades. The second statement bears proving; the first is self-evident. The writer would go on to show the existence of these features, not—as in the second case—the quality or value of those features. The writer of a main-point paper is reporting to or informing his or her audience; the writer of a thesis is attempting to sway the audience to his or her point of view.

## Key Sections to Recognize

In reading a particular passage, you want to identify what portions or sections of a whole essay you confront. Depending upon which section of an essay is offered, you may decide whether you are reading the writer's main point, thesis, purpose, or evidence.

**Introduction:** The introductory paragraph usually shows the writer's point of view, or thesis, and introduces that position with some lead-in or general data to support it. The thesis of an essay is the writer's stated or implied position on a particular issue or idea. The introduction often either contains or hints at the writer's purpose and point of view.

**Development:** This part consists of three or more middle paragraphs that prove the writer's position from different angles, using evidence from real-life experience and knowledge. Evidence may take the form of facts, examples, statistics, illustrations, opinions, or analogies.

In addition, each paragraph within the development section will have a stated or implied main point used to support the thesis of the whole passage. For example, a thesis might be "Dogs are better than cats." Having said that, a whole paragraph might be written with supporting examples to show a main point in support of that idea. The main point of the paragraph that needs support, then, might be as follows:

**First of all, dogs are more loyal than cats.**

The evidence that is summoned to support that point which, in turn, supports the overall thesis would therefore have to be facts, statistics, expert testimony, or anecdotal knowledge that shows that dogs are indeed more loyal than cats. For example: "The A.S.P.C.A. reports that 99 out of 100 dogs cannot adjust to new owners after the death of their original masters, while only 2 out of 100 cats cannot adjust in the same situation."

**Conclusion:** The last paragraph usually (but not always) sums up the writer's position and may add some final reminder of what the issue is, some speculation, or some call to action that the writer suggests.

# EVIDENCE

While reading, make a distinction between key ideas and the evidence for those ideas. *Evidence* is anything used to prove that an idea is true, real, correct, or probable.

## Types of Evidence

Only a few forms of evidence are available to the writer. The kinds of evidence that a writer can summon to support his or her position or point are as follows: (1) facts and statistics, (2) the testimony of an authority, (3) personal anecdote, (4) hypothetical illustrations, and (5) analogy. Strictly speaking, the last two in this list are not true evidence but only offer common-sense probability to the support of an argument. In fact, there is a hierarchy for evidence similar to that of purpose. The most powerful evidence is fact, supported by statistics; the least powerful is analogy. The following table suggests the relationship:

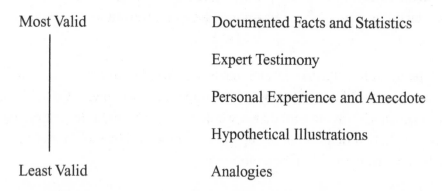

**Hierarchy of Validity of Evidence**

| Most Valid | Documented Facts and Statistics |
| | Expert Testimony |
| | Personal Experience and Anecdote |
| | Hypothetical Illustrations |
| Least Valid | Analogies |

*Documented facts and statistics* are the most powerful evidence a writer can bring to bear on proving an idea or supporting a main thesis. Documented facts and statistics must be used fairly and come from reliable sources. For example, *Funk and Wagnall's Encyclopedia* is a reliable source but Joe the plumber's *Guide to Waterfowl in Hoboken* is not. This is true because, first of all, Joe is a plumber, not an ornithologist (a bird scientist), and second, no one accepts Joe the plumber as an expert. Reliable sources for facts and statistics are the best information that can be offered.

*Expert testimony* is the reported positions, theses, or studies of people who are recognized experts in the field under discussion in the literature. A writer may use books, articles, essays, interviews, and so on by trained scientists and other professionals to support a thesis or position. Most often, this testimony takes the form of quotations from the expert or a paraphrasing of his or her important ideas or findings.

*Personal anecdote* is the evidence of a writer's own personal experience, or a "little story" about an event, person, or idea that exemplifies the point he or she is trying to make. It holds weight if the reader trusts the writer, and it is valuable; it is not as powerful or as conclusive as documented facts or the testimony of experts (unless the writer is a recognized authority in the field about which he or she has written).

*Hypothetical illustrations* are examples that suggest probable circumstances in which something would be true. Strictly speaking, a hypothetical illustration is not "hard" evidence, but rather evidence of probability. For example, to demonstrate that "people will do whatever they can get away with," a writer might bring up the hypothetical illustration of someone at a ticket counter who gets back more change than he or she paid for the ticket. The chances are, the writer might point out, that the person would pocket the extra money rather than be honest and return it. In this case, the writer is not naming anybody in particular or citing statistics to make the point, but rather is pointing to *a situation that is likely but is not an actual documented case.* This situation has either the weight of common sense for the reader or none at all.

*Analogy* is the last and weakest form of evidence. It is not actually evidence at all but certainly can serve as support. An analogy is simply a comparison between items that are different but that also have some striking similarities. Analogies often use the term "like" to show the relationship of ideas. For example, the writer might say, "Life is like'a tree: we start out struggling in the dirt, grow into the full bloom of youth, and become deeply rooted in our ways, until, in the autumn of our years, we lose our hair like leaves, and succumb ultimately to the bare winter of death."

While reading, determine what sort of evidence the writer is using and how effective it is in proving his or her point.

## Reasons for Evidence

To prove any thesis that the writer maintains is true, he or she may employ any one of the following seven strategies:

1. *show* that a process or a procedure does or should work step by step in time;

2. *compare or contrast* two or more things or ideas to show important differences or similarities;

3. *identify* a problem and then explain how to solve it;

4. *analyze* into its components, or *classify* by its types or categories, an idea or thing to show how it is put together, how it works, or how it is designed;

5. *explain* why something happens to produce a particular result or set of results;

6. *describe* the particular individual characteristics of a place, person, time, or idea;

7. *define* what a thing is or what an idea means.

# CAUSE AND EFFECT

Most people agree that conditions that exist have causes and that if factors are changed, it will result in some new effects. Cause-and-effect arguments are, however, difficult to prove because the exact relationship between two events is often difficult to establish.

Looking out for the use of such words as "consequently," "therefore," and "thus" will help you recognize when a cause-and-effect argument is being made.

# IDEAS IN OPPOSITION

To analyze the relationship between ideas in opposition (pro and con), first identify the claim each side is making. (Of course, in many situations there are more than two sides.) Pay attention to the intricacies of the position; many arguments are not simply for or against something, but instead are qualified positions with exceptions. For example, the claim that Medicare should pay for standard prescriptions is different from the claim that Medicare should pay for prescriptions. The word "standard" qualifies the argument; perhaps experimental drugs or preventative treatments are excluded from the proposal. In analyzing an argument, be sure to find the edges of the argument, where the arguer would not want to press the argument further.

After analyzing the argument, locate and evaluate the reasons that the author uses to support the claim. Ask yourself, "Why is the author's claim important?" Then examine the reasons the author gives: are they good reasons and are they connected to the claim? Finally, examine the evidence the author uses to support the reasons. The evidence should come from reliable sources and be pertinent to the reasons and claim. In examining two or more opposing arguments, you will judge which best supports its claim. However, the best argument may fail to convince its reader, especially on politically volatile topics such as abortion rights.

# LOGIC

## Induction, Deduction, and Fallacies

In formulating critical evaluations of a piece of writing, it is important to understand the problems, if any, with the logic of the piece that has been read. Does it make sense? If not, why doesn't it? It is up to the reader to find the errors in any piece of writing he or she reads. Of course, if the writer is effective, the reader won't find these fallacies. Be on the lookout for them because it is often a good way to refute, criticize, or counterargue if called upon to respond critically to any author's central idea, thesis, or main point. Make sure the evidence proves the writer's point and not something else.

Pay special attention to conclusions. The writer may not have proved the point. An essay is essentially a *syllogism* that proves something by *induction* or *deduction*. The *syllogism* is that *basic form of deductive reasoning* that is the cornerstone of most logic. It consists of a *major premise*, a *minor premise*, and a *conclusion*. Note how they are used in the discussion below. *Induction* is the sort of reasoning that arrives at a general conclusion based on the relationship among the contributing elements of an idea.

For example, a writer may observe under experimental conditions that whenever a spider begins to spin a web, it first rubs its back legs over its silk gland. The author may have observed 100,000 different species of spiders display this behavior. He or she may have also observed that they never rub their hind legs over the gland at any other time, only when they are about to put out silk to start a web. He or she may then *induce* from these observations that spiders must rub their hind legs over their silk glands in order to begin the production of silk to spin a web. Another individual may prove this theory wrong later because new evidence shows up to invalidate the induction. Until that happens, this will be the conclusion drawn from observations of the behavior of spiders.

*Deduction*, by way of contrast, reasons from the general to the particular. For example, an author may assert that all trees grow upward from the earth, not downward from the sky. Until someone finds a tree that grows from the sky to the earth, an individual will assume that every tree started growing out of the earth and base all other conclusions about the growth and flowering of trees upon this *deduction* as well.

Occasionally, however, the *premises* of a deductive argument are false or unprovable. The *premises* of an argument are those *definitions* or *assumptions* that are givens (concepts that do not stand in need of proof but are either self-evident, common knowledge, or agreed upon as terms between the writer and the reader). For example,

| | |
|---|---|
| **Major Premise:** | **All goats have beards.** |
| **Minor Premise:** | **Harry Jones has a beard.** |
| **Conclusion:** | **Therefore, Harry is a goat.** |

The conclusion is incorrect. It could be true if only goats have beards, but this is not the case; male human beings may have beards as well. Therefore, the conclusion is insupportable. In this example, we lack sufficient information to draw a conclusion about who or what Harry is.

## Typical Logical Fallacies

Below is a list of typical logical errors that weak writers commit. The list is not exhaustive. Know how they occur and practice finding them in others' arguments, either in conversation or in essays they may have written.

1. *Either/or:* The writer assumes only two opposing possibilities: "Either we abolish cars, or the environment is doomed." This argument is weak because other factors may contribute to the destruction of the environment as well.

2. *Oversimplification:* Here the author might first state, "Only motivated athletes become champions." Perhaps not; though unfortunate, unmotivated athletes who use enhancing steroids occasionally become champions, too.

3. *Begging the question:* The writer assumes he or she has proved something that has not been proven. "He is unintelligent because he is stupid." A lack of intelligence is almost synonymous with being stupid. It cannot be proven that he is stupid by saying he is unintelligent; that "he" is either or both of these is exactly what needs to be proved.

4. *Ignoring the issue:* An argument against the truth of a person's testimony in court shifts from what the witness observed to how the witness's testimony is inadmissible. "The witness is obviously unkempt and homeless." One has nothing to do with the other.

5. *Arguing against a person, not an idea:* The writer argues that somebody's idea has no merit because he or she is immoral or unintelligent: "John can't prove anything about dogs being faithful; he can't even understand basic mathematics."

6. *"It does not follow…"* or *non sequitur:* The writer leaps to a wrong conclusion: "John is tall; he must know a lot about mountains."

7. *Drawing the wrong conclusion from a sequence:* "He trained, read, then trained some more and, therefore, won the match." It is quite possible that other factors led to his winning the match.

---

# Drill 3

***Directions:*** Read the passages and answer the questions that follow.

Passage 1

The Matsushita Electric Industrial Company of Japan has developed a computer program that can use photographs of faces to predict the aging process and, also, how an unborn child may look. The system can show how a couple may look after 40 years of marriage and how newlyweds' future children may look. The computer analyzes facial characteristics from a photograph, based on shading and coloring differences, and then creates a three-dimensional model in its memory. The system consists of a personal computer with a program and circuit board. It will be marketed soon by Matsushita.

1. This passage is written from the point of view called

(A) first person.

(B) second person.

(C) third person.

(D) a combination of first and third person.

2. The intended purpose of this passage is to

   (A) persuade a couple to send in their photographs to use to predict their children's appearance.

   (B) explain how the aging process of adults and the appearance of their children can be predicted by a computer.

   (C) express an opinion about the technology of the future in Japan.

   (D) describe one way a computer uses photographs.

## Passage 2

As a farmer from Conrad, Montana, I might be the last person expected to invent and patent a motorcycle helmet. (No, I don't wear a helmet while I am driving my tractor.) The law in the United States requires that all cars sold must carry a third, high-mounted brake light on the rear of the vehicle. If cars need this light, I thought, how much safer life would be for motorcyclists if they, too, had such a light. The problem, however, was to install it "high-mounted." I have designed a helmet with a brake light in the rear. Thus, motorcyclists wearing a helmet like mine are much safer on the road.

3. The intended purpose of the passage is to

   (A) tell about a farmer in Montana.

   (B) explain a safety requirement for cars in the United States.

   (C) describe a man's motorcycle helmet invention that makes riding motorcycles safer.

   (D) show the versatility of some people.

4. The point of view of this passage is

   (A) first person.          (C) third person.

   (B) second person.          (D) first and third person.

---

**Drill 3 Answers**

1. (C)　　　　2. (B)　　　　3. (C)　　　　4. (A)

---

## Detailed Explanations of Answers

1. **(C)**　Choice (C) is the correct answer because the passage employs the point of view of an outsider through the use of pronouns such as *he, she,* and *it.*

2. **(B)**　The intended purpose is to explain. Although couples might be interested in sending in their photographs to see what their children may look like, choice (A), the passage is not encouraging this reaction from those who read it. Choice (C) is much too broad a response; also, the passage is not expressing an opinion. Choice (D) is too vague, although what it says is incomplete truth.

3. **(C)**　The focus of the passage is the motorcycle helmet, and the intended purpose is to explain why and how the helmet was invented. Choice (A) is a fact about the inventor—he is a farmer. Choice (B) is a true statement as well, but it is what prompted the writer's idea for a helmet. (D) is a general statement that is unrelated to this passage.

4. **(A)**　The personality of the speaker is revealed along with his ideas and actions. Notice also the use of the pronoun *I.* Choice (D) will attract some test-takers, but the first person point of view often uses third-person pronouns along with first-person pronouns.

## STRATEGIES FOR CRITICAL READING OF PASSAGES

Critical reading is a demanding process. Linguists and language philosophers speak passionately of the importance of true literacy in human affairs. It is not enough to merely comprehend; true literacy lies in the ability to make critical judgments, to analyze, and to evaluate. It is with this end in mind–true literacy–that any reader should approach a text.

### What Critical Readers Do

If you can summarize the main points of an essay, that's a start. If you can recall the plot twists in a short story or articulate the line of reasoning in an argument, that's a start. But if you are able to offer an informed opinion about the purpose and merits of a text, then you are on the road to true literacy.

The Communication and Literacy Skills Test seeks to identify critical readers who not only can describe *what* happened in a text they've read, but *why* it happened and *how* it happened. As a critical reader, you will be an active participant, not a passive recipient. It may help to envision yourself in a dialogue with the author and other critical readers. As rhetorician and critic Mikhail Bahktin argues, language operates in a dialogic mode, where receivers are just as essential as senders to the effective transmission of messages.

There are six strategies a critical reader can employ to participate fully in the "re-creative act" that is reading.

1. Get the facts straight.

2. Analyze the argument.

3. Identify basic features of style.

4. Explore your personal response.

5. Evaluate the text overall and determine its significance.

6. Compare and contrast related texts.

## 1. Get the Facts Straight

Listen and read actively, pencil in hand, underlining important phrases or noting key points in the margin. Briefly record your reactions, questions, and conclusions. Though you may not have time to annotate thoroughly during a test, if you rigorously practice annotating beforehand, you'll begin to do it less laboriously and with less written back-up.

Your first task as a critical reader is to learn everything you can about the text. You can begin by scrutinizing the implications of the title, trying to identify the author and general time period in which the text was written, and identifying the thesis. In short, a good reader looks for the main ideas, but also looks for other information (author, era, form) that may help him or her determine the slant of those ideas.

Once you have identified the essence of a passage, try to jot it down in your own words in a single sentence. This will help you focus on the meaning and purpose—useful information when the detailed multiple-choice questions present you with "blind alleys" or slightly off-base interpretation of text.

There are really four activities you perform in order to "get the facts straight":

a. **Previewing**–looking over a text to learn all you can *before* you start reading (This is, of course, much more difficult with excerpts.)

b. **Annotating**–marking up the text to record reactions, questions, and conclusions (Hint: It's especially useful to underline what you think the thesis is.)

c. **Outlining**–identifying the sequence of main ideas, often by *numbering* key phrases

d. **Summarizing**–stating the purpose and main idea of the passage

Once you have the facts straight, you are ready to tackle the analytic and evaluative aspects of critical reading. Before addressing those, let's test your ability to get the facts.

Following is an essay titled "Education of Women" by William Hazlitt, an essayist and scholar who wrote during the early nineteenth century. Try your hand at previewing, annotating, outlining, and summarizing it. Then look at the following pages, where a proficient critical reader has done those operations for you. Compare your responses and see where you can improve. Remember, you don't have to take copious notes to get to the essence of a text.

### "Education of Women"

We do not think a classical education proper for women. It may pervert their minds, but it cannot elevate them. It has been asked, Why a woman should not learn the dead languages as well as the modern ones? For this plain reason, that the one are still spoken, and may have immediate associations connected with them, and the other not. A woman may have a lover who is a Frenchman, or an Italian, or a Spaniard; and it is well to be provided against every contingency in that way. But what possible interest can she feel in those old-fashioned persons, the Greeks and Romans, or in what was done two thousand years ago? A modern widow would doubtless prefer Signor Tramezzani to Aeneas, and Mr. Conway would be a formidable rival to Paris.[1] No young lady in our days, in conceiving an idea of Apollo, can go a step beyond the image of her favorite poet: nor do we wonder that our old friend, the Prince Regent,[2] passes for a perfect Adonis in the circles of beauty and fashion. Women in general have no ideas, except personal ones. They are mere egoists. They have no passion for truth, nor any love of what is purely ideal. They hate to think, and they hate every one who seems to think of anything but themselves. Everything is to them a perfect nonentity which does not touch their senses, their vanity, or their interest.

Their poetry, their criticism, their politics, their morality, and their divinity, are downright affectation. That line in Milton is very striking—

"He for God only, she for God in him."

Such is the order of nature and providence; and we should be sorry to see any fantastic improvements on it. Women are what they were meant to be; and we wish for no alteration in their bodies or their minds. They are the creatures of the circumstances in which they are placed, of sense, of sympathy and habit. They are exquisitely susceptible of the passive impressions of things: but to form an idea of pure understanding or imagination, to feel an interest in the true and the good beyond themselves, requires an effort of which they are incapable. They want principle, except that which consists in an adherence to established custom; and this is the reason of the severe laws which have been set up as a barrier against every infringement of decorum and propriety in women. It has been observed by an ingenious writer of the present day, that women want imagination. This requires explanation. They have less of that imagination which depends on intensity of passion, on the accumulation of ideas and feelings round one object, on bringing all nature and all art to bear on a particular purpose, on continuity and comprehension of mind; but for the same reason, they have more fancy, that is greater flexibility of mind, and can more readily vary and separate their ideas at pleasure. The reason of the greater presence of mind which has been remarked in women is, that they are less in the habit of speculating on what is best to be done, and the first suggestion is decisive. The writer of this article confesses that he never met with any woman who could reason, and with but one reasonable woman. There is no instance of a woman having been a great mathematician or metaphysician or poet or painter: but they can dance and sing and act and write novels and fall in love, which last quality alone makes more than angels of them. Women are no judges of the characters of men, except as men. They have no real respect for men, or they never respect them for those qualities, for which they are respected by men. They in fact regard all such qualities as interfering with their own pretensions, and creating a jurisdiction different from their own. Women naturally wish to have their favourites all to themselves, and flatter their weaknesses to make them more dependent on their own good opinion, which, they think, is all they want. We have, indeed, seen instances of men, equally respectable and amiable, equally admired by the women and esteemed by the men, but who have been ruined by an excess of virtues and accomplishments.

—William Hazlitt (1815)

1. Hazlitt was a theatre critic and had accused a popular Italian tenor, Tramezzani, of overacting in his love scenes. He also criticized actor William Conway in the role of Romeo.
2. The Prince Regent was George, Prince of Wales.

### A. Previewing "Education of Women"

A quick look over the text of "Education of Women" reveals a few items worth mentioning. This short essay is probably most closely related to an Op-Ed (Opinion-Editorial) piece written in a newspaper. Published in the *Examiner* in 1815, the essay begins with a proclamation, "We do not think a classical education proper for women." The term "we" suggests the assurance of numbers and power. It's safe to assume Hazlitt believes he speaks for a significant group (perhaps educated men?). The year 1815 is relevant to our reading because it suggests a time when women did not enjoy the rights and privileges that are commonplace in the twenty-first century, at least in most of the major industrialized cultures. If the year were not stated, you could infer from the debate over educating women that the piece was written before the present time.

### B. Annotating "Education of Women"

An annotation records reactions, questions, and conclusions. Underlining key phrases may help you find the theme. Here is Hazlitt's essay with underlining and annotations alongside to facilitate easy reference:

**"Education of Women"**

<u>We do not think a classical education proper for women.</u> It may <u>pervert their minds,</u> but it <u>cannot elevate them.</u> It has been asked, Why a woman should not learn the dead languages as well as the <u>modern ones?</u> For this plain reason, that the one <u>are still spoken,</u> and may have immediate associations connected with them, and the other not. <u>A woman may have a lover who is a Frenchman, or an Italian, or a Spaniard;</u> and it is well to be provided against every contingency in that way. But <u>what possible interest</u> can she feel in those old-fashioned persons, the Greeks and Romans, or <u>in what was done two thousand years ago?</u> A modern widow would doubtless <u>prefer Signor Tramezzani to Aeneas, and Mr. Conway would be a formidable rival to Paris.</u>[1] No

1. The Thesis! But what was a "classical" education in 1815? Probably Latin and Greek, philosophy, and the "classics" of literature.

2. Perversion, not elevation, is the result of education of women; learning "taints" women.

3. Women learn modern languages only to be able to speak to their lovers; women have a shallow purpose for education.

4. Allusion to "poor" actors of the day (see footnote) who are preferable to historical figures (Aeneas, Paris); women have little interest in history or politics, only romantic self-gratification.

young lady in our days, in conceiving an idea of Apollo, can go a step beyond the image of her favorite poet: nor do we wonder that our old friend, the Prince Regent[2], passes for a perfect Adonis in the circles of beauty and fashion. <u>Women in general have no ideas, except personal ones.</u> They are mere egoists. They have no passion for truth, nor any love of what is purely ideal. <u>They hate to think,</u> and <u>they hate every one who seems to think of anything but themselves.</u> Everything is to them a perfect nonentity which does not touch their senses, their vanity, or their interest. Their poetry, their criticism, their politics, their morality, and their divinity, are downright affectation. That line in Milton is very striking—

"He for God only, she for God in him."

Such is the order of nature and providence; and we should be sorry to see any fantastic improvements on it. <u>Women are what they were meant to be;</u> and we wish for no alteration in their bodies or their minds. They are the <u>creatures of the circumstances in which they are placed,</u> of sense, <u>of sympathy and habit.</u> They are exquisitely susceptible of the passive impressions of things: but <u>to form an idea of pure understanding or imagination,</u> to feel an interest in the true and the good beyond themselves, <u>requires an effort of which they are incapable. They want principle,</u> except that which consists in an adherence to established custom; and this is the reason of the severe laws which have been set up as a barrier against every infringement of decorum and propriety in women. It has been observed by an ingenious writer of the present day, that <u>women want imagination.</u> This requires explanation. They have <u>less</u> of that imagination which depends on intensity of passion,

5. Women don't think; they are selfish and frivolous.

6. Women's destiny; they are creatures of circumstance, habit. Women can't change.

7. They have impressions, not ideas. So women only feel, can't think? They aren't interested in any truths beyond what is true for them.

8. They "want" principle... They "want" imagination... "Want" stresses a lack of something, not desire.

on the <u>accumulation of ideas and feelings round one object,</u> on bringing all nature and all art to bear on a particular purpose, on continuity and comprehension of mind; but for the same reason, <u>they have more fancy,</u> that is <u>greater flexibility of mind,</u> and <u>can more readily vary and separate their ideas at pleasure.</u> The reason of that greater presence of mind which has been remarked in women is, that they are <u>less in the habit of speculating on what is best to be done, and the first suggestion is decisive. The writer of this article confesses that he never met with any woman who could reason, and with but one reasonable woman. There is no instance of a woman having been a great mathematician or metaphysician or poet or painter: but they can dance and sing and act and write novels and fall in love,</u> which last quality alone makes more than angels of them. <u>Women are no judges of the characters of men, except as men. They have no real respect for men, or they never respect them for those qualities, for which they are respected by men.</u> They in fact regard all such qualities as interfering with their <u>own pretensions,</u> and creating a jurisdiction different from their own. Women naturally wish to have their favourites all to themselves, and flatter their weaknesses to make them more dependent on their own good opinion, which, they think, is all they want. We have, indeed, seen instances of <u>men,</u> equally respectable and amiable, equally admired by the women and esteemed by the men, but <u>who have been ruined by an excess of virtues and accomplishments.</u>

9. They don't synthesize ideas but rather "separate" them. Does this mean they can't compare issues and see things only in isolation?

10. Women go with the first idea and don't reason through alternatives. Where is his evidence?

11. Oh, here's the proof: he's met only one reasonable woman.

12. Women have accomplished little. Falling in love is their greatest skill. The double-standard is in action; women are restricted to "noncognitive" activity. The most they can aspire to is performing arts and romance.

13. Women ruin men.

As these annotations illustrate, a reader approaching Hazlitt's text would have several questions and perhaps express surprise at Hazlitt's opinionated judgments. Your notes should, as the sample annotations do, reflect your reactions as the text progresses. Make sure you include any conclusions you have drawn as well as the questions that occur to you. The lines you underline or highlight and the places where the text makes statement of "fact" will help you identify the main ideas later.

### C. Outlining "Education of Women"

Go back to the statements you have underlined. Paraphrase and list them in numerical order, with supporting statements subsumed under key statements. Hazlitt's essay could be said to have the following key points, extrapolated from the underlining and written in outline form.

1. Classical education is not proper for women.

   a. Modern language study better suits their romances.

   b. Women have no interest in history.

2. Education is wasted on them.

   a. Women have no ideas.

   b. Women have no passion for truth.

   c. Women hate to think.

3. Women are what they are meant to be: frivolous and superficial.

   a. They are creatures of circumstance, sympathy, and habit.

   b. They can't form ideas of understanding or imagination.

   c. They lack principle.

   d. They have fancy and flexibility of mind.

   e. They can't synthesize ideas but see ideas separately.

   f. They take the first suggestion rather than speculate on what's best.

   g. Women can't reason.

4. There are no examples of great women thinkers.

5. Women are frivolous creatures.

    a. Women are able only to dance, sing, act, write novels, and fall in love.

    b. Women cannot judge character.

    c. Women don't respect men for qualities considered good in women themselves. (They're hypocrites.)

### D. Summarizing "Education of Women"

Read in this outline form, Hazlitt's essay is clearly an opinionated discussion of why women are not suited to education. Women are "born to" certain frivolous qualities of mind and behavior and lack the mental capacity to reason, particularly in any principled fashion. The outline of key points and supporting statements leads the reader rather pointedly to this conclusion. Though at first Hazlitt's essay seems a disjointed litany of complaints, a sequence of reasons becomes more apparent after annotating and outlining the essay. It also becomes clearer how much Hazlitt relies on "accepted" opinion and his own experience rather than demonstrable proof.

We have just undertaken previewing, annotating, outlining, and summarizing the elements of "Get the Facts Straight." Very often at the conclusion of this stage of critical reading, the reader begins to get a handle on the text. The remaining five strategies after "Get the Facts Straight" seem to flow readily and speedily. Let's apply these remaining five strategies to Hazlitt's "Education of Women."

## 2. Analyze the Argument

An analysis examines a whole as the sum of its parts. Another brief look at the outline of "Education of Women" reveals the parts of Hazlitt's argument. In short, women should not be educated because they lack the qualities education enhances. They lack the capacity to entertain ideas because they have no passion for truth and hate to think. Women are naturally predisposed to acting precipitously rather than thoughtfully, with the use of reasoning. Evidence for these statements may be found in the lack of female contributions to human knowledge. Women can "perform," write novels (a less-than-respectable literary endeavor in 1815), and fall in love, but can do little else. In short, things that require judgment are not suitable activities for women.

Hazlitt's essay has a rather simple argumentative structure. He asserts that women are not educable and then provides "reasons" why. Hazlitt's "reasons" are primarily opinions, offered without any backing except the assertion that women have achieved little. The essay concludes with a final comment on the ability of women to ruin men, chiefly through flattery.

Analysis reveals that Hazlitt's essay has little to offer in support of the opinion it presents. Further, its statements seem more an emotional outpouring than a reasonable explanation. (The careful reader will also make note of how difficult it is to view Hazlitt's remarks in an unprejudiced fashion. The twenty-first century reader will, in all probability, find his assertions a bit ridiculous.)

## 3. Identify Basic Features of Style

Stylistically, Hazlitt's essay may be described as a series of blunt statements followed by reflection on how the statement is manifested in his culture. Hazlitt draws on anecdotal support—his observations of the women of his day, a line from Milton, and his own knowledge of the absence of women's accomplishments. Hazlitt's essay seems a collection of accepted or common knowledge: he writes as though his "reasons" are generally agreed upon, undisputed statements of fact. This structure suggests that because something is widely believed, readers should accept it. In all probability, readers in 1815 did. Thus, the tone is both authoritative and perhaps a bit annoyed (with the problems women present).

Hazlitt's diction is largely straightforward, more plain than flowery. A few of the words and phrases he chooses have powerful or dramatic connotations, such as "pervert," "mere egoists," "perfect nonentity," "downright affectation," "hate to think," and "no passion for truth." But he relies largely on ordinary language and sentence structure. Only occasionally does he indulge in a syntactic permutation. For example, in the sentence "The writer of this article confesses that he never met with any woman who could reason, and with but one reasonable woman," Hazlitt shifts the modal verb "could reason" to the adjective "reasonable" with memorable effect. By and large, however, his sentences are simple declaratives, not difficult to read or interpret and not especially memorable stylistically.

## 4. Explore Your Personal Response

While nineteenth-century readers would probably have nodded in agreement as Hazlitt offered reasons why women shouldn't be educated, contemporary readers are probably surprised, dismayed, and perhaps even angry. Review your responses in the annotations to the text. They will help recreate your personal reactions and the causes for those reactions. Do not always expect to agree with, or even appreciate, a writer's point of view. You will find yourself disagreeing with texts rather regularly. The important thing is to be certain you can account for the sources and causes of your disagreement. Much of reader disagreement with Hazlitt's essay rests in what we would consider a more enlightened, modern perspective on the abilities of women. An awareness of historical context does help explain "Education of Women," but probably doesn't increase twenty-first-century sympathy for Hazlitt's position.

## 5. Evaluate the Text Overall and Determine Its Significance

Hazlitt's essay "Education of Women" was a product of early nineteenth-century sensibilities. Its chief significance today is as a representative voice of its time, an indicator of a social and intellectual climate much different from our own. As a citizen of the romantic period preceding the Victorian age, Hazlitt expresses an understanding of women that today we would deem, at the very least, incomplete.

## 6. Compare and Contrast Related Texts

A complete analysis of Hazlitt's essay would include a comparison of other essays of his, if available, on the subject of women and education. It would also be useful to examine other early nineteenth-century essays on this subject and, lastly, to contrast Hazlitt's essay with contemporary essays that argue for and against the education of women. Through such comparison, a more complete understanding of Hazlitt's essay is possible. On the Communication and Literacy Skills Test, you might be asked to contrast opposing (or similar) views on a single subject, but only within very narrow parameters. For instance, you might be questioned about two distinct styles used to approach the same subject and the resulting effects.

Although you may experience certain points of departure from the previous discussion, most skilled readers will agree, in general, with its broad conclusions. This is because the text has been kept in mind and referred to throughout the discussion. If you read attentively, that is, if you attend to the text carefully, you are much more likely to reflect judiciously upon it. Thus, the components of our good-reading definition—to read attentively, reflectively, and judiciously—are all present in the six broad strategies described and employed.

The very *active* reading strategies employed in Hazlitt's essay "Education of Women" can be used with any text to help you "re-create" it with optimal effectiveness. That is to say, you as a reader should be able to very closely approximate the original authorial intentions, as well as understand the general audience response and your more particular individual response. Remember to work with the six strategies in sequence.

# Drill 4

*Directions:* Read the passages and answer the questions that follow.

## Passage 1

1    We laymen have always been intensely curious to know—like the cardinal who put a similar question to Ariosto—from what sources that strange being, the creative writer, draws his material, and how he manages to make such an impression on us with it and to arouse in us emotions of which, perhaps, we

5    had not even thought ourselves capable. Our interest is only heightened the more by the fact that, if we ask him, the writer himself gives us no explanation, or none that is satisfactory, and it is not at all weakened by our knowledge that not even the clearest insight into the determinants of his choice of material and into the nature of the art of creating imaginative form will ever help to make

10   creative writers of us.

If we could at least discover in ourselves or in people like ourselves an activity which was in some way akin to creative writing! An examination of it would then give us a hope of obtaining the beginnings of an explanation of the creative work of writers. And, indeed, there is some prospect of this being possible.

15   After all, creative writers themselves like to lessen the distance between their kind and the common run of humanity; they so often assure us that every man is a poet at heart and that the last poet will not perish till the last man does.

Should we not look for the first traces of imaginative activity as early as in childhood? The child's best-loved and most intense occupation is with his play

20   or games. Might we not say that every child at play behaves like a creative writer, in that he creates a world of his own, or, rather, rearranges the things of his world in a new way which pleases him? It would be wrong to think he does not take that world seriously; on the contrary, he takes play very seriously and he expends large amounts of emotion on it. The opposite of play is not what is

25   serious but what is real. In spite of all the emotion with which he cathects his world of play, the child distinguishes it quite well from reality; and he likes to link his imagined objects and situations to the tangible and visible things of the real world. This linking is all that differentiates the child's "play" from "fantasying."

1. What is the effect of the speaker's use of "we"?

   (A) It separates the speaker and his or her colleagues from the reader.

   (B) It involves the reader in the search for, yet distinguishes him or her from, the creative writer.

   (C) It creates a royal and authoritative persona for the speaker.

   (D) It makes the speaker the stand-in for all men.

2. What is the antecedent of "it" (line 4)?

   (A) "explanation"        (C) "interest"

   (B) "fact"               (D) "impression"

3. Which one of the following statements would the speaker be most likely to DISAGREE with?

   (A) A layperson cannot become a creative writer by studying the writer's methods.

   (B) All men are writers at heart.

   (C) Creative writers are fundamentally different from nonwriters.

   (D) Children understand the distinction between imagination and reality.

4. "Cathects" (line 25) can best be defined as

   (A) constructs.          (C) fantasizes.

   (B) distances.           (D) discourages.

5. The structure of the passage can best be described as

   (A) an initial paragraph that introduces an idea and two paragraphs that digress from that idea.

   (B) a series of paragraphs that answer the questions with which they begin.

   (C) a series of questions ascending in their inability to be answered.

   (D) paragraphs whose brevity parallels their narrowness of inquiry.

6. It can be inferred that the speaker believes that creative writing is

(A) an opposite of childhood play.

(B) unrelated to childhood play.

(C) a continuation of childhood play.

(D) similar to the fantasizing of childhood play.

## Passage 2

1    Under the strange nebulous envelopment, wherein our Professor has now
shrouded himself, no doubt but his spiritual nature is nevertheless progressive, and growing: for how can the "Son of Time," in any case, stand still? We
behold him, through those dim years, in a state of crisis, of transition: his mad
5    Pilgrimings, and general solution into aimless Discontinuity, what is all this but
a mad Fermentation; wherefrom, the fiercer it is, the clearer product will one
day evolve itself.

Such transitions are ever full of pain: thus the Eagle when he moults is sickly;
and, to attain his new beak, must harshly dash-off the old one upon rocks.
10    What Stoicism soever our Wanderer, in his individual acts and motions, may
affect, it is clear that there is a hot fever of anarchy and misery raging within;
coruscations of which flash out: as, indeed, how could there be other? Have we
not seen him disappointed, bemocked of Destiny, through long years? All that
the young heart might desire and pray for has been denied; nay, as in the last
15    worst instance, offered and then snatched away. Ever an "excellent Passivity";
but of useful, reasonable Activity, essential to the former as Food to Hunger,
nothing granted: till at length, in this wild Pilgrimage, he must forcibly seize
for himself an Activity, though useless, unreasonable. Alas, his cup of bitterness,
which had been filling drop by drop, ever since that first "ruddy morning" in
20    the Hinterschlag Gymnasium, was at the very lip; and then with that poison
drop, of the Towngood-and-Blumine business, it runs over, and even hisses over
in a deluge of foam.

He himself says once, with more justice than originality: "Man is, properly
speaking, based upon Hope, he has no other possession but Hope; this world
25    of his is emphatically the Place of Hope." What, then, was our Professor's possession? We see him, for the present, quite shutout from Hope; looking not into
the golden orient, but vaguely all round into a dim copper firmament, pregnant
with earthquake and tornado.

7. All of the following name the main character of the passage EXCEPT

   (A) our Wanderer.          (C) he/him.

   (B) the Eagle.             (D) our Professor.

8. Which phrase best summarizes the speaker's intent in examining this stage of the main character's life?

   (A) "Such transitions are ever full of pain" (line 8)

   (B) "Have we not seen him disappointed, bemocked of Destiny, through long years?" (lines 12–13)

   (C) "there is a hot fever of anarchy and misery raging within" (line 11)

   (D) "what is all this but a mad Fermentation; wherefrom, the fiercer it is, the clearer product will one day evolve itself" (lines 5–7)

9. "Emphatically" (line 29) can best be defined as

   (A) surprisingly.          (C) originally.

   (B) unimportantly.         (D) unequivocally.

10. What is the function of the clause introduced by "nay" in line 14?

   (A) It negates the clause that precedes it.

   (B) It contradicts the clause that precedes it.

   (C) It intensifies the clause that precedes it.

   (D) It restates the clause that precedes it.

---

**Drill 4 Answers**

| | | | |
|---|---|---|---|
| 1. (B) | 4. (C) | 7. (B) | 10. (C) |
| 2. (C) | 5. (B) | 8. (D) | |
| 3. (C) | 6. (D) | 9. (D) | |

## Detailed Explanations of Answers

1. **(B)** The term "we" is used to separate the speaker and his or her audience from creative writers. Rather than to create "a royal and authoritative persona" (C), the speaker uses the term "we" to relate to ordinary people, or "laymen."

2. **(C)** The speaker is referring to "our interest," as shown at the beginning of the sentence (line 6).

3. **(C)** This statement is contradicted in the second paragraph, in which the speaker discusses his or her hopes of finding similarities between "people like ourselves" and creative writers.

4. **(A)** Cathects means "to construct." Children are not distanced or discouraged from play, and in lines 34-35 we are told that "child's play" is different from "fantasying."

5. **(B)** Choice (A) cannot be correct because the writer builds upon, rather than digresses from, the idea. Only one question is asked, and it is, at least partially, answered at the conclusion of the passage. Finally, the supporting paragraphs are in no way either brief or narrow.

6. **(D)** The speaker finds "the first traces of imaginative activity" in childhood play, making choices (A) and (B) incorrect. Creative writing is more than a continuation of childhood play (choice C); it is imagination without a link to the "real world"—fantasizing.

7. **(B)** The main character is repeatedly referred to as he/him. The use of the word "our" before "Wanderer" and "Professor" lets the reader know that "Wanderer" and "Professor" are two names given to the main character. The main character is compared to "the Eagle," but they are not the same person.

8. **(D)** The "Discontinuity" and "mad Fermentation" mentioned in this sentence imply the speaker's intentions for the rest of the passage.

9. **(D)** This answer can be determined from the context of the sentence: "…he has no other possession but Hope; this world of his is emphatically the Place of Hope." It must mean "undoubtedly," or "unequivocally."

10. **(C)** The audience is told that the main character's desires are not only denied, but are actually offered and then taken away. The word "nay" thus initiates the intensification of the situation.

---

Following is another reading passage. Remember to use the four activities discussed on pages 77–78 to "get the facts straight."

## Step 1: Preview

A preview of the reading passage will give you a purpose and a reason for reading; previewing is a good strategy to use in test-taking. Before beginning to read the passage (usually a four-minute activity if you preview and review), you should take about 30 seconds to look over the passage and questions. An effective way to preview the passage is to read quickly the first sentence of each paragraph, the concluding sentence of the passage, and the questions–but not the answers–following the passage. A passage is given below. Practice previewing the passage by reading the first sentence of each paragraph and the last line of the passage.

> That the area of obscenity and pornography is a difficult one for the Supreme Court is well documented. The Court's numerous attempts to define obscenity have proven unworkable; they left the decision to the subjective preferences of the justices. Perhaps Justice Stewart put it best when, after refusing to define obscenity, he declared, "But I know it when I see it." Does the Court literally have to see it to know it? Specifically, what role does the fact-pattern, including the materials' medium, play in the Court's decision?
>
> Several recent studies employ fact-pattern analysis in modeling the Court's decision making. These studies examine the fact-pattern or case characteristics, often with ideological and attitudinal factors, as a determinant of the decision reached by the Court. In broad terms, these studies owe their theoretical underpinnings to attitude theory. As the name suggests, attitude theory views the Court's attitudes as an explanation of its decisions.
>
> These attitudes, however, do not operate in a vacuum. As Spaeth explains, "the activation of an attitude involves both an object and the situation in which that object is encountered." The objects to which the court directs its attitudes are litigants. The situation—the subject matter of the case—can be defined in broad or narrow terms. One may define the situation as an entire area of the law (e.g., civil liberties issues). On an even broader scale the situation may be

defined as the decision to grant certiorari or whether to defect from a minimum-winning coalition.

Defining the situation with such broad strokes, however, does not allow one to control for case content. In many specific issue areas, the cases present strikingly similar patterns. In examining the Court's search and seizure decisions, Segal found that a relatively small number of situational and case characteristic variables explain a high proportion of the Court's decisions.

Despite Segal's success, verification of the applicability of fact-pattern analysis in other issue areas has been slow in forthcoming. Renewed interest in obscenity and pornography by federal and state governments, the academic community, and numerous antipornography interest groups indicates the Court's decisions in this area deserve closer examination.

The Court's obscenity and pornography decisions also present an opportunity to study the Court's behavior in an area where the Court has granted significant decision-making authority to the states. In *Miller v. California* (1973) the Court announced the importance of local community standards in obscenity determinations. The Court's subsequent behavior may suggest how the Court will react in other areas where it has chosen to defer to the states (e.g., abortion).

## Questions

1. The main idea of the passage is best stated in which of the following?

   (A) The Supreme Court has difficulty convicting those who violate obscenity laws.

   (B) The current definitions for obscenity and pornography provided by the Supreme Court are unworkable.

   (C) Fact-pattern analysis is insufficient for determining the attitude of the Court toward the issues of obscenity and pornography.

   (D) Despite the difficulties presented by fact-pattern analysis, Justice Segal found the solution in the patterns of search and seizure decisions.

2. The main purpose of the writer in this passage is to

   (A) convince the reader that the Supreme Court is making decisions about obscenity based on their subjective views only.

   (B) explain to the reader how fact-pattern analysis works with respect to cases of obscenity and pornography.

   (C) define obscenity and pornography for the layperson.

   (D) demonstrate the role fact-pattern analysis plays in determining the Supreme Court's attitude about cases in obscenity and pornography.

3. Of the following, which fact best supports the writer's contention that the Court's decisions in the areas of obscenity and pornography deserve closer scrutiny?

   (A) The fact that a Supreme Court Justice said, "I know it when I see it."

   (B) The fact that recent studies employ fact-pattern analysis in modeling the Court's decision-making process

   (C) The fact that attitudes do not operate in a vacuum

   (D) The fact that federal and state governments, interest groups, and the academic community show renewed interest in the obscenity and pornography decisions made by the Supreme Court

4. Among the following statements, which states an opinion rather than a fact expressed by the writer?

   (A) The area of obscenity and pornography is a difficult one for the Supreme Court and is well documented.

   (B) The objects to which a court directs its attitudes are the litigants.

   (C) In many specific issue areas, the cases present strikingly similar patterns.

   (D) The Court's subsequent behavior may suggest how the Court will react in other legal areas.

5. The list of topics below that best reflects the organization of the topics of the passage is

(A)  I.    The difficulties of the Supreme Court
     II.   Several recent studies
     III.  Spaeth's definition of "attitude"
     IV.   The similar patterns of cases
     V.    Other issue areas
     VI.   The case of *Miller v. California*

(B)  I.    The Supreme Court, obscenity, and fact-pattern analysis
     II.   Fact-pattern analyses and attitude theory
     III.  The definition of "attitude" for the Court
     IV.   The definition of "situation"
     V.    The breakdown in fact-pattern analysis
     VI.   Studying Court behavior

(C)  I.    Justice Stewart's view of pornography
     II.   Theoretical underpinnings
     III.  A minimum-winning coalition
     IV.   Search and seizure decisions
     V.    Renewed interest in obscenity and pornography
     VI.   The importance of local community standards

(D)  I.    The Court's numerous attempts to define obscenity
     II.   Case characteristics
     III.  The subject matter of cases
     IV.   The Court's proportion of decisions
     V.    Broad-based factors
     VI.   Obscenity determination

6. Which paragraph below is the best summary of the passage?

(A) The Supreme Court's decision-making process with respect to obscenity and pornography has become too subjective. Fact-pattern analyses, used to determine the overall attitude of the Court, reveal only broad-based attitudes on the part of the Court toward the situations of obscenity cases. These patterns cannot fully account for the Court's attitudes toward case content. Research is not conclusive that fact-pattern analyses work when applied to legal areas. Renewed public and local interest suggests continued study and close examination of how the Court makes decisions. Delegating authority to the states may reflect patterns for Court decisions in other socially sensitive areas.

(B)  Though subjective, the Supreme Court's decisions are well documented. Fact-pattern analyses reveal the attitude of the Supreme Court toward its decisions in cases. Spaeth explains that an attitude involves both an object and a situation. For the Court, the situation may be defined as the decision to grant certiorari. Cases present strikingly similar patterns, and a small number of variables explain a high proportion of the Court's decisions. Segal has made an effort to verify the applicability of fact-pattern analysis with some success. The Court's decisions on obscenity and pornography suggest weak Court behavior, such as in *Miller v. California*.

(C)  To determine what obscenity and pornography mean to the Supreme Court, we must use fact-pattern analysis. Fact-pattern analysis reveals the ideas that the Court uses to operate in a vacuum. The litigants and the subject matter of cases are defined in broad terms (such as an entire area of law) to reveal the Court's decision-making process. Search and seizure cases reveal strikingly similar patterns, leaving the Court open to grant certiorari effectively. Renewed public interest in the Court's decisions proves how the Court will react in the future.

(D)  Supreme Court decisions about pornography and obscenity are under examination and are out of control. The Court has to see the case to know it. Fact-pattern analyses reveal that the Court can only define cases in narrow terms, thus revealing individual egotism on the part of the Justices. As a result of strikingly similar patterns in search and seizure cases, the Court should be studied further for its weakness in delegating authority to state courts, as in the case of *Miller v. California*.

7.  Based on the passage, the rationale for fact-pattern analyses arises out of what theoretical groundwork?

(A)  Subjectivity theory

(B)  The study of cultural norms

(C)  Attitude theory

(D)  Cybernetics

8. Based on data in the passage, what would most likely be the major cause for the difficulty in pinning down the Supreme Court's attitude toward cases of obscenity and pornography?

(A) The personal opinions of the Court Justices

(B) The broad nature of the situations of the cases

(C) The ineffective logistics of certiorari

(D) The inability of the Court to resolve the variables presented by individual case content

9. In the context of the passage, *subjective* (Sentence 2) might be most nearly defined as

(A) personal.

(C) focused.

(B) wrong.

(D) objective.

By previewing the passage, you should have read the following:

- The fact that the area of obscenity and pornography is a difficult one for the Supreme Court is well documented.

- Several recent studies employ fact-pattern analysis in modeling the Court's decision making.

- These attitudes, however, do not operate in a vacuum.

- Defining the situation with such broad strokes, however, does not allow one to control for case content.

- Despite Segal's success, verification of the applicability of fact-pattern analysis in other issue areas has been slow in forthcoming.

- The Court's obscenity and pornography decisions also present an opportunity to study the Court's behavior in an area where the Court has granted significant decision-making authority to the states.

- The Court's subsequent behavior may suggest how the Court will react in other areas where it has chosen to defer to the states (e.g., abortion).

These few sentences tell you much about the entire passage.

As you begin to examine the passage, you should first determine the main idea and underline it so that you can easily refer to it if a question requires you to do so (see Question 1). The main idea should be found in the first paragraph of the passage and may even be the first sentence. From what you have read thus far, you know that the main idea of this passage is that the Supreme Court has difficulty in making obscenity and pornography decisions.

In addition, you know that recent studies have used fact-pattern analysis in modeling the Court's decisions. You have learned also that attitudes do not operate independently and that case content is important. The feasibility of using fact-pattern analysis in other issue areas has not been quickly verified. To study the behavior of the Court in an area in which they have granted significant decision-making authority to the states, one only has to consider the obscenity and pornography decisions. In summary, the author suggests that the Court's subsequent behavior may suggest how the Court will react in those other areas in which decision-making authority has previously been granted to the states. As you can see, having this information will make the reading of the passage much easier.

## Step 2: Annotate

After you preview, you will be ready to read actively. This means that as you read, you will be engaged in such things as underlining important words, topic sentences, main ideas, and words denoting tone of the passage.

Read carefully the first sentence of each paragraph since this often contains the topic of the paragraph. You may wish to underline each topic sentence.

During this stage, you should also determine the writer's purpose in writing the passage (see Question 2), as this will help you focus on the main points and the writer's key points in the organization of a passage. You can determine the author's purpose by asking yourself, "Does *the relationship* between the writer's main idea plus evidence the writer uses answer one of four questions?":

- What is the writer's overall primary goal or objective?

- Is the writer trying primarily to persuade you by proving or using facts to make a case for an idea?

- Is the writer trying primarily to inform and enlighten you about an idea, object, or event?

- Is the writer attempting primarily to amuse you? Keep you fascinated? Laughing?

Make sure you examine all of the facts that the author uses to support his or her main idea. This will allow you to decide whether the writer has made a case and what sort of purpose he or she supports. Look for supporting details–facts, examples, illustrations, the testimony or research of experts—that are about the topic in question and that *show* what the writer *says* is so. In fact, paragraphs and theses consist of *show* and *tell*. The writer *tells* you something is so or not so and then *shows* you facts, illustrations, expert testimony, or experience to back up what he or she says is or is not so. As you determine where the author's supporting details are, you may want to label them so that you can refer to them easily when answering questions.

## Step 3: Outline

There may not be enough time for you to write a detailed outline for this test. However, you can organize the key points and ideas by numbering them in the text.

As you read, you should note the structure of the passage. There are several common structures for passages, some of which are described below.

## Main Types of Paragraph Structures

1. The structure is a main idea plus supporting arguments (examples).

2. The structure includes comparisons or contrasts.

3. There is a pro and a con structure.

4. The structure is chronological.

5. The structure has several different aspects of one idea.

By understanding the *relationship* among the main point, transitions, and supporting information, you may more readily determine the structure of organization and the writer's purpose in a given piece of writing.

## Step 4: Summarize

After you finish annotating and outlining, take 10 or 20 seconds to look over the main idea, the topic sentences that you have underlined, and the key words and phrases you have marked. At this point you have gathered enough information from the passage to answer questions dealing with main idea, purpose, support, fact vs. opinion, organization, summarization, recall, cause and effect, and definition. Let's look again at these questions.

## Main Idea Questions

Looking back at the questions that follow the passage, you see that Question 1 is a "main idea" question. In answering the question, you see that answer choice (C) is correct. The writer uses the second, third, fourth, and fifth paragraphs to show how fact-pattern analysis is an ineffective determinant of the attitude of the Court toward obscenity and pornography.

Answer (A) is incorrect. Nothing is ever said directly about "convicting" persons accused of obscenity, only that the Court has difficulty defining it.

Choice (B) is also incorrect. Though it is stated as a fact by the writer, it is used only as an effect that leads the writer to examine how fact-pattern analysis does or does not work to reveal the "cause" or attitude of the Court toward obscenity and pornography.

Finally, answer choice (D) is incorrect. The statement is contrary to what Segal found when he examined search and seizure cases.

## Purpose Questions

In examining Question 2, you see that you must determine the author's purpose in writing the passage. Looking at the answer choices, you see that choice (D) is correct. Though the writer never states it directly, he or she summons data consistently to show that fact-pattern analysis gives us only part of the picture; it cannot account for the attitude toward individual cases.

Choice (A) is incorrect. The writer doesn't try to convince us of this fact but merely states it as an opinion resulting from the evidence derived from the "well-documented" background to the problem.

(B) is also incorrect. The writer does not just explain the role of fact-pattern analysis but rather shows how it cannot fully apply.

The passage is about the Court's difficulty in defining these terms rather than what the definition is. Nowhere do definitions for these terms appear. Therefore, choice (C) is incorrect.

## Support Questions

Question 3 requires you to analyze the author's supporting details. To answer this question, let's look at the answer choices. Choice (D) must be correct. In the fifth paragraph, the writer states that the "renewed interest"—a real and observable fact—from these groups "indicates the Court's decisions…deserve closer examination," which is another way of saying scrutiny.

Answer (A) is incorrect. The writer uses this remark to show how the Court cannot effectively define obscenity and pornography but must rely on "subjective preferences" to resolve issues.

In addition, choice (B) is incorrect because the writer points to the data in (D), not fact-pattern analyses, to prove this.

(C), too, is incorrect. Although the statement is true, the writer makes this point to show how fact-pattern analysis doesn't help clear up the real-world "situation" in which the Court must make its decisions.

## Fact vs. Opinion Questions

By examining Question 4, you can see that you are required to know the difference between fact and opinion. Keeping in mind that an opinion is something that cannot be proven to hold true in all circumstances, you can determine that choice (D) is correct. It is the only statement among the four for which the evidence is yet to be gathered. It is the writer's opinion that this may be a way to predict the Court's attitudes.

(A), (B), and (C) are all taken from data or documentation already in existence in the world and are, therefore, incorrect.

## Organization Questions

Question 5 asks you to organize given topics to reflect the organization of the passage. After examining all of the choices, you will determine that choice (B) is the correct response. These topical areas lead directly to the implied thesis that the "role" of fact-pattern analysis is insufficient for determining the attitude of the Supreme Court in the areas of obscenity and pornography.

Answer (A) is incorrect because the first topic stated in the list is not the topic of the first paragraph. It is too global. The first paragraph is about the difficulties the Court has with defining obscenity and how fact-pattern analysis might be used to determine the Court's attitude and clear up the problem.

(C) is incorrect because each of the items listed in this topic list is supporting evidence or data for the real topic of each paragraph. [See the list in (B) for correct topics.] For example, Justice Stewart's statement about pornography is cited only to indicate the nature of the problem with obscenity for the Court. It is not the focus of the paragraph itself.

Finally, (D) is incorrect. As with choice (C), these are all incidental pieces of information or data used to make broader points.

## Summarization Questions

To answer Question 6, you must be able to summarize the passage. The paragraph that best and most accurately reports what the writer demonstrated based on the implied thesis is answer choice (C).

Choice (A) is incorrect. While it reflects some of the evidence presented in the passage, the passage does not imply that all Court decisions are subjective, just the ones about pornography and obscenity.

Response (B) is also incorrect. The writer repeatedly summons information to show how fact-pattern analysis cannot pin down the Court's attitude toward case content. Similarly, the writer does not suggest that delegating authority to the states, as in *Miller v. California,* is a sign of some weakness, but merely that it is worthy of study as a tool for predicting or identifying the Court's attitude.

(D) is incorrect. Nowhere does the writer say or suggest that the justice system is "out of control" or that the justices are "egotists," only that they are liable to make "subjective" decisions rather than decisions based on an identifiable shared standard.

At this point, the three remaining question types (recall questions, cause/effect questions, and definition questions) must be discussed. (See numbers 7, 8, and 9 on pages 91 and 92).

## Recall Questions

To answer Question 7, you must be able to recall information from the passage. The easiest way to answer this question is to refer to the passage. In the second paragraph, the writer states that recent studies using fact-pattern analyses "owe their theoretical underpinnings to attitude theory." Therefore, we can conclude that response (C) is correct.

Answer choices (A), (B), and (D) are incorrect, as they are never discussed or mentioned by the writer.

## Cause/Effect Questions

Question 8 requires you to analyze a cause-and-effect relationship. Choice (D) is correct because it is precisely what fact-pattern analyses cannot resolve.

Response (A) is incorrect because no evidence is presented for this; it is stated that they do make personal decisions but not how these decisions cause difficulty.

Answer choice (B) is incorrect because this is one way in which fact-pattern analysis can be helpful.

Finally, (C) is only a statement about certiorari being difficult to administer, but this was never claimed by the writer.

## Definition Questions

In question 9, choice (A) is best. By noting the example of Justice Stewart, we can see that Justice Stewart's comment is not an example of right or wrong. (He doesn't talk about right or wrong. He uses the verb "know"–whose root points to *know*ledge, primarily understanding or insight, not ethical considerations.) He probably doesn't mean "focused" by this because the focus is provided by the appearance or instance of the case itself. By noting the same word ending and the appearance of the root "object"–meaning an observable thing existing outside of ourselves in time and space, and comparing it with the root of subjective, "subject"–often pointing to something personally studied, we can begin to rule out "objective" as perhaps the opposite of "subjective." Most of the time if we are talking about people's "preferences," we are talking about taste or quality. These preferences are usually not a result of scientific study or clear reasoning, but they arise out of a combination of personal taste and idiosyncratic intuitions. Thus, (A) becomes the best choice.

Answer (B) is incorrect. Nothing is implied or stated about the rightness or wrongness of the decisions themselves. Rather, it is the definition of obscenity that seems "unworkable."

(C) is incorrect because the Court's focus is already in place: on obscenity and pornography.

(D) is also incorrect. *Objective* is the direct opposite of *subjective*. Reasoning based on the object of study (objective) is the opposite of reasoning based upon the beliefs, opinions, or ideas of the one viewing the object (subjective).

You may not have been familiar with the word subjective, but from your understanding of the writer's intent you should have been able to figure out what he or she was after. Surrounding words and phrases almost always offer you some clues in determining the meaning of a word. In addition, any examples that appear in the text may also provide some hints.

## INTERPRETATION OF GRAPHIC INFORMATION QUESTIONS

Although graphs, charts, and tables may not play a large part on the Communication and Literacy Skills Test, you should be familiar with them. You will likely encounter at least one passage that is accompanied by some form of graphic information. You will then be required to answer any question(s) based on the information presented in the graph, chart, or table.

Graphs are used to produce visual aids for given sets of information. Often, the impact of numbers and statistics is diminished by an overabundance of tedious numbers. A graph helps a reader visualize rapid or irregular information, as well as trace long periods of decline or increase. The following is a guide to reading the three principal graphic forms that you may encounter when taking the Communication and Literacy Skills Test.

### Line Graphs

Line graphs, like the one that follows, are used to track two elements of one or more subjects. One element is usually a time factor, over whose span the other element increases, decreases, or fluctuates. The lines that make up such a graph are composed of connected points that follow the chart through each integral stage. For example, look at the following graph.

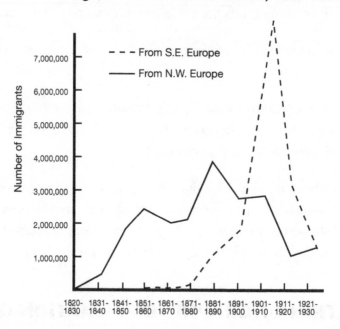

**Immigration to the United States, 1820–1930**

Source: U.S. Citizenship and Immigration Services, U.S. Department of Homeland Security

The average number of immigrants from 1820–1830 is represented at one point; the average number of immigrants from 1831–1840 is represented at the next. The line that connects these points is used only to ease the visual gradation between the points. It is not meant to give an accurate degree for every year between the two decades. If this were so, the line would hardly represent a straight, even progression from year to year. The sharp directness of the lines reveals otherwise. The purpose of the graph is to plot the average increases or decreases from point to point. When dealing with more than one subject, the line graph must use either different color lines or different types of lines. In the graph above, the continuous line represents immigration from northwestern Europe; the broken line represents immigration from southeastern Europe.

To read a line graph, find the point of change that interests you. For example, if you want to trace immigration from northwestern Europe from 1861–1870, you would find the position of the dark line on that point. Next, trace the position to the vertical information on the chart. In this instance, one would discover that approximately 2,000,000 immigrants arrived from northwestern Europe in the period of time from 1861–1870. If you wish to discover when the number of immigrants reached 4,000,000, you would read across from 4,000,000 on the vertical side of the graph and see that this number was reached in 1881–1890 from northwestern Europe and in 1891–1910 from southeastern Europe.

## Bar Graphs

Bar graphs are likewise used to plot two dynamic elements of a subject. However, unlike a line graph, the bar graph usually deals with only one subject. The other difference between a line graph and a bar graph is that a bar graph usually calls for a single element to be traced in terms of another, whereas a reader of a line graph usually plots either of the two elements with equal interest. For example, in the following bar graph, inflation and deflation are being marked over a span of years.

**INFLATION AND DEFLATION**

Inflation is a rise in the general level of prices.
Deflation is a decline in the general level of prices.

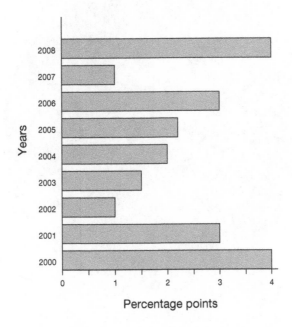

Percentage points are assigned to each year's level of prices, and that percentage decreases (deflation) from 2000 to 2002, and from 2006 to 2007. The price level is static from 2004 to 2005. The price level then increases (inflation) from 2007 to 2008. Therefore, it is obvious that the bar graph is read strictly in terms of the changes exhibited over a period of time. A line graph, conversely, is used to plot two dynamic elements of equal interest to the reader (e.g., either number of immigrants or the particular decade in question).

To read a bar graph, simply begin at the element at the base of a bar, and trace the bar its full length. Once reaching its length, cross-reference the other element of information that matches the length of the bar.

## Pie Charts

Pie charts differ greatly from line or bar graphs. Pie charts are used to help a reader visualize percentages of information with many elements to the subject. An entire "pie" represents 100% of a given quantity of information. The pie is then sliced into measurements that correspond to their respective shares of the whole. For example, in the following pie chart Heena's rent occupies a slice greater than any other in the pie, because no other element equals or exceeds 31% of Heena's monthly budget.

**HEENA'S MONTHLY BUDGET**

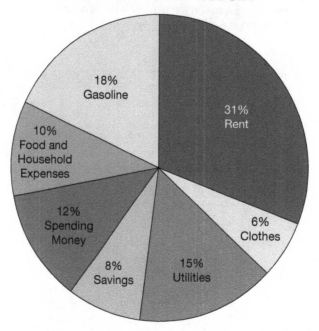

Another aspect of pie charts is that the smaller percentage elements are moved consecutively to the larger elements. Therefore, the largest element in the chart will necessarily be adjacent to the smallest element in the chart, and the line that separates them is the beginning or endpoint of the chart. From this point the chart fans out to the other elements of the chart, going from the smallest percentages to the largest.

To read a pie chart, choose the element of the subject that interests you, and compare its size to those of the other elements. In cases where the elements are similar in size, do not assume they are equal. The exact percentage of the element will be listed within that slice of the chart. For example, Heena's utilities, food and household, and spending money are all similar in size, but it is clear when reading the chart that each possesses a different value.

## Reading Tables

Tables such as the one below are useful because they relate to large bodies of information within a confined area. To read a table, cross index the headings that run horizontally across the top of the table with the headings that run vertically down the left side of the table. Scanning the table for the overall information within is usually done by reading line by line as if reading regular text, although with a table the reader is constantly referring to the appropriate headings at the top of the table to interpret the information listed.

| Summary of Plant Tissues | | |
|---|---|---|
| **Tissue** | **Location** | **Functions** |
| Epidermal | Root | Protection; Increases absorption area |
| | Stem | Protection; Reduces $H_2O$ loss |
| | Leaf | Protection; Reduces $H_2O$ loss; Regulates gas exchange |
| Parenchyma | Root, stem, leaf | Storage of food and $H_2O$ |
| Sclerenchyma | Stem and leaf | Support |
| Chlorenchyma | Leaf and young stems | Photosynthesis |
| Vascular a. Xylem | Root, stem, leaf | Upward transport of fluid |
| b. Phloem | Leaf, stem, root | Downward transport of fluid |
| Meristematic | Root and stem | Growth; Formation of xylem, phloem, and other tissues |

To use the table on the previous page, simply choose a particular plant tissue and then find the appropriate information needed about that tissue through the headings listed at the top of the table. For example, the one function of chlorenchyma tissue is photosynthesis.

## Helpful Hints

You should approach any graphic information you encounter as a key to a larger body of information in abbreviated form. Be sure to use the visual aids of the graphics (e.g., the size of slices on pie charts) as aids only; do not ignore the written information listed on the graph, table, etc. Note especially the title and headings so that you know exactly at what you are looking. Also, be aware of the source of the information, where applicable. Know what each element of the graphic information represents; this will help you compare how drastic or subtle any changes are, and over what span of time they take place. Be sure you realize what the actual numbers represent, whether they be dollars, thousands of people, millions of shares, etc. Finally, note the way in which the graphic information relates to the text it seeks to illustrate; know in what ways the graphic information supports the arguments of the author of the given passage.

## Drill 5

*Directions:* Read the passage and answer the questions that follow.

Immigration

The influx of immigrants that America had been experiencing slowed during the conflicts with France and England, but the flow increased between 1815 and 1837, when an economic downturn sharply reduced their numbers. Thus, the overall rise in population during these years was due more to incoming foreigners than to natural increase. Most of the newcomers were from Britain, Germany, and southern Ireland. The Germans usually fared best because they brought more money and more skills. Discrimination, primarily directed against the Catholics, was common in the job market. "Irish Need Not Apply" signs were common. However, the persistent labor shortage prevented the natives from totally excluding the foreign elements. These newcomers huddled in ethnic neighborhoods in the cities, or those who could moved out West to try their hands at farming.

In 1790, 5% of the U.S. population lived in cities of 2,500 or more. By 1860, that figure had risen to 25%. This rapid urbanization created an array of problems.

The rapid growth in urban areas was not matched by the growth of services. Clean water, trash removal, housing, and public transportation all lagged behind, and the wealthy got them first. Bad water and poor sanitation produced poor health, and epidemics of typhoid fever, typhus, and cholera were common. Police and fire protection were usually inadequate and the development of professional forces was resisted because of the cost and the potential for political patronage and corruption.

Rapid growth helped to produce a wave of violence in the cities. In New York City in 1834, the Democrats fought the Whigs with such vigor that the state militia was summoned. New York and Philadelphia witnessed race riots in mid-1830s, and a Charlestown, Massachusetts, mob sacked a Catholic convent in 1834. In the 1830s, 115 major incidents of mob violence were recorded. Street crime was common in all the major cities.

### SOURCES OF IMMIGRATION, 1820–1840

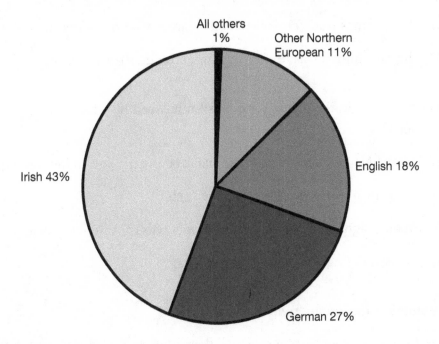

1. The author's purpose for writing this essay is

    (A) to bring to light the poor treatment of immigrants.

    (B) to show the violent effects of overpopulation.

    (C) to trace the relation of immigration to the problems of rapid urban growth.

    (D) to dissuade an active life in big cities.

2. Which of the following best defines the word *sacked* as it is used in the last paragraph?

    (A) Robbed

    (B) Carried

    (C) Trespassed on

    (D) Vandalized

3. Which of the following statements best summarizes the main idea of the fourth paragraph?

   (A) Racial tensions caused riots in New York City and Philadelphia.

   (B) The rapid growth in urban population sowed the seeds of violence in U.S. cities.

   (C) Street crimes were far worse in urban areas than race riots and political fights.

   (D) The state militia was responsible for curbing urban violence.

4. Ideas presented in the passage are most influenced by which of the following assumptions?

   (A) Urban life was more or less controllable before the flow of immigration in 1820.

   (B) The British had more skills than the Irish.

   (C) Ethnic neighborhoods had always been a part of American society.

   (D) France and England often held conflicts.

5. According to the graph, from 1820–1840

   (A) there were more Irish immigrants than all other nationalities combined.

   (B) the combined number of immigrants from England and Germany exceeded those from Ireland.

   (C) 1% of the immigrants were from Italy.

   (D) there was an equal number of English and German immigrants.

---

**Drill 5 Answers**

1.  (C)        3.  (B)        5.  (B)
2.  (D)        4.  (A)

## Detailed Explanations of Answers

1. **(C)** While the author does mention poor treatment (such as discrimination) and violence, those examples are used only as support for his or her purpose, which is to trace the relation of immigration to the problems of rapid urban growth. The author makes no attempt to dissuade an active life in big cities.

2. **(D)** Choices (A), (C), and (D) have similar meanings, but only "vandalized," choice (D), is a synonym of "sacked."

3. **(B)** Choices (A), (C), and (D) each account for only one issue. Choice (B) summarizes the problems discussed throughout the entire paragraph.

4. **(A)** The issues presented in this passage are not dependent on (B) the skill-level of immigrants, (C) the history of ethnic neighborhoods in America, or (D) conflict between France and England.

5. **(B)** Although this answer is not immediately clear from visually interpreting the graph, (B) is proven to be the correct answer when the numbers are added. The number of English and German immigrants at this time were 18% and 27%, respectively. The total from these two countries is 45%, 2% more than were from Ireland.

# MTEL Communication and Literacy Skills

## CHAPTER 3:
## Writing Subtest Review

# Writing Subtest Review

I. Written Mechanics

II. Grammar and Usage

III. Written Composition

## I. Written Mechanics

### SENTENCE ORDER AND SEQUENCE OF IDEAS IN A PARAGRAPH

The order of sentences within a paragraph is important. The sentences should be ordered so that the writer presents ideas logically and effectively. Several patterns of organizing sentences and ideas are available for the writer's use.

**Chronological Order** presents events in the order in which they occurred. This type of order is also called time order.

**Emphatic Order** moves from least important to most important or most important to least important. This type of order is also known as order of importance.

**Spatial Order** is used to describe a person, object, or place. This type of order is also called space order because the subject is being described from top to bottom or from left to right.

## Drill 1

*Directions:* Read the following sentences and determine the sequence you think would be best.

(1) The computer can be a great help in planning a trip. (2) The best routes to drive to the area are mapped for the traveler. (3) Once a traveler selects a destination, information about the area chosen is available. (4) The major attractions of the area are described. (5) Where to eat and sleep as well as the history of the area is provided. (6) Alternate routes for driving to the area can be the most rapid or the most scenic. (7) Sometimes discounts to special sites are offered in the form of computer print-outs. (8) The computer as a "travel agent" provides all of these services without cost.

### Drill 1 Answer

The recommended sequence of the sentences is 1, 3, 2, 6, 5, 4, 7, and 8.

## TRANSITIONS

As you review the passage a second time, look for and circle transitions that reveal the connections among the writer's ideas. Transitions show how the writer is reasoning to get to the point—perhaps it is a cause/effect pattern or a problem/solution discussion in which the writer provides the solution. He or she may use transitions either at the beginnings of paragraphs or to show connections among ideas within a single paragraph.

Here are some typical transitional words and phrases:

### Linking Similar Ideas

For explanation, analogy, and accruing factual evidence or opinions for a point of view.

| | | |
|---|---|---|
| again | besides | further |
| also | equally important | furthermore |
| and | for example | in addition |
| another | for instance | in like manner |

| | | |
|---|---|---|
| likewise | nor | similarly |
| moreover | of course | too |

EXAMPLE    Neither Emerson *nor* any of the others were real observers of the moral life.

## Linking Dissimilar/Contradictory Ideas

To show comparison or contrast among similar or opposing notions.

| | | |
|---|---|---|
| although | however | on the other hand |
| and yet | in spite of | otherwise |
| as if | instead | provided that |
| but | nevertheless | still |
| conversely | on the contrary | yet |

EXAMPLE    *Although* he did not mention Hawthorne by name, the reference was unmistakable.

## Indicating Cause, Purpose, or Result

Causes may be immediate or remote: The immediate cause for my spilling the glass of water was that I knocked it over with my hand. The remote cause might be that I was trying to put on my hat, and in the process I lost my focus on the glass of water in line with my sweeping hand, which was reaching for my hat across the table.

To show the solutions to a problem or the outcome of a certain series of causes.

| | | |
|---|---|---|
| as a result | for this reason | then |
| as for | hence | therefore |
| because | since | thus |
| consequently | so | |

EXAMPLE    *As a result* of the romantic movement, we have almost forgotten that poetry can deal with epistemology.

*distinguishes justified belief from opinion*

## Indicating Time or Position

Used in process and procedure explanations or chronological narratives to show a sequence in time or place.

| | | |
|---|---|---|
| above | before | meanwhile |
| across | beyond | next |
| afterward | eventually | presently |
| around | finally | second |
| at once | first | thereafter |
| at the present time | here | thereupon |

EXAMPLE    At first clearly symbolizing Hester's adulterousness, the scarlet letter *eventually* represents multiple meanings for the townspeople.

## Indicating an Example or Summary

Used to point to supporting evidence or explanatory material and to complete an idea within a paragraph or within a whole essay.

| | | |
|---|---|---|
| as a result | in any event | in other words |
| as I have said | in brief | in short |
| for example | in conclusion | on the whole |
| for instance | in fact | to sum up |
| in any case | | |

EXAMPLE    *In other words,* he must devise a structure that can combine the story of whaling, Ahab's tragedy, and his own speculations on human destiny.

# II. Grammar and Usage

The requirements for informal spoken English are far more relaxed than the rigid rules for what MTEL test administrators term "edited written English." The contents of this section on grammar and usage will help you master the Written Mechanics portion of the Communications and Literacy Skills Test. In this test section, the newest addition to the test, you will be called on to spot and correct spelling, capitalization, and punctuation errors. Other sections of the test will require you to deal with structural facets of grammar and usage, as covered in the pages that follow.

## WORD CHOICE SKILLS

### Denotative and Connotative Meanings

The *denotative* meaning of a word is its literal, dictionary definition: what the word denotes or "means." The *connotative* meaning of a word is what the word connotes or "suggests"; it is a meaning apart from what the word literally means. A writer should choose a word based on the tone and context of the sentence; this ensures that a word bears the appropriate connotation while still conveying some exactness in denotation. For example, a gift might be described as "cheap," but the directness of this word has a negative connotation—something cheap is something of little or no value. The word "inexpensive" has a more positive connotation, though "cheap" is a synonym for "inexpensive." Decisions of this type require you to determine the appropriateness of words and phrases for the context of a sentence.

### Wordiness and Conciseness

Effective writing is concise. Wordiness, on the other hand, decreases the clarity of expression by cluttering sentences with unnecessary words.

Effective writing demands that you avoid redundancies (unnecessary repetitions), circumlocution (failure to get to the point), and padding with loose synonyms.

Notice the difference in impact between the first and second sentences in the following pairs:

> **INCORRECT:** The medical exam that he gave me was entirely complete.

> **CORRECT:** The medical exam he gave me was complete.

INCORRECT: Larry asked his friend John, who was a good, old friend, if he would join him and go along with him to see the foreign film made in Japan.

CORRECT: Larry asked his good, old friend John if he would join him in seeing the Japanese film.

INCORRECT: I was absolutely, totally happy with the present that my parents gave to me at 7 A.M. on the morning of my birthday.

CORRECT: I was happy with the present my parents gave me on the morning of my birthday.

# Drill 2

*Directions:* Read each sentence and replace the underlined words with the appropriate answer.

1. His <u>principal</u> reasons for resigning were his <u>principles</u> of right and wrong.

   (A) principal . . . principals

   (B) principle . . . principals

   (C) principle . . . principles

   (D) No change is necessary.

2. The book tells about Alzheimer's disease—how it <u>affects</u> the patient and what <u>effect</u> it has on the patient's family.

   (A) effects . . . affect

   (B) affects . . . affect

   (C) effects . . . effects

   (D) No change is necessary.

3. The <u>amount</u> of homeless children we can help depends on the <u>number</u> of available shelters.

   (A) number . . . number

   (B) amount . . . amount

   (C) number . . . amount

   (D) No change is necessary.

4. All students are <u>suppose to</u> pass the test before <u>achieving</u> upper-division status.

    (A) supposing to . . . achieving

    (B) suppose to . . . being achieved

    (C) supposed to . . . achieving

    (D) No change is necessary.

5. The reason he <u>succeeded</u> is <u>because</u> he worked hard.

    (A) succeeded . . . that         (C) succede . . . because of

    (B) seceded . . . that           (D) No change is necessary.

---

***Directions:*** Select the sentence that clearly and effectively states the idea and has no structural errors.

6. (A) South of Richmond, the two roads converge together to form a single highway.

    (B) South of Richmond, the two roads converge together to form an interstate highway.

    (C) South of Richmond, the two roads converge to form an interstate highway.

    (D) South of Richmond, the two roads converge to form a single interstate highway.

7. (A) The student depended on his parents for financial support.

    (B) The student lacked the ways and means to pay for his room and board, so he depended on his parents for this kind of money and support.

    (C) The student lacked the ways and means or the wherewithal to support himself, so his parents provided him with the financial support he needed.

    (D) The student lacked the means to pay for his room and board, so he depended on his parents for financial support.

8. (A) Vincent van Gogh and Paul Gauguin were close personal friends and companions who enjoyed each other's company and frequently worked together on their artwork.

   (B) Vincent van Gogh and Paul Gauguin were friends who frequently painted together.

   (C) Vincent van Gogh was a close personal friend of Paul Gauguin's, and the two of them often worked together on their artwork because they enjoyed each other's company.

   (D) Vincent van Gogh, a close personal friend of Paul Gauguin's, often worked with him on their artwork.

9. (A) A college education often involves putting away childish thoughts, which are characteristic of youngsters, and concentrating on the future, which lies ahead.

   (B) A college education involves putting away childish thoughts, which are characteristic of youngsters, and concentrating on the future.

   (C) A college education involves putting away childish thoughts and concentrating on the future.

   (D) A college education involves putting away childish thoughts and concentrating on the future which lies ahead.

10. (A) I had the occasion to visit an Oriental pagoda while I was a tourist on vacation and visiting in Kyoto, Japan.

    (B) I visited a Japanese pagoda in Kyoto.

    (C) I had occasion to visit a pagoda when I was vacationing in Kyoto, Japan.

    (D) On my vacation, I visited a Japanese pagoda in Kyoto.

---

### Drill 2 Answers

| | | | | | | | |
|---|---|---|---|---|---|---|---|
| 1. | (D) | 4. | (C) | 7. | (A) | 10. | (B) |
| 2. | (D) | 5. | (A) | 8. | (B) | | |
| 3. | (A) | 6. | (C) | 9. | (C) | | |

## Grammatical Terms

In order to better understand the role of grammar in sentence structure, it is necessary to know and be able to define grammatical terms. For this reason, one section of the Communication and Literacy Skills Test will ask you to define selected grammatical terms. Study the following list of words and their definitions; knowledge of these terms will help you not only in this section but throughout the entire test.

**absolute phrase**—a phrase that is related to a sentence in meaning, though it has no grammatical relationship to the sentence

**abstract noun**—a noun that names a quality or mental concept; something intangible that exists only in our minds

**active voice sentence**—a sentence in which the subject performs the action

**adjective**—a word that describes or modifies a noun or pronoun

**adjective clause**—a clause that functions as an adjective and usually begins with a relative pronoun that is often omitted

**antecedent**—the noun, usually before the pronoun, that the pronoun replaces

**case**—groupings of nouns and pronouns that tell how the words in question are related to the other words used with them

**clause**—a group of related words containing both a subject and a predicate

**collective noun**—a noun that describes a group of people or things that are considered a single unit

**comma splice**—an incorrect sentence construction in which two independent clauses are fused together with a comma

**common noun**—a noun that does not name a specific person, place, thing, or idea

**comparative adjective**—compares two persons, places, things, or ideas

**complement**—a word often used to complete the meaning of an intransitive verb without receiving the intransitive verb's action and with copulative (linking) verbs to describe state of being

**compound sentence**—a sentence with at least two verbs and two subjects

**concrete noun**—a noun that names a member of a class; a group of people, places, or things that is physical, visible, and tangible

**conjunction**—a word that connects other words to each other

**countable noun**—a noun that can be made plural via changing the ending, usually by adding "s"

**declarative statement**—a sentence that makes a statement

**demonstrative pronoun**—a pronoun that points to or identifies a noun without explicitly naming it

**dependent clause**—a group of connected words that have both a predicate and a subject but still cannot stand alone

**direct object**—a word that receives a direct action from the subject of a sentence

**elliptical clause**—an instance in which clause elements are omitted if the context makes clear what is being indicated

**exclamatory statement**—a sentence that communicates a strong emotion or surprise

**first person**—indicates an "I" or "we" as the subject of the sentence

**future tense**—an expression of action that takes place in a time to follow the present

**idiom**—an expression that is characteristic of a particular language

**imperative**—a verb used as a command

**imperative statement**—a sentence that makes a command

**indefinite pronoun**—a pronoun that has an unknown or ambiguous antecedent

**independent (or main) clause**—a clause that can stand by itself as a simple sentence

**indicative mood**—a verb used to state a fact or ask a question

**indirect object**—a word that receives the action of the subject of the sentence indirectly

**infinitive**—the basic form of the verb, usually preceded by the preposition "to"

**interjection**—used to express strong emotion or surprise

**interrogative pronoun**—a pronoun that poses a question

**interrogative statement**—a sentence that asks a question

**intransitive verb**—a verb that does not take an object

**misplaced modifier**—a modifier that is not placed near the word it modifies

**mood**—indicates the tone of a verb

*nominal* **of a sentence**—a word or group of words that can function as a noun

**nominative case**—when a noun or pronoun is the subject of the verb

**noncountable noun**—a noun that cannot be made plural via changing the ending, usually by adding "s"

**noun**—a person, place, thing, animal, action, or quality

**noun compound**—a group of words (usually two) that functions as a single part of speech

*object* **of the preposition**—the noun after the preposition

**objective case**—when a noun or pronoun is used as the direct object, indirect object, or object of a preposition

**participial phrase**—a phrase that contains a participle and its modifiers, which is used as an adjective to modify a noun or pronoun

**passive voice sentence**—a sentence in which the subject receives the action

**past tense**—an expression of action that is completed at a definite moment before the present

**person**—indicates who is speaking and whether the subject is singular or plural

**personal pronoun**—a pronoun that refers to beings and objects. The basic personal pronouns are *I, you, he, she, we, they*

**phrase**—a group of connected words without a subject or predicate

**positive adjective**—describes a noun or pronoun on its own terms, without comparing it to anything else

**possessive case**—a noun or pronoun used to show ownership

**predicate**—the action of the sentence or what is said about the subject

**preposition**—a word that demonstrates the relationship between its object and another word in the sentence

**prepositional phrase**—a phrase that begins with a preposition and contains a noun and its modifiers

**present tense**—an expression of action that goes on in the current time or with regularity

**pronoun**—a word that replaces a noun

**proper noun**—the official name of a particular person, place, or thing

**regular verb**—a verb that forms the past tense by adding "ed" to the basic verb

**relative pronoun**—a pronoun that relates one part of a sentence to a word in another part of the sentence

**run-on sentence**—two complete sentences totally fused

**second person**—indicates a "you" singular or "you" plural as the subject of the sentence

**sentence**—a group of words that contains a subject and a predicate and ends with a period, exclamation point, or question mark

**sentence fragment**—part of a sentence; usually missing a predicate or a subject

**split infinitive**—an instance in which the words that make up an infinitive are separated by one or more words

**subject of the sentence**—the part of a sentence about which something is said

**subjunctive**—an uncommon construction used to express with exactitude how a verb usage is to be interpreted

**superlative**—compares three or more persons, places, or things

**third person**—indicates "he," "she," "it," or "they" as the subject of the sentence

**transitive verb**—a verb that takes an object to complete its meaning

**verb**—a word showing action or state of being

# SENTENCE STRUCTURE SKILLS

## Parallelism

Parallel structure is used to express matching ideas. It refers to the grammatical balance of a series of any of the following:

## Phrases:

The squirrel ran *along the fence, up the tree,* and *into his burrow* with a mouthful of acorns.

## Adjectives:

The job market is flooded with *very talented, highly motivated,* and *well-educated* young people.

## Nouns:

You will need a *notebook, pencil,* and *dictionary* for the test.

## Clauses:

The children were told to decide *which toy they would keep* and *which toy they would give away.*

## Verbs:

The farmer *plowed, planted,* and *harvested* his corn in record time.

## Verbals:

*Reading, writing,* and *calculating* are fundamental skills that all of us should possess.

## Correlative Conjunctions:

*Either* you will do your homework *or* you will fail.

## Repetition of Structural Signals:

Structural signals include articles, auxiliaries, prepositions, and conjunctions.

> **INCORRECT:** I have quit my job, enrolled in school, and am looking for a reliable babysitter.

> **CORRECT:** I *have quit* my job, *have enrolled* in school, and *am looking* for a reliable babysitter.

Note: Repetition of prepositions is considered formal and is unnecessary.

> You can travel *by car, by plane, or by train*; it's all up to you.

> **OR**

> You can travel *by car, plane, or train*; it's all up to you.

When a sentence contains items in a series, check for both punctuation and sentence balance. When you check for punctuation, make sure the commas are used correctly. When you check for parallelism, make sure that the conjunctions connect similar grammatical constructions, such as all adjectives or all clauses.

## Misplaced and Dangling Modifiers

A misplaced modifier is one that is in the wrong place in the sentence. Misplaced modifiers come in all forms—words, phrases, and clauses. Sentences containing misplaced modifiers are often very comical: *Mom made me eat the spinach instead of my brother.* Misplaced modifiers, like the one in this sentence, are usually too far away from the word or words they modify. This sentence should read: *Mom made me, instead of my brother, eat the spinach.*

Modifiers like *only*, *nearly*, and *almost* should be placed next to the word they modify and not in front of some other word, especially a verb, that they are not intended to modify.

A modifier is misplaced if it appears to modify the wrong part of the sentence or if we cannot be certain what part of the sentence the writer intended it to modify. To correct a misplaced modifier, move the modifier next to the word it describes.

> **INCORRECT:** She served hamburgers to the men on paper plates.
>
> **CORRECT:** She served hamburgers on paper plates to the men.

Split infinitives also result in misplaced modifiers. Infinitives consist of the marker *to* plus the plain form of the verb. The two parts of the infinitive make up a grammatical unit that should not be split. Splitting an infinitive is placing an adverb between the *to* and the verb.

> **INCORRECT:** The weather service expects temperatures to not rise.
>
> **CORRECT:** The weather service expects temperatures not to rise.

Sometimes a split infinitive may be natural and preferable, and though it may still bother some readers, it has become acceptable in formal writing.

> **EXAMPLE** Several U.S. industries expect *to* more than *triple* their use of robots within the next decade.

A squinting modifier is one that may refer to either a preceding or a following word, leaving the reader uncertain about what it is intended to modify. Correct a squinting modifier by moving it next to the word it is intended to modify.

> **INCORRECT:** Snipers who fired on the soldiers often escaped capture.
>
> **CORRECT:** Snipers who often fired on the soldiers escaped capture.
>
> **OR** Snipers who fired on the soldiers escaped capture often.

A dangling modifier is a modifier or verb in search of a subject: the modifying phrase (usually an *-ing* word group, an *-ed* or *-en* word group, or a *to + a verb* word group—participle phrase or infinitive phrase respectively) either appears to modify the wrong word or has nothing to modify. It is literally dangling at the beginning or the end of a sentence. The sentences often look and sound correct: *To be a student government officer, your grades must be above average.* (However, the verbal modifier has nothing to describe. Who is *to be* *a student government officer?* Your grades?) Questions of this type require you to determine whether a modifier has a headword or whether it is dangling at the beginning or the end of the sentence.

To correct a dangling modifier, reword the sentence by either: 1) changing the modifying phrase to a clause with a subject or 2) changing the subject of the sentence to the word that should be modified. The following are examples of a dangling participle and a dangling infinitive:

INCORRECT: Shortly after leaving home, the accident occurred.

Who is <u>leaving home</u>, the accident?

CORRECT: Shortly after we left home, the accident occurred.

---

INCORRECT: To get up on time, a great effort was needed.

<u>To get up</u> needs a subject.

CORRECT: To get up on time, I made a great effort.

## Fragments

A fragment is an incomplete construction that may or may not have a subject and a verb. Specifically, a fragment is a group of words pretending to be a sentence. Not all fragments appear as separate sentences, however. Often, fragments are separated by semicolons.

INCORRECT: Traffic was stalled for ten miles on the freeway. Because repairs were being made on potholes.

CORRECT: Traffic was stalled for ten miles on the freeway because repairs were being made on potholes.

---

INCORRECT: It was a funny story; one that I had never heard before.

CORRECT: It was a funny story, one that I had never heard before.

## Run-on/Fused Sentences

A run-on/fused sentence is not necessarily a long sentence or a sentence that the reader considers too long; in fact, a run-on may be two short sentences: *Dry ice does not melt it evaporates*. A run-on results when the writer fuses or runs together two separate sentences without using any correct mark of punctuation to separate them.

INCORRECT: **Knowing how to use a dictionary is no problem each dictionary has a section in the front of the book telling how to use it.**

CORRECT: **Knowing how to use a dictionary is no problem. Each dictionary has a section in the front of the book telling how to use it.**

Even if one or both of the fused sentences contains internal punctuation, the sentence is still a run-on.

INCORRECT: **Bob bought dress shoes, a suit, and a nice shirt he needed them for his sister's wedding.**

CORRECT: **Bob bought dress shoes, a suit, and a nice shirt. He needed them for his sister's wedding.**

## Comma Splices

A comma splice is the unjustifiable use of only a comma to combine what really is two separate sentences.

INCORRECT: **One common error in writing is incorrect spelling, the other is the occasional use of faulty diction.**

CORRECT: **One common error in writing is incorrect spelling; the other is the occasional use of faulty diction.**

Both run-on sentences and comma splices may be corrected in one of the following ways:

RUN-ON: **Neal won the award he had the highest score.**

COMMA SPLICE: **Neal won the award, he had the highest score.**

Separate the sentences with a period:

**Neal won the award. He had the highest score.**

Separate the sentences with a comma and a coordinating conjunction such as *and, but, or, nor, for, yet,* or *so:*

**Neal won the award, for he had the highest score.**

Separate the sentences with a semicolon:

**Neal won the award; he had the highest score.**

Separate the sentences with a subordinating conjunction such as *although, because, since,* or *if*:

**Neal won the award because he had the highest score.**

## Subordination, Coordination, and Predication

Suppose, for the sake of clarity, you wanted to combine the information in these two sentences to create one statement:

**I studied a foreign language. I found English quite easy.**

How you decide to combine this information should be determined by the relationship you'd like to show between the two facts. *I studied a foreign language, and I found English quite easy* seems rather illogical. The **coordination** of the two ideas (connecting them with the coordinating conjunction *and*) is ineffective. Using **subordination** instead (connecting the sentences with a subordinating conjunction) clearly shows the degree of relative importance between the expressed ideas:

**After I studied a foreign language, I found English quite easy.**

When using a conjunction, be sure that the sentence parts you are joining are in agreement.

**INCORRECT:** She loved him dearly but not his dog.

**CORRECT:** She loved him dearly, but she did not love his dog.

A common mistake that is made is to forget that each member of the pair must be followed by the same kind of construction.

INCORRECT: They complimented them both for their bravery and they thanked them for their kindness.

CORRECT: They both complimented them for their bravery and thanked them for their kindness.

*While* refers to time and should not be used as a substitute for *although*, *and*, or *but*.

INCORRECT: While I'm usually interested in Fellini movies, I'd rather not go tonight.

CORRECT: Although I'm usually interested in Fellini movies, I'd rather not go tonight.

*Where* refers to a place and should not be used as a substitute for *that*.

INCORRECT: We read in the paper where they are making great strides in DNA research.

CORRECT: We read in the paper that they are making great strides in DNA research.

After words like *reason* and *explanation*, use *that*, not *because*.

INCORRECT: His explanation for his tardiness was because his alarm did not go off.

CORRECT: His explanation for his tardiness was that his alarm did not go off.

# Drill 3

***Directions:*** Select the sentence that clearly and effectively states the idea and has no structural errors.

1. (A) Many gases are invisible, odorless, and they have no taste.

   (B) Many gases are invisible, odorless, and have no taste.

   (C) Many gases are invisible, odorless, and tasteless.

2. (A) Everyone agreed that she had neither the voice or the skill to be a speaker.

   (B) Everyone agreed that she had neither the voice nor the skill to be a speaker.

   (C) Everyone agreed that she had either the voice nor the skill to be a speaker.

3. (A) The mayor will be remembered because he kept his campaign promises and because of his refusal to accept political favors.

   (B) The mayor will be remembered because he kept his campaign promises and because he refused to accept political favors.

   (C) The mayor will be remembered because of his refusal to accept political favors and he kept his campaign promises.

4. (A) While taking a shower, the doorbell rang.

   (B) While I was taking a shower, the doorbell rang.

   (C) While taking a shower, someone rang the doorbell.

5. (A) He swung the bat while the runner stole second base.

   (B) The runner stole second base while he swung the bat.

   (C) While he was swinging the bat, the runner stole second base.

---

**Directions:** Choose the correct replacement for the underlined words.

6. Nothing grows as well in Mississippi as <u>cotton. Cotton</u> being the state's principal crop.

   (A) cotton, this          (C) cotton cotton

   (B) cotton; cotton         (D) No change is necessary.

7. It was a heartwrenching <u>movie; one</u> that I had never seen before.

   (A) movie and

   (B) movie, one

   (C) movie. One

   (D) No change is necessary.

8. Traffic was stalled for three miles on the <u>bridge. Because</u> repairs were being made.

   (A) bridge because

   (B) bridge; because

   (C) bridge, because

   (D) No change is necessary.

9. The ability to write complete sentences comes with <u>practice writing</u> run-on sentences seems to occur naturally.

   (A) practice, writing

   (B) practice. Writing

   (C) practice and

   (D) No change is necessary.

10. Even though she had taken French classes, she could not understand native French <u>speakers they</u> all spoke too fast.

   (A) speakers, they

   (B) speakers. They

   (C) speaking

   (D) No change is necessary.

---

**Drill 3 Answers**

| | | | |
|---|---|---|---|
| 1. (C) | 4. (B) | 7. (B) | 10. (B) |
| 2. (B) | 5. (A) | 8. (A) | |
| 3. (B) | 6. (A) | 9. (B) | |

# EFFECTIVE USE OF NEGATIVES IN A SENTENCE

The use of negative words and phrases in forming effective sentences falls into two categories: the avoidance of common nonstandard uses of negative words and the use of negative wording to achieve a special purpose in a sentence.

## Common nonstandard negative expressions

The most common error in forming sentences with negative words and phrases is the use of a *double negative*, or two negative terms used for the same purpose. A double negative is nonstandard English. The following are examples of double negatives:

1. The adverbs, such as *never* and *nowhere*, combined with a verb and the negative word *not* to form a contraction.

   INCORRECT:   Marty *don't never* listen to all of the directions before he starts a project.

   CORRECT:   Marty *doesn't ever* listen to all of the directions before he starts a project.

   Marty *never* listens to all of the directions before he starts a project.

   The sentences are made correct by removing one of the negative words.

2. The pronouns, such as *no one, none, nobody, nothing,* or *neither,* combined with a verb and the negative word *not* to form a contraction.

   INCORRECT:   We *don't* know *nobody* who can do the task.

   CORRECT:   We *don't* know *anybody* who can do the task.

   We know *nobody* who can do the task.

   The sentences are made correct by removing one of the negative words.

3. The words *hardly, scarcely,* or *barely* combined with a verb and the negative word *not* to form a contraction.

> **INCORRECT:** Surely the hot temperature *can't hardly* last much longer.

> **CORRECT:** Surely the hot temperature *can't* last much longer.

> Surely the hot temperature *can hardly* last much longer.

The sentence is made correct in the second example by changing the first negative (*can't*) to a positive (*can*).

> **INCORRECT:** The travelers became lost when they *couldn't barely* see the road.

> **CORRECT:** The travelers became lost when they *could barely* see the road.

> The travelers became lost when they *couldn't* see the road.

The sentence is made correct by removing one of the negative words.

4. The words *only* or *but* combined with a verb and the negative word *not.*

> **INCORRECT:** The astronaut *can't help but try* to avert the accident.

> **CORRECT:** The astronaut *can't help trying* to avert the accident

> The astronaut *must try* to avert the accident.

The sentence is made correct by removing the word *but* and changing the negative to a positive.

## Drill 4

*Directions:* Underline the double negative in the following sentences.

1. The neighbors didn't see nobody parked in the driveway.

2. A series of thunderstorms can't help but bring relief after the long drought.

3. Neither of the programs won't be held at a time when most of us can attend.

4. Listening for the doorbell, Irene don't never fall alseep.

5. The science lesson can't barely cover all of the material in the assignment.

6. A few witnesses didn't give no possible cause for the accident.

7. The students in the class don't like no change in the daily routine.

8. The club members do not allow no one to be late to a meeting.

9. The principal can't do nothing about the required fire drills.

10. The Broadway play doesn't have no more tickets for tonight's performance.

## Drill 4 Answers

1. The neighbors <u>didn't</u> see <u>nobody</u> parked in the driveway.

2. A series of thunderstorms <u>can't</u> help <u>but</u> bring relief after the long drought.

3. <u>Neither</u> of the programs <u>won't</u> be held at a time when most of us can attend.

4.  Listening for the doorbell, Irene <u>don't never</u> fall alseep.

5.  The science lesson <u>can't barely</u> cover all of the material in the assignment.

6.  A few witnesses <u>didn't</u> give <u>no</u> possible cause for the accident.

7.  The students in the class <u>don't</u> like <u>no</u> change in the daily routine.

8.  The club members do <u>not</u> allow <u>no</u> one to be late to a meeting.

9.  The principal <u>can't</u> do <u>nothing</u> about the required fire drills.

10.  The Broadway play <u>doesn't</u> have <u>no</u> more tickets for tonight's performance.

## Effective negative wording for sentence variety

Some special sentence structures using negative wording can be quite effective. Of course, no double negative expressions occur in these sentence patterns.

1.  Provide a definition by giving examples of what a term is not.

EXAMPLE   The speaker's special technique of appealing to his audience—*not* by using meaningless examples, *not* by providing boring details, *not* by trying to impress with his experience—centered on his awareness of their interests and career goals.

2.  Use a series of negative introductory phrases.

EXAMPLE   *Never* late to class, *never* poorly prepared for the day's lesson, *never* unresponsive to his students' interests, the teacher easily involved them in the class focus.

3. Use two or more negatives that do not create a double negative within the sentence because each refers to a separate verb or serves another purpose in the sentence.

**EXAMPLES**   A loud chorus of *nays* indicated the senators did *not* favor the amendment.

(*Nays* is a noun, the subject of *indicated; did not favor* is a verb, the predicate of the noun *senators*.)

*Never* resisting the array of desserts, Joey could *not* lose weight.

(*Never resisting* is a participial phrase modifying the subject *Joey; could not lose* is the predicate verb of *Joey*.)

A problem *never* before encountered did *not* interfere with the results of the race.

(The participial phrase *never before encountered* describes *problem; did not interfere* is the predicate verb for the subject *problem*.)

# VERBS

## Verb Forms

This section covers the principal parts of some irregular verbs including *lie* and *lay*. The use of regular verbs like *look* and *receive* poses no real problem to most writers because the past and past participle forms end in *-ed*; it is the irregular forms that pose the most serious problems—for example, *seen*, *written*, and *begun*.

## Regular Verbs

Regular verbs form the past tense by adding -ed to the present tense.

| Present | Past | Past Perfect |
|---------|------|--------------|
| walk | walked | had walked |
| study | studied | had studied |

**EXAMPLES**   I *walk* to school.

Yesterday, I *walked* to the store.

Yesterday I *had walked* to school before I *walked* to the store.

## Irregular Verbs

Irregular verbs form the past tense in a number of different ways. Many commonly used verbs are irregular, such as the verb *to be*.

| Present | Past | Past Perfect |
|---------|------|--------------|
| am | was | had been |
| begin | began | had begun |
| choose | chose | had chosen |
| drink | drank | had drunk |
| see | saw | had seen |
| write | wrote | had written |

The commonly used verbs above are probably familiar to you. Most errors in usage result from a confusion of the past and past perfect forms.

**EXAMPLES**   She *sees* stars.

We *saw* a new film.

After we *had seen* the film, we *went* out to dinner.

---

I *drink* eight glasses of water a day.

Yesterday I *drank* ten glasses of Perrier.

After I *had drunk* ten glasses of water, I *was* no longer thirsty.

## Transitive and Intransitive Verbs

The verbs *lay* and *lie*, *set* and *sit*, and *raise* and *rise* are often confused. This is probably because the verbs in each pair have similar meanings; however, one takes a direct object (transitive) to complete its meaning, and the other stands alone (intransitive). Some of the verbs are regular and some irregular. The only way to be sure to use them correctly is to memorize them. The present progressive tense is also given below because students often find this form confusing as well. (The present progressive tense signals an ongoing action in the present.)

| Present | Past | Past Perfect | Present Progressive |
|---|---|---|---|
| lay (to place something) | laid | had laid | is laying |
| lie (to rest) | lay | had lain | is lying |

**to lay** (transitive)

Please *lay* the books on the table.

She is *laying* the table for dinner.

He *laid* the books on the floor.

After he *had laid* the books on the floor, he *was told* to clean his room.

**to lie** (intransitive)

Go *lie* down.

Whose books *are lying* on the floor?

His books *lay* on the floor all day.

After the books *had lain* on the floor all day, he *picked* them up.

| Present | Past | Past Perfect |
|---|---|---|
| set (to place something) | set | had set |
| sit (to be seated) | sat | had sat |

**to set** (transitive)

Just *set* that down anywhere.

I *set* the table yesterday.

Because I *had set* the table, you *had to do* the dishes.

**to sit** (intransitive)

Please *sit* down.

They *sat* down to dinner.

After they *had sat* down to dinner, they *realized* that the glasses were not crystal clear.

| Present | Past | Past Perfect |
|---|---|---|
| raise (to move something to a higher position) | raised | had raised |
| rise (to stand up, to ascend) | rose | had risen |

---

**to raise** (transitive)

I *raise* the flag every morning.

I *raised* my hand in class yesterday.

After I *had raised* my hand, the teacher *called* on me.

---

**to rise** (intransitive)

I *rise* at eight.

The price of milk *rose* by eight percent last year.

After the dough *had risen*, I *baked* it.

Remember: *Lay, set,* and *raise* are transitive verbs. They transfer their action to an object, which is present in the sentence. *Lie, sit,* and *rise* are intransitive verbs. Their action is limited to the subject of the sentence.

## Verb Tenses

Tense sequence indicates a logical time sequence.

## Use Present Tense

in statements about the present:

I *am* tired.

in statements about habitual conditions:

I *go* to bed at 10:30 *every night.*

in statements of universal truth:

> I learned that the sun *is* 90 million miles from the earth.

in statements about the contents of literature and other published works:

> In this book, Sandy *becomes* a nun and *writes* a book on psychology.

## Use Past Tense

in statements of the finished past:

> He *wrote* his first book in 1949, and it *was published* in 1952.

## Use Future Tense

in statements to indicate an action or condition expected in the future:

> I *will graduate* next year.

## Use Present Perfect Tense

for an action that began in the past but continues into the future:

> I *have lived* here all my life.

## Use Past Perfect Tense

for an earlier action that is mentioned in a later action:

> Cindy ate the apple that she *had picked.*

(First she picked it; then she ate it.)

## Use Future Perfect Tense

for an action that will have been completed at a specific future time:

> By May, I *shall have graduated.*

## Use a Present Participle

for action that occurs at the same time as the verb:

*Speeding* **down the interstate, I saw a cop's flashing lights.**

## Use a Perfect Participle

for action that occurred before the main verb:

*Having read* **the directions, I started the test.**

## Use the Subjunctive Mood

to express a wish or state a condition contrary to fact:

*If it were not raining,* **we could have a picnic.**

in *that* clauses after verbs like *request, recommend, suggest, ask, require*, and *insist* and after such expressions as *it is important* and *it is necessary*:

**It is necessary that all papers** *be submitted* **on time.**

# SUBJECT-VERB AGREEMENT

Agreement is the grammatical correspondence between the subject and the verb of a sentence: *I do; we do; you do; they do; he, she, it does.*

Every English verb has five forms, two of which are the bare form (plural) and the *-s* form (singular). Usually, singular verb forms end in *-s;* plural forms do not.

## Rules Governing Subject-Verb Agreement

A verb must agree with its subject, not with any additive phrase in the sentence such as a prepositional or verbal phrase. Ignore such phrases.

**Your** *copy* **of the rules** *is* **on the desk.**

**Ms. Craig's** *record* **of community service and outstanding teaching** *qualifies* **her for a promotion.**

In an inverted sentence beginning with a prepositional phrase, the verb still agrees with its subject.

> **At the end of the summer** *come* **the best** *sales*.

> **Under the house** *are* **some old Mason** *jars*.

Prepositional phrases beginning with compound prepositions such as *along with, together with, in addition to,* and *as well as* should be ignored because they do not affect subject-verb agreement.

> *Gladys Knight,* **as well as the Pips,** *is* **riding the midnight train to Georgia.**

A verb must agree with its subject, not its subject complement.

> *Taxes are* **a problem.**

> **A** *problem is* **taxes.**

When a sentence begins with an expletive such as *there, here,* or *it,* the verb agrees with the subject, not the expletive.

> **Surely, there** *are* **several** *alumni* **who would be interested in forming a group.**

> **There** *are* **50** *students* **in my English class.**

> **There** *is* **a horrifying** *study* **on child abuse in** *Psychology Today*.

Indefinite pronouns such as *each, either, one, everyone, everybody,* and *everything* are singular.

> *Somebody* **in Detroit** *loves* **me.**

> *Does either* **[one] of you have a pencil?**

> *Neither* **of my brothers** *has* **a car.**

Indefinite pronouns such as *several, few, both,* and *many* are plural.

> *Both* **of my sorority sisters** *have* **decided to live off campus.**

> *Few seek* **the enlightenment of transcendental meditation.**

Indefinite pronouns such as *all, some, most,* and *none* may be singular or plural depending on their referents.

> *Some* of the food *is* cold.
>
> *Some* of the vegetables *are* cold.
>
> I can think of some retorts, but *none seem* appropriate.
>
> *None* of the children *is* as sweet as Sally.

Fractions such as *one-half* and *one-third* may be singular or plural depending on the referent.

> *Half* of the mail *has* been delivered.
>
> *Half* of the letters *have* been read.

Subjects joined by *and* take a plural verb unless the subjects are thought to be one item or unit.

> *Jim* and *Tammy were* televangelists.
>
> *Simon and Garfunkel is* my favorite group.

In cases when the subjects are joined by *or, nor, either…or,* or *neither…nor,* the verb must agree with the subject closer to it.

> Either the teacher or the *students are* responsible.
>
> Neither the students nor the *teacher is* responsible.

Relative pronouns such as *who, which,* or *that,* which refer to plural antecedents, require plural verbs. However, when the relative pronoun refers to a singular subject, the pronoun takes a singular verb.

> She is one of the girls *who cheer* on Friday nights.
>
> She is the only cheerleader *who has* a broken leg.

Subjects preceded by *every, each,* and *many a* are singular.

> *Every* man, woman, and child *was* given a life preserver.
>
> *Each* undergraduate *is* required to pass a proficiency exam.
>
> *Many a* tear *has* to fall before one matures.

A collective noun, such as *audience, faculty, jury,* etc., requires a singular verb when the group is regarded as a whole, and a plural verb when the members of the group are regarded as individuals.

The *jury has* made its decision.

The *faculty are* preparing their grade rosters.

Subjects preceded by *the number of* or *the percentage of* are singular, while subjects preceded by *a number of* or *a percentage of* are plural.

The *number of* vacationers in Florida *increases* every year.

A *number of* vacationers *are* young couples.

Titles of books, companies, name brands, and groups are singular or plural depending on their meaning.

*Great Expectations is* my favorite novel.

The *Rolling Stones are* performing in the Super Dome.

Certain nouns of Latin and Greek origin have unusual singular and plural forms.

| Singular | Plural |
| --- | --- |
| criterion | criteria |
| alumnus | alumni |
| datum | data |
| medium | media |

The *data are* available for inspection.

The only *criterion* for membership *is* a high GPA.

Some nouns, such as *deer*, *shrimp*, and *sheep,* have the same spellings for both their singular and plural forms. In these cases, the meaning of the sentence will determine whether they are singular or plural.

*Deer are* beautiful animals.

The spotted *deer is* licking the sugar cube.

Some nouns, like *scissors*, *jeans*, and *wages,* have plural forms but no singular counter-parts. These nouns almost always take plural verbs.

> The *scissors are* on the table.

> My new *jeans fit* me like a glove.

Words used as examples, not as grammatical parts of the sentence, require singular verbs.

> *Can't is* the contraction for "cannot."

> *Cats is* the plural form of "cat."

Mathematical expressions of subtraction and division require singular verbs, but expressions of addition and multiplication take either singular or plural verbs.

> **Ten divided by two equals five.**

> **Five times two equals ten.**

OR  **Five times two equal ten.**

Nouns expressing time, distance, weight, and measurement are singular when they refer to a unit and plural when they refer to separate items.

> *Fifty yards is* a short distance.

> *Ten years have* passed since I finished college.

Expressions of quantity are usually plural.

> *Nine out of ten* dentists *recommend* that their patients floss.

Some nouns ending in *-ics,* such as *economics* and *ethics*, take singular verbs when they refer to principles or a field of study; however, when they refer to individual practices, they usually take plural verbs.

> *Ethics is* being taught in the spring.

> His unusual business *ethics are* what got him into trouble.

Some nouns, like *measles*, *news*, and *calculus,* appear to be plural but are actually singular in number. These nouns require singular verbs.

> *Measles is* a very contagious disease.

> *Calculus requires* great skill in algebra.

A verbal noun (infinitive or gerund) serving as a subject is treated as singular, even if the object of the verbal phrase is plural.

> *Hiding* your mistakes *does* not make them go away.

> *To run* five miles *is* my goal.

A noun phrase or clause acting as the subject of a sentence requires a singular verb.

> *What I need is* to be loved.

> *Whether there* is any connection between them *is* unknown.

Clauses beginning with *what* may be singular or plural depending on the meaning, that is, whether *what* means "the thing" or "the things."

> *What I want for Christmas* is a new motorcycle.

> *What matters* are his ideas.

A plural subject followed by a singular appositive requires a plural verb; similarly, a singular subject followed by a plural appositive requires a singular verb.

> When the girls throw a party, *they* each *bring* a gift.

> The *board,* all ten members, *is* meeting today.

---

# Drill 5

*Directions:* Choose the correct replacement for the underlined words.

1. If you <u>had been concerned</u> about Marilyn, you <u>would have went</u> to greater lengths to ensure her safety.

   (A) had been concern . . . would have gone

   (B) was concerned . . . would have gone

   (C) had been concerned . . . would have gone

   (D) No change is necessary.

2. Susan <u>laid</u> in bed too long and missed her class.

   (A) lays

   (B) lay

   (C) lied

   (D) No change is necessary.

3. The Great Wall of China <u>is</u> fifteen hundred miles long; it <u>was built</u> in the third century B.C.

   (A) was . . . was built

   (B) is . . . is built

   (C) has been . . . was built

   (D) No change is necessary.

4. The professor <u>was retiring</u> in February.

   (A) is retiring

   (B) has retired

   (C) is retired

   (D) No change is necessary.

5. The ceiling of the Sistine Chapel <u>was</u> painted by Michelangelo; it <u>depicted</u> scenes from the Creation in the Old Testament.

   (A) was . . . depicts

   (B) is . . . depicts

   (C) has been . . . depicting

   (D) No change is necessary.

6. After Christmas <u>comes</u> the best sales.

   (A) has come

   (B) come

   (C) is coming

   (D) No change is necessary.

7. The bakery's specialty <u>are</u> wedding cakes.

   (A) is

   (B) were

   (C) be

   (D) No change is necessary.

8. Every man, woman, and child <u>were given</u> a life preserver.

    (A) have been given         (C) was given

    (B) had gave               (D) No change is necessary.

9. Hiding your mistakes <u>don't</u> make them go away.

    (A) doesn't               (C) have not

    (B) do not               (D) No change is necessary.

10. The Board of Regents <u>has recommended</u> a tuition increase.

    (A) have recommended       (C) had recommended

    (B) has recommend          (D) No change is necessary.

## Drill 5 Answers

| | | | | | | | |
|---|---|---|---|---|---|---|---|
| 1. | (C) | 4. | (A) | 7. | (A) | 10. | (D) |
| 2. | (B) | 5. | (A) | 8. | (C) | | |
| 3. | (D) | 6. | (B) | 9. | (A) | | |

# PRONOUNS

## Pronoun Case

Appropriate pronoun case is essential to effective, understandable essay writing. Pronoun case can either be nominative or objective.

| Nominative Case | Objective Case |
|---|---|
| I | me |
| he | him |
| she | her |
| we | us |
| they | them |
| who | whom |

This review section answers the most frequently asked grammar questions: when to use *I* and when to use *me*; when to use *who* and when to use *whom*. Some writers avoid *whom* altogether, and instead of distinguishing between *I* and *me*, many writers incorrectly use *myself*.

## Use the Nominative Case (Subject Pronouns)

for the subject of a sentence:

> *We* **students studied until early morning for the final.**
>
> **Alan and *I* "burned the midnight oil," too.**

for pronouns in apposition to the subject:

> **Only two students, Alex and *I*, were asked to report on the meeting.**

for the predicate nominative/subject complement:

> **The actors nominated for the award were *she* and *I*.**

for the subject of an elliptical clause:

> **Molly is more experienced than *he*.**

for the subject of a subordinate clause:

> **Robert is the driver *who* reported the accident.**

for the complement of an infinitive with no expressed subject:

> **I would not want to be *he*.**

## Use the Objective Case (Object Pronouns)

for the direct object of a sentence:

> **Mary invited *us* to her party.**

for the object of a preposition:

> **The books that were torn belonged to *her*.**
>
> **Just between you and *me*, I'm bored.**

for the indirect object of a sentence:

> **Walter gave a dozen red roses to** *her*.

for the appositive of a direct object:

> **The committee elected two delegates, Barbara and** *me*.

for the object of an infinitive:

> **The young boy wanted to help** *us* **paint the fence.**

for the object of a gerund:

> **Enlisting** *him* **was surprisingly easy.**

for the object of a past participle:

> **Having called the other students and** *us,* **the secretary went home for the day.**

for a pronoun that precedes an infinitive (the subject of an infinitive):

> **The supervisor told** *him* **to work late.**

for the complement of an infinitive with an expressed subject:

> **The fans thought the best player to be** *him*.

for the object of an elliptical clause:

> **Susan writes Shawn oftener than** *me*.

When a conjunction connects two pronouns or a pronoun and a noun, remove the "and" and the other pronoun or noun to determine the correct pronoun form:

> **Mom gave** ~~Tom and~~ **myself a piece of cake.**
>
> **Mom gave** ~~Tom and~~ **I a piece of cake.**
>
> **Mom gave** ~~Tom and~~ **me a piece of cake.**

Removal of these words reveals what the correct pronoun should be:

**Mom gave *me* a piece of cake.**

The only pronouns that are acceptable after *between* and other prepositions are *me, her, him, them,* and *whom.* When deciding between *who* and *whom,* try substituting *he* for *who* and *him* for *whom;* then follow these easy transformation steps:

1. Isolate the *who* clause or the *whom* clause:

   **whom we can trust**

2. Invert the word order, if necessary. Place the words in the clause in the natural order of an English sentence, with the subject followed by the verb:

   **we can trust whom**

3. Read the final form with the *he* or *him* inserted:

   **We can trust ~~whom~~ him.**

When a pronoun follows a comparative conjunction like *than* or *as,* complete the elliptical construction to help you determine which pronoun is correct.

EXAMPLE    **She has more credit hours than me [do].**

**She has more credit hours than I [do].**

## Pronoun-Antecedent Agreement

Using the appropriate pronoun antecedent is very important to the effective essay. Pronouns must agree with their antecedent in number, gender, and person. An antecedent is a noun or pronoun to which another noun or pronoun refers.

Here are the two basic rules for pronoun reference-antecedent agreement:

1. Every pronoun must have a conspicuous antecedent.

2. Every pronoun must agree with its antecedent in number, gender, and person.

When an antecedent is one of dual gender, like *student, singer, artist, person, citizen,* etc., use *his or her.* Some careful writers change the antecedent to a plural noun to avoid using the sexist, singular masculine pronoun *his:*

**INCORRECT:**  **Everyone hopes that he will win the lottery.**

**CORRECT:**  **Most people hope that they will win the lottery.**

Ordinarily, the relative pronoun *who* is used to refer to people, *which* and *that* to refer to things and places, and *where* to refer to places. The distinction between *that* and *which* is a grammatical distinction. When differentiating something from a larger class of which it is a member, use "that." When the subject is not being distinguished from a larger class, use "which."

**EXAMPLE**  **I bought the sweater *that* was on sale.**

**EXAMPLE**  **There were many sweaters, all of *which* were on sale.**

Many writers prefer to use *that* to refer to collective nouns.

**EXAMPLE**  **A family *that* traces its lineage is usually proud of its roots.**

Many writers are not sure when to use the reflexive case pronoun and when to use the possessive case pronoun. The rules governing the usage of the reflexive case and the possessive case are quite simple.

## Use the Possessive Case

before a noun in a sentence:

**Our friend moved during the semester break.**

**My dog has fleas, but *her* dog doesn't.**

before a gerund in a sentence:

**Her running helps to relieve stress.**

**His driving terrified her.**

as a noun in a sentence:

*Mine* **was the last test graded that day.**

to indicate possession:

**Karen never allows anyone else to drive** *her* **car.**

**Brad thought the book was** *his,* **but it was someone else's.**

## Use the Reflexive Case

as a direct object to rename the subject:

**I kicked** *myself.*

as an indirect object to rename the subject:

**Henry bought** *himself* **a tie.**

as an object of a prepositional phrase:

**Tom and Lillie baked the pie for** *themselves.*

as a predicate pronoun:

**She hasn't been** *herself* **lately.**

Do not use the reflexive in place of the nominative pronoun:

**INCORRECT:  Both Randy and** *myself* **plan to go.**

**CORRECT:  Both Randy and** *I* **plan to go.**

---

**INCORRECT:**  *Yourself* **will take on the challenges of college.**

**CORRECT:**  *You* **will take on the challenges of college.**

---

**INCORRECT:  Either James or** *yourself* **will paint the mural.**

**CORRECT:  Either James or** *you* **will paint the mural.**

Watch out for careless use of the pronoun form:

> INCORRECT: George *hisself* told me it was true.

> CORRECT: George *himself* told me it was true.

---

> INCORRECT: They washed the car *theirselves*.

> CORRECT: They washed the car *themselves*.

Notice that reflexive pronouns are not set off by commas:

> INCORRECT: Mary, *herself*, gave him the diploma.

> CORRECT: Mary *herself* gave him the diploma.

---

> INCORRECT: I will do it, *myself*.

> CORRECT: I will do it *myself*.

---

## Pronoun Reference

Pronoun reference requires you to determine whether the antecedent is conspicuously written in the sentence or whether it is remote, implied, ambiguous, or vague, none of which results in clear writing. Make sure that every italicized pronoun has a conspicuous antecedent and that one pronoun substitutes only for another noun or pronoun, not for an idea or a sentence.

## Pronoun Reference Problems Occur

when a pronoun refers to either of two antecedents:

> INCORRECT: Joanna told Kim that *she* was getting fat.

> CORRECT: Joanna told Kim, "I'm getting fat."

when a pronoun refers to a remote antecedent:

> INCORRECT: A strange car followed us closely, and *he* kept blinking his lights at us.

CORRECT:   A strange car followed us closely, and its driver kept blinking his lights at us.

when *this*, *that*, and *which* refer to the general idea of the preceding clause or sentence rather than the preceding word:

INCORRECT:   The students could not understand the pronoun reference handout, *which* annoyed them very much.

CORRECT:   The students could not understand the pronoun reference handout, a fact which annoyed them very much.

OR   The students were annoyed because they could not understand the pronoun reference handout.

when a pronoun refers to an unexpressed but implied noun:

INCORRECT:   My husband wants me to knit a blanket, but I'm not interested in *it*.

CORRECT:   My husband wants me to knit a blanket, but I'm not interested in knitting.

when *it* is used as something other than an expletive to postpone a subject:

INCORRECT:   *It* says in today's paper that the newest shipment of cars from Detroit, Michigan, seems to include outright imitations of European models.

CORRECT:   Today's paper says that the newest shipment of cars from Detroit, Michigan, seems to include outright imitations of European models.

INCORRECT:   The football game was canceled because *it* was bad weather.

CORRECT:   The football game was canceled because the weather was bad.

when *they* or *it* is used to refer to something or someone indefinitely, and there is no definite antecedent:

INCORRECT:   At the job placement office, *they* told me to stop wearing ripped jeans to my interviews.

CORRECT:   At the job placement office, the interviewer told me to stop wearing ripped jeans to my interviews.

when the pronoun does not agree with its antecedent in number, gender, or person:

INCORRECT:   Any graduate student, if *they* are interested, may attend the lecture.

CORRECT:   Any graduate student, if he or she is interested, may attend the lecture.

OR   All graduate students, if they are interested, may attend the lecture.

---

INCORRECT:   Many Americans are concerned that the overuse of slang and colloquialisms is corrupting *the* language.

CORRECT:   Many Americans are concerned that the overuse of slang and colloquialisms is corrupting their language.

---

INCORRECT:   The Board of Regents will not make a decision about tuition increase until *their* March meeting.

CORRECT:   The Board of Regents will not make a decision about tuition increase until its March meeting.

when a noun or pronoun has no expressed antecedent:

INCORRECT:   In the President's address to the union, *he* promised no more taxes.

CORRECT:   In his address to the union, the President promised no more taxes.

## Indefinite Pronouns

**Some indefinite pronouns are always singular, some are always plural**, and others may be singular or plural depending on their use.

| Singular | Plural | Singular or Plural |
|----------|--------|---------------------|
| Another, anyone, anybody, anything, each, either, everybody, everyone, everything, neither, nobody, no one, nothing, one, other, somebody, someone, something | Both, few, many, others, several | All, any, enough, most, much, none, some |

**Singular indefinite pronouns** require singular verbs and **plural indefinite** pronouns require plural verbs. For those indefinite pronouns that can be either singular or plural, subject-verb agreement depends on the nouns to which they refer:

EXAMPLE     *Everyone wants* a ticket to the concert. (singular)

*Few* of us *believe* we will get tickets. (plural)

*Most* of the stadium *was* completely full. (*most* refers to the singular noun *stadium*)

*Most* of the attendees *were* young adults. (*most* refers to the plural noun *attendees*)

# Drill 6

*Directions:* Choose the correct replacement for the underlined words.

1. My friend and <u>myself</u> bought tickets for *Cats*.

    (A) I

    (B) me

    (C) us

    (D) No change is necessary.

2. Alcohol and tobacco are harmful to <u>whomever</u> consumes them.

    (A) whom

    (B) who

    (C) whoever

    (D) No change is necessary.

3. Everyone is wondering <u>whom</u> her successor will be.

   (A) who

   (B) whose

   (C) who'll

   (D) No change is necessary.

4. Rosa Lee's parents discovered that it was <u>her who</u> wrecked the family car.

   (A) she who

   (B) she whom

   (C) her whom

   (D) No change is necessary.

5. A student <u>who</u> wishes to protest <u>his or her</u> grades must file a formal grievance in the Dean's office.

   (A) that . . . their

   (B) which . . . his

   (C) whom . . . their

   (D) No change is necessary.

6. One of the best things about working for this company is that <u>they pay</u> big bonuses.

   (A) it pays

   (B) they always pay

   (C) they paid

   (D) No change is necessary.

7. Every car owner should be sure that <u>their</u> automobile insurance is adequate.

   (A) your

   (B) his or her

   (C) its

   (D) No change is necessary.

8. My mother wants me to become a teacher, but I'm not interested in <u>it</u>.

   (A) this

   (B) teaching

   (C) that

   (D) No change is necessary.

9. Since I had not paid my electric bill, <u>they</u> sent me a delinquency notice.

   (A) the power company

   (B) he

   (C) it

   (D) No change is necessary.

10. Margaret seldom wrote to her sister when <u>she</u> was away at college.

   (A) who

   (B) her

   (C) her sister

   (D) No change is necessary.

---

**Drill 6 Answers**

| | | | |
|---|---|---|---|
| 1. (A) | 4. (A) | 7. (B) | 10. (C) |
| 2. (C) | 5. (D) | 8. (B) | |
| 3. (A) | 6. (A) | 9. (A) | |

# WRONG OR MISSING PREPOSITIONS

Prepositions are usually quite short and their importance is often overlooked. But, they can dramatically change the meaning of what is intended by the writer or speaker. You can readily see the difference between throwing something **to** a person and **at** a person! It is important to be comfortable with the most common prepositions and their uses.

## Prepositions for Time, Place, and Introducing Objects

### Time

Prepositions that indicate time are:

> **on** is used with days

> **at** is used with noon, night, midnight, and with the time of day

> **in** is used with other parts of the day, with months, with years, with seasons

EXAMPLES **on** Monday

**at** noon

**in** the afternoon, **in** July, **in** 2012, **in** summer

**Since, for, by, from—to, from—until, during, within** are used for extended time.

EXAMPLES    gone **since** Friday (*He left on Friday and hasn't returned.*)

**for a** month. (*He will spend a month there.*)

**from** May **to** June. (*beginning in May and ending in June*)

**from** summer **until** fall (*beginning in summer and ending in fall*)

**during** the morning (*for some period of time in the morning*)

**within** a week. (*no longer than a week.*)

## Place or Location or Spatial Relationship

Some prepositions that indicate where something is are: **in, inside, on, at, over, above, under, beneath, underneath, below, near, next to, by, between, among, opposite**

EXAMPLES    **in** the soup             **beneath** the covers

**at** the beach           **underneath** the sink

**over** the fence          **below** the window

**above** the couch        **near** the fireplace

**under** the table         **next to** the fire engine

**by** the factory door      **beside** the silo

**between** the trucks      **from** the store

**among** the radishes     **in front of** the window

**opposite** the refrigerator  **inside** the basket

**across** the road         **near** the library

**against** the wall        **off** the porch

**ahead of** the pack      **out of** the trunk

**along** the shore        **through** the looking glass

**among** the vegetables   **toward** the sunrise

**around** the corner      **within** a room

**behind** the shed

## Introduction of the Objects of Verbs

Some prepositions that point to the objects of a verb are: **at, of, for.**

EXAMPLES    glance **at**, laugh **at**, look **at**, rejoice **at**, smile **at**, stare **at**

approve **of**, consists **of**, smells **of**, think **of**

call **for**, hope **for**, look **for**, wait **for**, watch **for**, wish **for**

## Prepositions that Indicate Direction:

The basic preposition of a direction is **to. To** is used to indicate a movement toward a goal. With many active verbs, **on** and **in** have a directional meaning and can be used along with **onto** and **into**.

EXAMPLES    walked **to** the river

drove **onto** the ramp

ran **into** the tunnel

the train traveled **on**

the police officer ran **in** pursuit

## DRILL 7

*Directions:* Choose the correct replacement for the underlined words.

1. You can buy your movie tickets <u>by</u> the ticket booth in the mall.

   (A) in                  (C) at

   (B) on                  (D) with

2. She baked her chocolate cake <u>at</u> the morning.

   (A) during              (C) from

   (B) within              (D) at

3. Jessie's prom gown was stored <u>by</u> her bedroom closet.

    (A)  in                    (C)  into

    (B)  inside of          (D)  over at

4. The group sauntered <u>by</u> the river.

    (A)  off                 (C)  to

    (B)  at                 (D)  along

5. When we camped, we could hear the wolves howling late <u>to</u> night.

    (A)  into              (C)  in

    (B)  from            (D)  at

6. My daughter hasn't called me <u>by</u> over a month!

    (A)  at                (C)  in

    (B)  from            (D)  within

7. The woman <u>by</u> us complained all of the time that we waited in line to buy the concert tickets.

    (A)  above           (C)  along

    (B)  in front of      (D)  across

8. When I went to purchase my shoes, there was no one <u>by</u> the cash register.

    (A)  at                (C)  on

    (B)  in                (D)  with

9. His cry of surprise caused me to glance <u>on</u> his newspaper.

    (A)  at                (C)  to

    (B)  about          (D)  for

10. When I opened the cooler it smelled <u>with</u> rotten eggs.

    (A) for                 (C) from

    (B) after               (D) of

---

**Drill 7 Answers**

| | | | | | | | |
|---|---|---|---|---|---|---|---|
| 1. | (C) | 4. | (D) | 7. | (B) | 10. (D) | |
| 2. | (A) | 5. | (A) | 8. | (A) | | |
| 3. | (A) | 6. | (C) | 9. | (A) | | |

# ADJECTIVES AND ADVERBS

## Correct Usage

Adjectives are words that modify nouns or pronouns by defining, describing, limiting, or qualifying those nouns or pronouns.

Adverbs are words that modify verbs, adjectives, or other adverbs. They express ideas such as time, place, manner, cause, and degree. Use adjectives as subject complements with linking verbs; use adverbs with action verbs.

| EXAMPLE | The old man's speech was *eloquent.* | ADJECTIVE |
|---|---|---|
| | Mr. Brown speaks *eloquently.* | ADVERB |
| | Please be *careful.* | ADJECTIVE |
| | Please drive *carefully.* | ADVERB |

## Good or Well

*Good* is an adjective; its use as an adverb is colloquial and nonstandard.

INCORRECT:  He plays *good.*

CORRECT:  He looks *good* for an octogenarian.

The quiche tastes very *good.*

*Well* may be either an adverb or an adjective. As an adjective, *well* means "in good health."

| | | |
|---|---|---|
| CORRECT: | He plays *well.* | ADVERB |
| | My mother is not *well.* | ADJECTIVE |

## Bad or Badly

*Bad* is an adjective used after sense verbs such as *look, smell, taste, feel,* or *sound,* or after linking verbs such as *is, am, are, was,* or *were.*

INCORRECT: I feel *badly* about the delay.

CORRECT: I feel *bad* about the delay.

*Badly* is an adverb used after all other verbs.

INCORRECT: It doesn't hurt very *bad.*

CORRECT: It doesn't hurt very *badly.*

## Real or Really

*Real* is an adjective; its use as an adverb is colloquial and nonstandard. It means "genuine."

INCORRECT: He writes *real* well.

CORRECT: This is *real* leather.

*Really* is an adverb meaning "very."

INCORRECT: This is *really* diamond.

CORRECT: Have a *really* nice day.

| EXAMPLES | This is *real* amethyst. | ADJECTIVE |
|---|---|---|
| | This is *really* difficult. | ADVERB |
| | This is a *real* crisis | ADJECTIVE |
| | This is *really* important. | ADVERB |

## Sort Of and Kind Of

*Sort of* and *kind of* are often misused in written English by writers who actually mean *rather* or *somewhat*.

INCORRECT: Jan was *kind of* saddened by the results of the test.

CORRECT: Jan was *somewhat* saddened by the results of the test.

## Drill 8

*Directions:* Choose the correct replacement for the underlined words.

1. Although the band performed <u>badly</u>, I feel <u>real bad</u> about missing the concert.

   (A) badly . . . real badly

   (B) bad . . . badly

   (C) badly . . . very bad

   (D) No change is necessary.

2. These reports are <u>relative simple</u> to prepare.

   (A) relatively simple

   (B) relative simply

   (C) relatively simply

   (D) No change is necessary.

3. He did <u>very well</u> on the test although his writing skills are not <u>good</u>.

   (A) real well . . . good

   (B) very good . . . good

   (C) good . . . great

   (D) No change is necessary.

4. Shake the medicine bottle <u>good</u> before you open it.

   (A) very good

   (B) real good

   (C) well

   (D) No change is necessary.

5. Though she speaks <u>fluently</u>, she writes <u>poorly</u> because she doesn't observe <u>closely</u> or think <u>clear</u>.

    (A) fluently . . . poorly . . . closely . . . clearly

    (B) fluent . . . poor . . . close . . . clear

    (C) fluently . . . poor . . . closely . . . clear

    (D) No change is necessary.

---

### Drill 8 Answers

| | | | |
|---|---|---|---|
| 1. | (C) | 4. | (C) |
| 2. | (A) | 5. | (A) |
| 3. | (D) | | |

## Faulty Comparisons

Most problems with adjectives and adverbs concern what is commonly called the use of degrees of comparison. There are three forms of modifiers: positive, comparative, and superlative.

| Positive | Comparative | Superlative |
|---|---|---|
| good | better | best |
| old | older | oldest |
| friendly | friendlier | friendliest |
| lonely | lonelier | loneliest |
| talented | more talented | most talented |
| beautiful | more beautiful | most beautiful |

The *positive* form of a modifier describes a thing, action, or quality without comparing it to another.

EXAMPLES    Jan and her mother have a *close* relationship.

Kurt is a *talented* musician.

A professional mountaineer always climbs *carefully*.

The *comparative* form of a modifier compares a thing, action, or quality to one other thing, action, or quality.

EXAMPLES    The relationship between Jan and her sister is *closer* than the relationship between Jan and her mother.

Kurt is a *more talented* musician than Frank.

A professional mountaineer climbs *more carefully* than a typical weekend mountain climber.

The *superlative* form of a modifier compares a thing, quality, or action to two or more other things, qualities, or actions. Often the comparison is indicated by the words "of all."

EXAMPLES    The *closest* relationship *of all* between siblings often occurs with twins.

The *most talented* artists still have difficulty making a living by selling their work.

Anthony is the *most experienced* in the Piedmont Mountain Climbing Club.

Most adjectives and adverbs of one- and two-syllable words add "-er" or "-est" to form the comparative and superlative forms. Modifiers of three syllables or more use "more" or "less" for the comparative form and "most" or "least" for the superlative form.

Common errors occur when a speaker or writer uses both methods of forming the comparative or superlative forms for a description or uses the wrong method to form the appropriate degree.

INCORRECT: Jack is *more taller* than Gordon. (As a one-syllable adjective, *tall* forms the comparative degree by adding only *-er.*)

CORRECT: Jack is *taller* than Gordon.

INCORRECT: The fall leaves are *beautifuler* this year than last. (As a three-syllable word, *beautiful* forms the comparative degree with *more* or *less.*)

CORRECT: The fall leaves are *more beautiful* this year than last.

INCORRECT: The *most shortest* poem is the one I want to memorize. (*Short*, a one-syllable word, forms the superlative degree with *-er* or *-est.*)

CORRECT: The *shortest* poem is the one I want to memorize.

A few adjectives and adverbs have irregular forms for the comparative and superlative degrees. The descriptive word changes to a new word for the following:

| Adjective/Adverb | Comparative | Superlative |
| --- | --- | --- |
| good or well | better | best |
| many or much | more | most |
| ill, bad, or badly | worse | worst |
| far | farther or further | farthest or furthest |
| little | less or littler | least or littlest |

A dictionary indicates the correct formation of comparative and superlative degrees of words and the occasion for the use of each.

**EXAMPLES**   We must walk *far* to get enough exercise.

We must walk *farther* than we have already to lose a pound this week.

Whoever reads *furthest* in the novel tonight will lead the class discussion tomorrow.

Some adjectives and adverbs cannot be used in comparative or superlative forms. These words are called *absolutes*. The meaning of an absolute has no potential for comparison or superlative. Frequently used absolute modifiers are "dead," "empty," "full," "perfect," "unique," "false," "final," and "true." Sometimes, however, an absolute can be used with "nearly."

**EXAMPLES**   A *nearly empty* gas tank caused Jorge to be late.

---

# Drill 9

*Directions:* Correct any error in the form of adjective or adverb used in the following sentences.

1. The recent tornado caused the most dreadfulest damage of any recent storm.

2. The new machine works goodest for me than for other employees.

3. A last-minute change made the hike further than we had expected.

4. Your feeling worst today than yesterday concerns me.

5. Who is the best informed, Beth or Ricky?

6. Often in August the most warmest weather of all the months occurs.

---

***Directions:*** Put the following words into the appropriate comparative and superlative forms.

7. high                                9. courteous

8. much                                10. smoothly

---

## Drill 9 Answers

1. The recent tornado caused the <u>most dreadful</u> damage of any recent storm.

2. The new machine works <u>better</u> for me than for other employees.

3. A last-minute change made the hike <u>farther</u> than we had expected.

4. Your feeling <u>worse</u> today than yesterday concerns me.

5. Who is the <u>better</u> informed, Beth or Ricky?

6. Often in August the <u>warmest</u> weather of all the months occurs.

| Positive | Comparative | Superlative |
|----------|-------------|-------------|
| 7. high | higher | highest |
| 8. much | more | most |
| 9. courteous | more or less courteous | most or least courteous |
| 10. smoothly | more or less smoothly | most or least smoothly |

# PUNCTUATION

## Commas

Commas should be placed according to standard rules of punctuation for purpose, clarity, and effect. The proper use of commas is explained in the following rules and examples.

In a series, when more than one adjective describes a noun, use a comma to separate and emphasize each adjective. The comma takes the place of the word "and" in the series.

> **the long, dark passageway**
>
> **another confusing, sleepless night**
>
> **an elaborate, complex, brilliant plan**
>
> **the old, gray, crumpled hat**

Some adjective-noun combinations are thought of as one word. In these cases, the adjective in front of the adjective-noun combination needs no comma. If you inserted *and* between the adjective-noun combination, it would not make sense.

> **a stately oak tree**
>
> **an exceptional wine glass**
>
> **my worst report card**
>
> **a china dinner plate**

The comma is also used to separate words, phrases, and whole ideas (clauses); it still takes the place of *and* when used this way.

> **an apple, a pear, a fig, and a banana**
>
> **a lovely lady, an elegant dress, and many admirers**
>
> **She lowered the shade, closed the curtain, turned off the light, and went to bed.**

The only question that exists about the use of commas in a series is whether or not one should be used before the final item. It is standard usage to do so although many newspapers and magazines have stopped using the final comma. Occasionally, the omission of the comma can be confusing.

| INCORRECT: | He got on his horse, tracked a rabbit and a deer and rode on to Canton. |
|---|---|
| CORRECT: | He got on his horse, tracked a rabbit and a deer, and rode on to Canton. |

| INCORRECT: | We planned the trip with Mary and Harold, Susan, Dick and Joan, Gregory and Jean and Charles. |
|---|---|
| CORRECT: | We planned the trip with Mary and Harold, Susan, Dick and Joan, Gregory and Jean, and Charles. |

Usually if a dependent clause or a phrase of more than five or six words precedes the subject at the beginning of a sentence, a comma is used to set it off.

**After last night's fiasco at the disco, she couldn't bear the thought of looking at him again.**

**Whenever I try to talk about politics, my wife leaves the room.**

**Provided you have said nothing, they will never guess who you are.**

It is not necessary to use a comma with a short sentence.

**In January she will go to Switzerland.**

**After a rest I'll feel better.**

**During the day no one is home.**

If an introductory phrase includes a verb form that is being used as another part of speech (a verbal), it must be followed by a comma.

| INCORRECT: | When eating Mary never looked up from her plate. |
|---|---|
| CORRECT: | When eating, Mary never looked up from her plate. |

| INCORRECT: | Because of her desire to follow her faith in James wavered. |
|---|---|
| CORRECT: | Because of her desire to follow, her faith in James wavered. |

| INCORRECT: | Having decided to leave Mary James wrote her a letter. |
|---|---|
| CORRECT: | Having decided to leave Mary, James wrote her a letter. |

To separate sentences with two main ideas, you need to be able to recognize compound sentences. When a sentence contains more than two subjects and verbs (clauses) and when the two clauses are joined by a conjunction *(and, but, or, nor, for,* or *yet)*, use a comma before the conjunction to show that another clause is coming.

I thought I knew the poem by heart, but he showed me three lines I had forgotten.

Are we really interested in helping the children, or are we more concerned with protecting our good names?

He is supposed to leave tomorrow, but he is not ready to go.

Jim knows you are disappointed, and he has known it for a long time.

If the two parts of the sentence are short and closely related, it is not necessary to use a comma.

He threw the ball and the dog ran after it.

Jane played the piano and Michael danced.

Be careful not to confuse a sentence that has a compound verb and a single subject with a compound sentence. If the subject is the same for both verbs, there is no need for a comma.

| INCORRECT: | Charles sent some flowers, and wrote a long letter explaining why he had not been able to attend. |
|---|---|
| CORRECT: | Charles sent some flowers and wrote a long letter explaining why he had not been able to attend. |

INCORRECT: Last Thursday we went to the concert with Julia, and afterwards dined at an old Italian restaurant.

CORRECT: Last Thursday we went to the concert with Julia and afterwards dined at an old Italian restaurant.

---

INCORRECT: For the third time, the teacher explained that the literacy level for high school students was much lower than it had been in previous years, and this time wrote the statistics on the board for everyone to see.

CORRECT: For the third time, the teacher explained that the literacy level for high school students was much lower than it had been in previous years and this time wrote the statistics on the board for everyone to see.

In general, words and phrases that stop the flow of the sentence or are unnecessary for the main idea are set off by commas. This includes

## Abbreviations after Names:

Did you invite John Paul, Jr., and his sister?

Martha Harris, Ph.D., will be the speaker tonight.

## Interjections (an Exclamation Without Added Grammatical Connection):

Oh, I'm so glad to see you.

I tried so hard, alas, to do it.

Hey, let me out of here.

## Direct Address:

Roy, won't you open the door for the dog?

I can't understand, Mother, what you are trying to say.

May I ask, Mr. President, why you called us together?

Hey, lady, watch out for that car!

## Tag Questions:

I'm really hungry, aren't you?

Jerry looks like his father, doesn't he?

## Geographical Names and Addresses:

The concert will be held in Chicago, Illinois, on August 12.

The letter was addressed to Mrs. Marion Heartwell, 1881 Pine Lane, Palo Alto, California 95824.

(Note: No comma is needed before the zip code because it is already clearly set off from the state name.)

## Transitional Words and Phrases:

On the other hand, I hope he gets better.

In addition, the phone rang constantly this afternoon.

I am, nevertheless, going to the beach on Sunday.

You'll find, therefore, that no one is more loyal than I am.

## Parenthetical Words and Phrases:

You will become, I believe, a great statesman.

We know, of course, that this is the only thing to do.

The Mannes affair was, to put it mildly, a surprise.

## Unusual Word Order:

The dress, new and crisp, hung in the closet.

Intently, she stared out the window.

## Nonrestrictive Elements:

Parts of a sentence that modify other parts are sometimes essential to the meaning of the sentence and sometimes not. When a modifying word or group of words is not vital to the meaning of the sentence, it is set off by commas. Since it does not restrict the meaning of the words it modifies, it is called "nonrestrictive." Modifiers that are essential to the meaning of the sentence are called "restrictive" and are not set off by commas.

| | |
|---|---|
| **ESSENTIAL:** | The girl *who wrote the story* is my sister. |
| **NONESSENTIAL:** | My sister, *the girl who wrote the story*, has always loved to write. |

---

| | |
|---|---|
| **ESSENTIAL:** | John Milton's *Paradise Lost* tells a remarkable story. |
| **NONESSENTIAL:** | Dante's greatest work, *The Divine Comedy,* marked the beginning of the Renaissance. |

---

| | |
|---|---|
| **ESSENTIAL:** | The cup *that is on the piano* is the one I want. |
| **NONESSENTIAL:** | The cup, *which my brother gave me last year*, is on the piano. |

---

| | |
|---|---|
| **ESSENTIAL:** | The people *who arrived late* were not seated. |
| **NONESSENTIAL:** | George, *who arrived late*, was not seated. |

## Direct Quotations:

Most direct quotes or quoted materials are set off from the rest of the sentence by commas.

"Please read your part more loudly," the director insisted.

"I won't know what to do," said Michael, "if you leave me."

The teacher said sternly, "I will not dismiss this class until I have silence."

Who was it who said, "Do not ask for whom the bell tolls; it tolls for thee"?

Note: Commas always go inside the closing quotation mark, even if the comma is not part of the material being quoted.

Be careful not to set off indirect quotes or quotes that are used as subjects or complements.

> She said she would never come back. (indirect quote)
>
> "To be or not to be" is the famous beginning of a soliloquy in Shakespeare's *Hamlet.* (subject)
>
> Back then my favorite poem was "Evangeline." (complement)

## Contrasting Elements:

> Her intelligence, not her beauty, got her the job.
>
> Your plan will take you a little further from, rather than closer to, your destination.
>
> It was a reasonable, though not appealing, idea.
>
> He wanted glory, but found happiness instead.

## Dates:

Both forms of the date are acceptable.

> She will arrive on April 6, 2012.
>
> He left on 5 December 2010.
>
> In January 2009, he handed in his resignation.
>
> On October 22, 2008, Frank and Julie were married.

Usually, when a subordinate clause is at the end of a sentence, no comma is necessary preceding the clause. However, when a subordinate clause introduces a sentence, a comma should be used after the clause.

Some common subordinating conjunctions are

| | | |
|---|---|---|
| after | even though | till |
| although | if | unless |
| as | inasmuch as | until |
| as if | since | when |
| because | so that | whenever |
| before | though | while |

## Semicolons

Correct semicolon usage requires you to be able to distinguish between the semicolon, the comma, and the colon. This review section covers the basic uses of the semicolon: to separate independent clauses not joined by a coordinating conjunction, to separate independent clauses separated by a conjunctive adverb, and to separate items in a series containing internal commas. It is important to be consistent; if you use a semicolon between *any* of the items in the series, you must use semicolons to separate *all* of the items in the series.

Usually a comma follows the conjunctive adverb. Note also that a period can be used to separate two sentences joined by a conjunctive adverb. Some common conjunctive adverbs are

| | | |
|---|---|---|
| accordingly | indeed | now |
| besides | in fact | on the other hand |
| consequently | moreover | otherwise |
| finally | nevertheless | perhaps |
| furthermore | next | still |
| however | nonetheless | therefore |

*Then* is also used as a conjunctive adverb, but it is not usually followed by a comma.

## Use the Semicolon

to separate independent clauses that are not joined by a coordinating conjunction:

**I understand how to use commas; the semicolon I have not yet mastered.**

to separate two independent clauses connected by a conjunctive adverb:

**He took great care with his work; *therefore*, he was very successful.**

to combine two independent clauses connected by a coordinating conjunction if either or both of the clauses contain other internal punctuation:

**Success in college, some maintain, requires intelligence, industry, and perseverance; *but* others, fewer in number, assert that only personality is important.**

to separate items in a series when each item has internal punctuation:

> I bought an old, dilapidated chair; an antique table that was in beautiful condition; and a new, ugly, blue and white rug.

> Call our customer service line for assistance: Arizona, 1-800-555-6020; New Mexico, 1-800-555-5050; California, 1-800-555-3140; or Nevada, 1-800-555-3214.

## Do Not Use the Semicolon

to precede an explanation or summary of the first clause:

> **WEAK:** The first week of camping was wonderful; we lived in cabins instead of tents.

> **BETTER:** The first week of camping was wonderful: we lived in cabins instead of tents.

Note: Although the sentences above are punctuated correctly, the use of the semicolon provides a miscue, suggesting that the second clause is merely an extension, not an explanation, of the first clause. The colon provides a better clue.

to separate a dependent and an independent clause:

> **INCORRECT:** You should not make such statements; even though they are correct.

> **CORRECT:** You should not make such statements even though they are correct.

to separate an appositive phrase or clause from a sentence:

> **INCORRECT:** His immediate aim in life is centered around two things; becoming an engineer and learning to fly an airplane.

> **CORRECT:** His immediate aim in life is centered around two things: becoming an engineer and learning to fly an airplane.

to substitute for a comma:

> INCORRECT:  **My roommate also likes sports; particularly football, basketball, and baseball.**
>
> CORRECT:  **My roommate also likes sports, particularly football, basketball, and baseball.**

to set off other types of phrases or clauses from a sentence:

> INCORRECT:  **Being of a cynical mind; I should ask for a recount of the ballots.**
>
> CORRECT:  **Being of a cynical mind, I should ask for a recount of the ballots.**

---

> INCORRECT:  **The next meeting of the club has been postponed two weeks; inasmuch as both the president and vice president are out of town.**
>
> CORRECT:  **The next meeting of the club has been postponed two weeks, inasmuch as both the president and vice president are out of town.**

Note that the semicolon is not a terminal mark of punctuation; therefore, it should not be followed by a capital letter unless the first word in the second clause ordinarily requires capitalization.

## Colons

While it is true that a colon is used to precede a list, one must also make sure that a complete sentence precedes the colon. The colon signals the reader that a list, explanation, or restatement of the preceding will follow. It is like an arrow, indicating that something is to follow. The difference between the colon and the semicolon and between the colon and the period is that the colon is an introductory mark, not a terminal mark. Look at the following examples:

> **The Constitution provides for a separation of powers among the three branches of government.**
>
> *government.* The period signals a new sentence.

*government*; The semicolon signals an interrelated sentence.

*government*, The comma signals a coordinating conjunction followed by another independent clause.

*government*: The colon signals a list.

**The Constitution provides for a separation of powers among the three branches of government: executive, legislative, and judicial.**

Observe the following rules to ensure that a complete sentence precedes a colon.

Use the colon to introduce a list (one item may constitute a list):

**I hate this one course: English.**

**Three plays by William Shakespeare will be presented in repertory this summer at the University of Michigan: *Hamlet, Macbeth,* and *Othello.***

To introduce a list preceded by *as follows* or *the following*:

**The reasons he cited for his success are as follows: integrity, honesty, industry, and a pleasant disposition.**

To separate two independent clauses, when the second clause is a restatement or explanation of the first:

**All of my high school teachers said one thing in particular: college is going to be difficult.**

To introduce a word or word group that is a restatement, explanation, or summary of the first sentence:

**These two things he loved: an honest man and a beautiful woman.**

To introduce a formal appositive:

**I am positive there is one appeal that you can't overlook: money.**

To separate the introductory words from a quotation that follows, if the quotation is formal, long, or paragraphed separately:

**The actor then stated: "I would rather be able to adequately play the part of Hamlet than to perform a miraculous operation, deliver a great lecture, or build a magnificent skyscraper."**

The colon should be used only after statements that are grammatically complete.

Do *not* use a colon after a verb:

INCORRECT: My favorite holidays are: Christmas, New Year's Eve, and Halloween.

CORRECT: My favorite holidays are Christmas, New Year's Eve, and Halloween.

Do *not* use a colon after a preposition:

INCORRECT: I enjoy different ethnic foods such as: Greek, Chinese, and Italian.

CORRECT: I enjoy different ethnic foods such as Greek, Chinese, and Italian.

Do *not* use a colon interchangeably with a dash:

INCORRECT: Mathematics, German, English: These gave me the greatest difficulty of all my studies.

CORRECT: Mathematics, German, English—these gave me the greatest difficulty of all my studies.

Information preceding the colon should be a complete sentence regardless of the explanatory information following the clause.

Do *not* use the colon before the words *for example, namely, that is,* or *for instance* even though these words may be introducing a list.

INCORRECT: We agreed to it: namely, to give him a surprise party.

CORRECT: We agreed to it, namely, to give him a surprise party.

Colon-usage questions test your knowledge of the colon preceding a list, restatement, or explanation. These questions also require you to be able to distinguish between the colon and the period, the colon and the comma, and the colon and the semicolon.

## Apostrophes

Apostrophes require you to know when an apostrophe has been used appropriately to make a noun possessive, not plural. Remember the following rules when considering how to show possession.

Add *'s* to singular nouns and indefinite pronouns:

> **Tiffany's flowers**
>
> **a dog's bark**
>
> **everybody's computer**
>
> **at the owner's expense**
>
> **today's paper**

Add *'s* to singular nouns ending in *s,* unless this distorts the pronunciation:

> **Delores's paper**
>
> **the boss's pen**
>
> **for righteousness' sake**
>
> **Dr. Evans's office OR Dr. Evans' office**

Add *an apostrophe* to plural nouns ending in *s* or *es:*

> **two cents' worth**
>
> **ladies' night**
>
> **thirteen years' experience**
>
> **two weeks' pay**

Add *'s* to plural nouns not ending in *s:*

> **men's room**
>
> **children's toys**

Add *'s* to the last word in compound words or groups:

> **brother-in-law's car**
>
> **someone else's paper**

Add *'s* to the last name when indicating joint ownership:

**Joe and Edna's home**

**Julie and Kathy's party**

**women and children's clinic**

Add *'s* to both names if you intend to show ownership by each person:

**Joe's and Edna's trucks**

**Julie's and Kathy's pies**

**Ted's and Jane's marriage vows**

Possessive pronouns change their forms *without* the addition of an apostrophe:

**her, his, hers**

**your, yours**

**their, theirs**

**it, its**

Use the possessive form of a noun preceding a gerund:

**His driving annoys me.**

**My bowling a strike irritated him.**

**Do you mind our stopping by?**

**We appreciate your coming.**

Add *'s* to letters, numbers, words referred to as words, and abbreviations with periods to show that they are plural:

**no if's, and's, or but's**

**the do's and don't's of dating**

**three A's**

**Ph.D.'s are granted by universities.**

Add *s* to decades, symbols, and abbreviations without periods to show that they are plural:

TVs

VCRs

the 1800s

the returning POWs

## Quotation Marks

It is important to have an understanding of the proper use of quotation marks with other marks of punctuation, with titles, and with dialogue.

The most common use of double quotation marks (") is to set off quoted words, phrases, and sentences.

> "If everybody minded their own business," said the Duchess in a hoarse growl, "the world would go round a great deal faster than it does."
>
> "Then you would say what you mean," the March Hare went on.
>
> "I do," Alice hastily replied: "at least—at least I mean what I say—that's the same thing, you know."
>
> —from Lewis Carroll's *Alice in Wonderland*

Single quotation marks are used to set off quoted material within a quote.

> "Shall I bring 'Rime of the Ancient Mariner' along with us?" she asked her brother.
>
> Mrs. Green said, "The doctor told me, 'Go immediately to bed when you get home!'"
>
> "If she said that to me," Katherine insisted, "I would tell her, 'I never intend to speak to you again! Goodbye, Susan!'"

When writing dialogue, begin a new paragraph each time the speaker changes.

> "Do you know what time it is?" asked Jane.
>
> "Can't you see I'm busy?" snapped Mary.
>
> "It's easy to see that you're in a bad mood today!" replied Jane.

Use quotation marks to enclose words used as words. (Sometimes italics are used for this purpose.)

"Judgment" has always been a difficult word for me to spell.

Do you know what "abstruse" means?

"Horse and buggy" and "bread and butter" can be used either as adjectives or as nouns.

If slang is used within more formal writing, the slang words or phrases should be set off with quotation marks.

Harrison's decision to leave the conference and to "stick his neck out" by flying to Jamaica was applauded by the rest of the conference attendees.

When words are meant to have an unusual or specific significance to the reader, for instance irony or humor, they are sometimes placed in quotation marks.

For years, women were not allowed to buy real estate in order to "protect" them from unscrupulous dealers.

The "conversation" resulted in one black eye and a broken nose.

To set off titles of TV shows, poems, stories, and book chapters, use quotation marks. (Book, motion picture, newspaper, and magazine titles are underlined when handwritten.)

The article "Moving South in the Southern Rain," by Jergen Smith in the *Southern News*, attracted the attention of our editor.

The assignment is "Childhood Development," Chapter 18 of *Human Behavior*.

My favorite essay by Montaigne is "On Silence."

"Happy Days" led the TV ratings for years, didn't it?

You will find Keats' "Ode on a Grecian Urn" in Chapter 3, "The Romantic Era," in Lastly's *Selections from Great English Poets*.

## Errors to Avoid

Be sure to remember that quotation marks always come in pairs. Do not make the mistake of using only one set.

|  |  |
|---|---|
| INCORRECT: | "You'll never convince me to move to the city, said Thurman. I consider it an insane asylum." |
| CORRECT: | "You'll never convince me to move to the city," said Thurman. "I consider it an insane asylum." |

---

|  |  |
|---|---|
| INCORRECT: | "Idleness and pride tax with a heavier hand than kings and parliaments," Benjamin Franklin is supposed to have said. If we can get rid of the former, we may easily bear the latter." |
| CORRECT: | "Idleness and pride tax with a heavier hand than kings and parliaments," Benjamin Franklin is supposed to have said. "If we can get rid of the former, we may easily bear the latter." |

When a quote consists of several sentences, do not put the quotation marks at the beginning and end of each sentence; put them at the beginning and end of the entire quotation.

|  |  |
|---|---|
| INCORRECT: | "It was during his student days in Bonn that Beethoven fastened upon Schiller's poem." "The heady sense of liberation in the verses must have appealed to him." "They appealed to every German."—John Burke |
| CORRECT: | "It was during his student days in Bonn that Beethoven fastened upon Schiller's poem. The heady sense of liberation in the verses must have appealed to him. They appealed to every German."—John Burke |

Instead of setting off a long quote with quotation marks, if it is longer than five or six lines, you may want to indent and single space it. If you do indent, do not use quotation marks.

> In his *First Inaugural Address,* Abraham Lincoln appeals to the war-torn American people:
>
> > We are not enemies, but friends. We must not be enemies. Though passion may have strained, it must not break, our bonds of affection. The mystic chords of memory, stretching from every battlefield and patriot grave to every living heart and hearthstone all over this broad land, will yet swell the chorus of the Union when again touched, as surely they will be, by the better angels of our nature.

Be careful not to use quotation marks with indirect quotations.

> INCORRECT:  Mary wondered "if she would get over it."

> CORRECT:  Mary wondered if she would get over it.

---

> INCORRECT:  The nurse asked "how long it had been since we had visited the doctor's office."

> CORRECT:  The nurse asked how long it had been since we had visited the doctor's office.

When you quote several paragraphs, it is not sufficient to place quotation marks at the beginning and end of the entire quote. Place quotation marks at the *beginning of each paragraph* but only at the *end of the last paragraph*. Here is an abbreviated quotation for an example:

> "Here begins an odyssey through the world of classical mythology, starting with the creation of the world...
>
> "It is true that themes similar to the classical may be found in any corpus of mythology...Even technology is not immune to the influence of Greece and Rome...
>
> "We need hardly mention the extent to which painters and sculptors...have used and adapted classical mythology to illustrate the past, to reveal the human body, to express romantic or antiromantic ideals, or to symbolize any particular point of view."

Remember that commas and periods are *always* placed inside the quotation marks even if they are not actually part of the quote.

INCORRECT: "Life always gets colder near the summit", Nietzsche is purported to have said, "—the cold increases, responsibility grows".

CORRECT: "Life always gets colder near the summit," Nietzsche is purported to have said, "—the cold increases, responsibility grows."

INCORRECT: "Get down here right away", John cried. "You'll miss the sunset if you don't."

CORRECT: "Get down here right away," John cried. "You'll miss the sunset if you don't."

INCORRECT: "If my dog could talk", Mary mused, "I'll bet he would say, 'Take me for a walk right this minute'".

CORRECT: "If my dog could talk," Mary mused, "I'll bet he would say, 'Take me for a walk right this minute.' "

Other marks of punctuation, such as question marks, exclamation points, colons, and semicolons, go inside the quotation marks if they are part of the quoted material. If they are not part of the quotation, however, they go outside the quotation marks. Be careful to distinguish between the guidelines for the comma and period, which always go inside the quotation marks, and those for other marks of punctuation.

INCORRECT: "I'll always love you"! he exclaimed happily.

CORRECT: "I'll always love you!" he exclaimed happily.

INCORRECT: Did you hear her say, "He'll be there early?"

CORRECT: Did you hear her say, "He'll be there early"?

INCORRECT: She called down the stairs, "When are you going"?

CORRECT: She called down the stairs, "When are you going?"

INCORRECT: "Let me out"! he cried. "Don't you have any pity"?

CORRECT: "Let me out!" he cried. "Don't you have any pity?"

Remember to use only one mark of punctuation at the end of a sentence ending with a quotation mark.

INCORRECT: She thought out loud, "Will I ever finish this paper in time for that class?".

CORRECT: She thought out loud, "Will I ever finish this paper in time for that class?"

INCORRECT: "Not the same thing a bit!", said the Hatter. "Why, you might just as well say that 'I see what I eat' is the same thing as 'I eat what I see'!".

CORRECT: "Not the same thing a bit!" said the Hatter. "Why, you might just as well say that 'I see what I eat' is the same thing as 'I eat what I see'!"

# Drill 10

*Directions:* Choose the correct replacement for the underlined words.

1. Indianola, <u>Mississippi, where B.B. King and my father grew up,</u> has a population of less than 50,000 people.

   (A) Mississippi where, B.B. King and my father grew up,

   (B) Mississippi where B.B. King and my father grew up,

   (C) Mississippi; where B.B. King and my father grew up,

   (D) No change is necessary.

2. John Steinbeck's best known novel *The Grapes of Wrath* is the story of the <u>Joads an Oklahoma family</u> who were driven from their dustbowl farm and forced to become migrant workers in California.

   (A) Joads, an Oklahoma family

   (B) Joads, an Oklahoma family,

   (C) Joads; an Oklahoma family

   (D) No change is necessary.

3. All students who are interested in student teaching next <u>semester, must submit an application to the Teacher Education Office.</u>

   (A) semester must submit an application to the Teacher Education Office.

   (B) semester, must submit an application, to the Teacher Education Office.

   (C) semester: must submit an application to the Teacher Education Office.

   (D) No change is necessary.

4. Whenever you travel by <u>car, or plane, you</u> must wear a seatbelt.

   (A) car or plane you          (C) car or plane, you

   (B) car, or plane you         (D) No change is necessary.

5. Wearing a seatbelt is not just a good <u>idea, it's</u> the law.

   (A) idea; it's               (C) idea. It's

   (B) idea it's                (D) No change is necessary.

6. Senators and representatives can be reelected <u>indefinitely; a</u> president can only serve two terms.

   (A) indefinitely but a       (C) indefinitely a

   (B) indefinitely, a          (D) No change is necessary.

7. Students must pay a penalty for overdue library <u>books, however, there</u> is a grace period.

    (A) books; however, there

    (B) books however, there

    (C) books: however, there

    (D) No change is necessary.

8. Among the states that seceded from the Union to join the Confederacy in 1860–1861 <u>were:</u> Mississippi, Florida, and Alabama.

    (A) were

    (B) were;

    (C) were.

    (D) No change is necessary.

9. The art exhibit displayed works by many famous <u>artists such as:</u> Dali, Picasso, and Michelangelo.

    (A) artists such as;

    (B) artists such as

    (C) artists. Such as

    (D) No change is necessary.

10. The National Shakespeare Company will perform <u>the following plays:</u> *Othello*, *Macbeth*, *Hamlet*, and *As You Like It*.

    (A) the following plays,

    (B) the following plays;

    (C) the following plays

    (D) No change is necessary.

---

**Drill 10 Answers**

| | | | |
|---|---|---|---|
| 1. (D) | 4. (C) | 7. (A) | 10. (D) |
| 2. (A) | 5. (A) | 8. (A) | |
| 3. (A) | 6. (D) | 9. (B) | |

# CAPITALIZATION

When a word is capitalized, it calls attention to itself. This attention should be for a good reason. There are standard uses for capital letters. In general, capitalize (1) all proper nouns, (2) the first word of a sentence, and (3) the first word of a direct quotation.

## You Should Also Capitalize

Names of ships, aircraft, spacecraft, and trains:

| | |
|---|---|
| *Apollo 13* | *Mariner IV* |
| DC-10 | *S.S. United States* |
| *Sputnik II* | Boeing 707 |

Names of deities:

| | |
|---|---|
| God | Jupiter |
| Allah | Holy Ghost |
| Buddha | Venus |
| Jehovah | Shiva |

Geological periods:

| | |
|---|---|
| Neolithic age | Cenozoic era |
| late Pleistocene times | Ice Age |

Names of astronomical bodies:

| | |
|---|---|
| Mercury | Big Dipper |
| the Milky Way | Halley's comet |
| Ursa Major | North Star |

Personifications:

Reliable Nature brought her promised Spring.

Bring on Melancholy in his sad might.

She believed that Love was the answer to all her problems.

Historical periods:

| | |
|---|---|
| Middle Ages | World War I |
| Reign of Terror | Great Depression |
| Christian Era | Roaring Twenties |
| Age of Louis XIV | Renaissance |

Organizations, associations, and institutions:

| | |
|---|---|
| Girl Scouts | North Atlantic Treaty Organization |
| Kiwanis Club | League of Women Voters |
| Boston Red Sox | Unitarian Church |
| Smithsonian Institution | Common Market |
| Library of Congress | Franklin Glen High School |
| New York Philharmonic | Harvard University |

Government and judicial groups:

| | |
|---|---|
| Senate | United States Court of Appeals |
| Parliament | Committee on Foreign Affairs |
| Peace Corps | Boston City Council |
| Census Bureau | Massachusetts Supreme Court |
| Department of State | House of Representatives |

A general term that accompanies a specific name is capitalized if it follows the specific name. If it stands alone or comes before the specific name, it is usually (but not always) put in lowercase:

| | |
|---|---|
| Washington State | the state of Washington |
| Senator Durbin | the senator from Illinois |
| Central Park | the park |
| Golden Gate Bridge | the bridge |
| President Obama | the president of the United States |
| Pope Benedict | the pope |

| | |
|---|---|
| Queen Elizabeth I | the queen of England |
| Tropic of Capricorn | the tropics |
| Monroe Doctrine | the doctrine of expansion |
| Mississippi River | the river |
| Easter Day | the day |
| Treaty of Versailles | the treaty |
| Webster's Dictionary | the dictionary |
| Equatorial Current | the equator |

Use a capital letter to start a sentence:

**Our car would not start.**

**When will you leave? I need to know right away.**

**Never!**

**Let me in! Please!**

When a sentence appears within a sentence, start it with a capital letter:

**We had only one concern: When would we eat?**

**My sister said, "I'll find the Monopoly game."**

**He answered, "We can only stay a few minutes."**

The most important words of titles are capitalized. Those words not capitalized are conjunctions (*and, or, but*) and short prepositions (*of, on, by, for*). The first and last word of a title must always be capitalized:

| | |
|---|---|
| *A Man for All Seasons* | *Crime and Punishment* |
| *Of Mice and Men* | *Rise of the West* |
| *Strange Life of Ivan Osokin* | "Blue Suede Shoes" |
| "Amazing Grace" | "Ode to Billy Joe" |
| "Rubaiyat of Omar Khayyam" | "NCIS—Los Angeles" |

Capitalize newspaper and magazine titles:

*U.S. News & World Report*

*National Geographic*

*The New York Times*

*The Boston Globe*

Capitalize radio and TV station call letters:

| | |
|---|---|
| ABC | NBC |
| WNEW | WBOP |
| CNN | HBO |

Do not capitalize compass directions or seasons:

| | |
|---|---|
| west | north |
| east | south |
| spring | winter |
| autumn | summer |

Capitalize regions:

| | |
|---|---|
| the South | the Northeast |
| the West | Eastern Europe |

BUT:  the south of France

the eastern part of town

Capitalize specific military units:

the U.S. Army

the 7th Fleet

the German Navy

the 1st Infantry Division

Capitalize political groups and philosophies:

| | |
|---|---|
| Democratic party | Communist party |
| Marxist party | Nazi party |
| Whig party | Federalist party |
| Existentialism | Transcendentalism |

BUT do not capitalize systems of government or individual adherents to a philosophy:

| | |
|---|---|
| democracy | communism |
| fascist | agnostic |
| existentialist | transcendentalist |

---

## Drill 11

*Directions:* Choose the correct replacement for the underlined words.

1. Mexico is the southernmost country in <u>North America</u>. It borders the United States on the north; it is bordered on the <u>south</u> by Belize and Guatemala.

   (A) north America . . . South

   (B) North America . . . South

   (C) North america . . . south

   (D) No change is necessary.

2. The <u>Northern Hemisphere</u> is the half of the <u>earth</u> that lies north of the <u>Equator.</u>

   (A) Northern hemisphere . . . earth . . . equator

   (B) Northern hemisphere . . . Earth . . . Equator

   (C) Northern Hemisphere . . . Earth . . . equator

   (D) No change is necessary.

3. Aphrodite (<u>Venus in Roman Mythology</u>) was the <u>Greek</u> goddess of love.

   (A) Venus in Roman mythology . . . greek

   (B) venus in roman mythology . . . Greek

   (C) Venus in Roman mythology . . . Greek

   (D) No change is necessary.

4. The <u>Koran</u> is considered by <u>Muslims</u> to be the holy word.

   (A) koran . . . muslims

   (B) koran . . . Muslims

   (C) Koran . . . muslims

   (D) No change is necessary.

5. At the <u>spring</u> graduation ceremonies, the university awarded over 2,000 <u>bachelor's</u> degrees.

   (A) Spring . . . Bachelor's

   (B) spring . . . Bachelor's

   (C) Spring . . . bachelor's

   (D) No change is necessary.

6. The fall of the <u>Berlin wall</u> was an important symbol of the collapse of <u>Communism</u>.

   (A) berlin Wall . . . communism

   (B) Berlin Wall . . . communism

   (C) Berlin Wall . . . Communism

   (D) No change is necessary.

7. A photograph of <u>mars</u> was printed in <u>The *New York Times*</u>.

   (A) Mars . . . *The New York Times*

   (B) mars . . . *The New York times*

   (C) mars . . . *the New York Time*s

   (D) No change is necessary.

**Directions:** Select the sentence that clearly and effectively states the idea and has no structural errors.

8. (A) Until 1989, Tom Landry was the only Coach the Dallas cowboys ever had.

   (B) Until 1989, Tom Landry was the only coach the Dallas Cowboys ever had.

   (C) Until 1989, Tom Landry was the only Coach the Dallas Cowboys ever had.

9. (A) My favorite works by Ernest Hemingway are "The Snows of Kilamanjaro," *The Sun Also Rises,* and *For Whom the Bell Tolls.*

   (B) My favorite works by Ernest Hemingway are "The Snows Of Kilamanjaro," *The Sun Also Rises,* and *For Whom The Bell Tolls.*

   (C) My favorite works by Ernest Hemingway are "The Snows of Kilamanjaro," *The Sun also Rises,* and *For whom the Bell Tolls.*

10. (A) The freshman curriculum at the community college includes english, a foreign language, Algebra I, and history.

    (B) The freshman curriculum at the community college includes English, a foreign language, Algebra I, and history.

    (C) The Freshman curriculum at the Community College includes English, a foreign language, Algebra I, and History.

---

**Drill 11 Answers**

| 1. (D) | 4. (D) | 7. (A) | 10. (B) |
|--------|--------|--------|---------|
| 2. (C) | 5. (D) | 8. (B) | |
| 3. (C) | 6. (B) | 9. (A) | |

## SPELLING

Spelling questions test your ability to recognize misspelled words. This section reviews spelling tips and rules to help you spot incorrect spellings. Problems such as the distinction between "to" and "too" and "lead" and "led" are covered in the vocabulary review at the beginning of this book.

- Remember, "i" before "e" except after "c," or when sounded as "a" as in "neighbor" and "weigh."

- There are only three words in the English language that end in "-ceed":

    **proceed, succeed, exceed**

- There are several words that end in "-cede":

    **secede, recede, concede, precede**

- There is only one word in the English language that ends in "-sede":

    **supersede**

Many people learn to read English phonetically; that is, by sounding out the letters of the words. However, many English words are not pronounced the way they are spelled, and those who try to spell English words phonetically often make spelling "errors." It is better to memorize the correct spelling of English words rather than to rely on phonetics to spell correctly.

### Frequently Misspelled Words

The following is a list of frequently misspelled words. Study the spelling of each word by having a friend or teacher drill you on the words. Then mark down the words that you misspelled and study those select ones again. (The words appear in their most popular spellings.)

| A | a lot  ability  absence  absent  abundance  accept  acceptable  accident  accommodate  accompanied  accomplish  accumulation  accuse  accustomed  ache  achieve  achievement  acknowledge  acquaintance  acquainted  acquire  across  address  addressed  adequate  advantage  advantageous  advertise  advertisement  advice  advisable  advise  advisor  aerial  affect  affectionate  again  against  aggravate  aggressive  agree  aisle  all right  almost  already  although  altogether  always  amateur  American  among  amount  analysis  analyze  angel  angle  annual  another  answer  antiseptic  anxious  apologize  apparatus  apparent  appear  appearance  appetite  application  apply  appreciate  appreciation  approach  appropriate  approval  approve  approximate  argue  arguing  argument  arouse  arrange  arrangement  article  artificial  ascend  assistance  assistant  associate  association  attempt  attendance  attention  audience  August  author  automobile  autumn  auxiliary  available  avenue  awful  awkward |
|---|---|
| B | bachelor  balance  balloon  bargain  basic  beautiful  because  become  before  beginning  being  believe  benefit  benefited  between  bicycle  board  bored  borrow  bottle  bottom  boundary  brake  breadth  breath  breathe  brilliant  building  bulletin  bureau  burial  buried  bury  bushes  business |
| C | cafeteria  calculator  calendar  campaign  capital  capitol  captain  career  careful  careless  carriage  carrying  category  ceiling  cemetery  cereal  certain  changeable  characteristic  charity  chief  choose  chose  cigarette  circumstance  citizen  clothes  clothing  coarse  coffee  collect  college  colonel  column  comedy  comfortable  commitment  committed  committee  communicate  company  comparative  compel  competent  competition  compliment  conceal  conceit  conceivable  conceive  concentration  conception  condition  conference  confident  congratulate  conquer  conscience  conscientious  conscious  consequence  consequently  considerable  consistency  consistent  continual  continuous  controlled  controversy  convenience  convenient  conversation  cooperate  corporal  corroborate  council  counsel  counselor  courage  courageous  course  courteous  courtesy  criticism  criticize  crystal  curiosity  curriculum  cylinder |

| D | daily  daughter  daybreak  death  deceive  December  deception  decide  decision  decisive  deed  definite  delicious  dependent  deposit  derelict  descend  descent  describe  description  desert  desirable  despair  desperate  dessert  destruction  determine  develop  development  device  dictator  died  difference  different  dilemma  dinner  direction  disappear  disappoint  disappointment  disapproval  disapprove  disastrous  discipline  discover  discriminate  disease  dissatisfied  dissection  dissipate  distance  distinction  division  doctor  dollar  doubt  dozen |
|---|---|
| E | earnest  easy  ecstasy  ecstatic  education  effect  efficiency  efficient  eight  either  eligibility  eligible  eliminate  embarrass  embarrassment  emergency  emphasis  emphasize  enclosure  encouraging  endeavor  engineer  English  enormous  enough  entrance  envelope  environment  equipment  equipped  especially  essential  evening  evident  exaggerate  exaggeration  examine  exceed  excellent  except  exceptional  exercise  exhausted  exhaustion  exhilaration  existence  exorbitant  expense  experience  experiment  explanation  extreme |
| F | facility  factory  familiar  fascinate  fascinating  fatigue  February  financial  financier  flourish  forcibly  forehead  foreign  formal  former  fortunate  fourteen  fourth  frequent  friend  frightening  fundamental  further |
| G | gallon  garden  gardener  general  genius  government  governor  grammar  grateful  great  grievance  grievous  grocery  guarantee  guess  guidance |
| H | half  hammer  handkerchief  happiness  healthy  heard  heavy  height  heroes  heroine  hideous  himself  hoarse  holiday  hopeless  hospital  humorous  hurried  hurrying |
| I | ignorance  imaginary  imbecile  imitation  immediately  immigrant  incidental  increase  independence  independent  indispensable  inevitable  influence  influential  initiate  innocence  inoculate  inquiry  insistent  instead  instinct  integrity  intellectual  intelligence  intercede  interest  interfere  interference  interpreted  interrupt  invitation  irrelevant  irresistible  irritable  island  its  it's  itself |

| J | January   jealous   journal   judgment |
|---|---|
| K | kindergarten   kitchen   knew   knock   know   knowledge |
| L | labor   laboratory   laid   language   later   latter   laugh   leisure length   lesson   library   license   light   lightning   likelihood likely   literal   literature   livelihood   loaf   loneliness   loose lose   losing   loyal   loyalty |
| M | magazine   maintenance   maneuver   marriage   married marry   match   material   mathematics   measure   medicine millennium   million   miniature   minimum   miracle miscellaneous   mischief   mischievous   misspelled   mistake momentous   monkey   monotonous   moral   morale mortgage   mountain   mournful   muscle   mysterious   mystery |
| N | narrative   natural   necessary   needle   negligence   neighbor neither   newspaper   newsstand   niece   noticeable |
| O | o'clock   obedient   obstacle   occasion   occasional   occur occurred   occurrence   ocean   offer   often   omission   omit once   operate   opinion   opportune   opportunity   optimist optimistic   origin   original   oscillate   ought   ounce   overcoat |
| P | paid   pamphlet   panicky   parallel   parallelism   particular partner   pastime   patience   peace   peaceable   pear   peculiar pencil   people   perceive   perception   perfect   perform performance   perhaps   period   permanence   permanent perpendicular   perseverance   persevere   persistent   personal personality   personnel   persuade   persuasion   pertain   pianist picture   piece   plain   playwright   pleasant   please   pleasure pocket   poison   policeman   political   population   portrayal positive   possess   possession   possessive   possible   post office potatoes   practical   prairie   precede   preceding   precise predictable   prefer   preference   preferential   preferred prejudice   preparation   prepare   prescription   presence president   prevalent   primitive   principal   principle   privilege probably   procedure   proceed   produce   professional professor   profitable   prominent   promise   pronounce pronunciation   propeller   prophet   prospect   psychology pursue   pursuit |

| Q | quality  quantity  quarreling  quart  quarter  quiet  quite |
|---|---|
| R | raise  realistic  realize  reason  rebellion  recede  receipt receive  recipe  recognize  recommend  recuperate  referred rehearsal  reign  relevant  relieve  remedy  renovate repeat  repetition  representative  requirements  resemblance resistance  resource  respectability  responsibility  restaurant rhythm  rhythmical  ridiculous  right  role  roll  roommate |
| S | sandwich  Saturday  scarcely  scene  schedule  science scientific  scissors  season  secretary  seize  seminar  sense separate  service  several  severely  shepherd  sheriff  shining shoulder  shriek  siege  sight  signal  significance  significant similar  similarity  sincerely  site  soldier  solemn  sophomore soul  source  souvenir  special  specified  specimen  speech stationary  stationery  statue  statute  stockings  stomach straight  strength  strenuous  stretch  striking  studying substantial  succeed  successful  sudden  superintendent suppress  surely  surprise  suspense  sweat  sweet  syllable symmetrical  sympathy  synonym |
| T | technical  telegram  telephone  temperament  temperature tenant  tendency  tenement  therefore  thorough  through title  together  tomorrow  tongue  toward  tragedy transferred  treasury  tremendous  tries  truly  twelfth twelve  tyranny |
| U | undoubtedly  United States  university  unnecessary  unusual useful  usual |
| V | vacuum  valley  valuable  variety  vegetable  vein vengeance  versatile  vicinity  vicious  view  village  villain visitor  voice  volume |
| W | waist  waste  weak  wear  weather  Wednesday  week weigh  weird  whether  which  while  whole  wholly whose  wretched |

## Drill 12

*Directions:* Identify the misspelled word in each set.

1. (A) probly

    (B) accommodate

    (C) acquaintance

2. (A) auxiliary

    (B) atheletic

    (C) beginning

3. (A) environment

    (B) existence

    (C) Febuary

4. (A) ocassion

    (B) occurrence

    (C) omitted

5. (A) perspiration

    (B) referring

    (C) priviledge

*Directions:* Choose the correct replacement for the underlined words.

6. <u>Preceding</u> the <u>business</u> session, lunch will be served in a <u>separate</u> room.

    (A) preceeding . . . business . . . seperate

    (B) proceeding . . . bussiness . . . seperate

    (C) proceeding . . . business . . . seperite

    (D) No change is necessary.

7. Monte <u>inadvertently</u> left <u>several</u> of his <u>libary</u> books in the cafeteria.

    (A) inadverdently . . . serveral . . . libery

    (B) inadvertently . . . several . . . library

    (C) inadvertentely . . . several . . . librery

    (D) No change is necessary.

8. Sam wished he had more <u>liesure</u> time so he could <u>persue</u> his favorite hobbies.

    (A) leisure . . . pursue        (C) leisure . . . persue

    (B) Liesure . . . pursue        (D) No change is necessary.

9. One of my <u>favrite</u> <u>charecters</u> in <u>litrature</u> is Bilbo from *The Hobbit*.

    (A) favrite . . . characters . . . literature

    (B) favorite . . . characters . . . literature

    (C) favourite . . . characters . . . literature

    (D) No change is necessary.

10. Even <u>tho</u> Joe was badly hurt in the <u>accidant</u>, the company said they were not <u>lible</u> for damages.

   (A) though . . . accidant . . . libel

   (B) though . . . accident . . . liable

   (C) though . . . acident . . . liable

   (D) No change is necessary.

---

**Drill 12 Answers**

| | | | | | | | |
|---|---|---|---|---|---|---|---|
| 1. | (A) | 4. | (A) | 7. | (B) | 10. | (B) |
| 2. | (B) | 5. | (C) | 8. | (A) | | |
| 3. | (C) | 6. | (D) | 9. | (B) | | |

# COMMON ERRORS IN THE USE OF HOMONYMS

**Homonyms** are words that have the same sound and often the same spellings but have different meanings. **Homophones** are words that are pronounced the same but are different in meaning, origin, and sometimes spelling. Often the two terms are used interchangeably. However, some teachers prefer to differentiate between the two. They reserve homonyms for those words that have the same spelling and homophones for those that sound the same but have different spellings. Both homonyms and homophones are often used incorrectly. Here are some of the most common ones.

## Examples

### Homonyms

**fair** (appearance), **fair** (fun place with rides and exhibits); **its**, (belongs to it), **it's** (it is)

### Homophones

cite, sight, and site; sea and see; your and you're; bow and bough; bear, bare; horse, hoarse; fourth, forth; know, no; new knew; principle; principal; their, they're; to, too, two;

who's, whose; your, you're; blue, blew; rode, rowed; new, gnu; band, banned; ways, weighs; isle, aisle; won, one.

*Note:* The MTEL test does not differentiate between homonyms and homophones, and gives examples of both in their sample for homonyms.

## DRILL 13

**Directions:** Choose the correct homonym for the blank in the sentence.

1. The boat was out of ___ of land.

    site                          sight

2. Diane's new __dress was very appropriate for the occasion.

    blue                          blew

3. The bird had broken __ wing.

    its                           it's

4. The tiger paced back and __ in its cage.

    fourth                        forth

5. The bride refused to walk down the __.

    isle                          aisle

6. The new __ looked out at her gathered students.

    principal                     principle

7. The hunter raised his __ and arrow to shoot at the deer.

    bough                         bow

8. Are you able to __ several instances of the misuse of homonyms?

   sight                     cite

9. Looking at the __, they decided to cancel the game.

   weather                   whether

10. Mel's voice was a bit __ after shouting for his team.

    Horse                    hoarse

---

**Drill 13 Answers**

| | | | | | | | |
|---|---|---|---|---|---|---|---|
| 1. | sight | 4. | forth | 7. | bow | 10. | hoarse |
| 2. | blue | 5. | aisle | 8. | cite | | |
| 3. | its | 6. | principal | 9. | weather | | |

# III. Written Composition

## PRE-WRITING/PLANNING

Before you begin to write, there are certain preliminary steps you should take. A few minutes spent planning pay off—your final essay will be more focused, better-developed, and clearer. For a 30-minute essay, you should spend about five minutes on the pre-writing process.

## Understand the Question

Read the essay question very carefully and ask yourself the following questions:

- What is the meaning of the topic statement?

- Is the question asking me to persuade the reader of the validity of a certain opinion?

- Do I agree or disagree with the statement? What will be my thesis?

- What kinds of examples can I use to support my thesis? Explore personal experiences, historical evidence, current events, and literary subjects.

## Choosing a Topic

You may be assigned a topic to write about or you may be able to choose your own. A *topic* is any subject of study, inquiry, or discussion that is addressed for the sake of an audience. A topic, however, is not a main point or a thesis. Remember that a *topic* is the subject about which the author writes. Books, cars, people, sports, rainbows, fish, potato chips—*anything* can be a topic of inquiry, study, or discussion. The point is to choose one and begin to focus on writing about it.

Some topics are too broad to deal with in a short 500-word essay, so you may be asked to narrow the topic. Narrowing a topic means limiting it and becoming more specific about what is to be discussed in the paper, making it a manageable length and scope. For example, suppose the chosen topic is "books." Before writing, decide on the *purpose* in writing and the *audience* that is going to read the work. Decide on some relevant characteristics that the reader(s) may have.

## Getting Ideas on Paper Quickly

Often the most difficult question in writing is how to begin. Several techniques for becoming *fluent* are recommended by experts. This section explores some of the major ones available. In the reading process, the reader must determine what his or her purpose for reading is and what the writer's purpose for writing is.

Similarly, in the writing process, the writer must decide what the purpose for writing is going to be. This technique will help the writer get started and, at the same time, will help narrow down the topic. What does the author want to explain when writing about "books"? Does the author wish to describe (that is, talk about what physical qualities the books possess), explain what they are, inform readers about some issue or quality about them, or persuade readers about something in relation to "books"?

More often than not, the writer is asked to *persuade* the reader(s) of something about the topic. This calls for the use of *argumentation*, or persuasive composition, to make the point.

Suppose the writer wants to persuade the reader that books are difficult to read. *Audience* is the next important consideration. The writer must decide on the person or group of people that would, or should, be persuaded by the argument. Once the author determines the audience, his or her focus for persuasion changes. *Audience awareness often determines the direction and content of writing.* If a student attempts to persuade his or her professors that books are difficult to read, then he or she will have to summon a great deal of information because most professors would disagree. On the other hand, if the audience consists of students, the writer may be able to limit his or her evidence and convince them using fewer examples.

It would be impossible, however, to discuss in a 500-word essay, or even in a short research paper, how all the books on the whole earth are difficult to read. The writer needs to narrow the subject of discussion even further. The way to do this is to use specific adjectives to condense the field of thinking and discussion. Thus, instead of claiming that books are difficult to read and leaving open an encyclopedia of trouble, narrow the field.

**History textbooks are difficult for first-year college students to read.**

Admittedly, however, *some* first-year students will not find reading history textbooks difficult. Therefore, do not claim that this statement is true for all by not *qualifying the thesis.* Instead, narrow the topic even further:

**Many history textbooks are difficult to read for selected first-year college students.**

Obviously, this topic can be narrowed even further.

## Freewriting

Through a technique called *freewriting*, the writer can also begin the writing process. Freewriting is putting down on paper whatever comes to mind at the time. When utilizing this technique, be sure not to worry about technical matters such as spelling, punctuation, paragraphing, etc. The writer often develops interesting and novel ideas during this stage. The important aspect about freewriting is the "flow" of the writing, however imperfect the technical aspects of sentence structure and grammar may be at the moment. Correcting these errors comes later in the process.

## Brainstorming

*Brainstorming* is the technique by which the author takes a few minutes to list, in random order, all the ideas and thoughts he or she has about a topic. When brainstorming a topic, the writer acts as a reporter would act and uses the *reporter's heuristic* for getting the "lead" to the story. A good reporter asks key questions of any event in order to write the "lead" or beginning to a story: What happened? Who was there? When did it happen? How did it happen? Where did it happen? Why did it happen? When confronting a topic, the writer asks similar related questions of the topic and writes down the answers to the relevant questions as quickly as he or she thinks of them. The author must simply write down ideas as they come out and not censor them. By the end of this process, the writer will have conceived many ideas and concepts.

## Clustering

*Clustering* involves writing a topic in the center of a piece of blank, unlined paper around which the writer writes down all the things about the topic that he or she can think of, thus creating little "rays" of thought that stem from the topic. Following is an illustration of how this might look.

### Clustering: A Pre-writing Technique

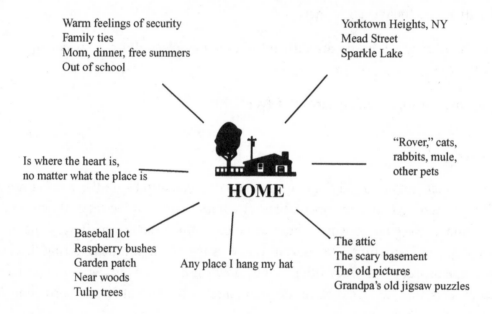

Warm feelings of security
Family ties
Mom, dinner, free summers
Out of school

Yorktown Heights, NY
Mead Street
Sparkle Lake

"Rover," cats, rabbits, mule, other pets

Is where the heart is, no matter what the place is

**HOME**

"Rover," cats,
rabbits, mule,
other pets

Baseball lot
Raspberry bushes
Garden patch
Near woods
Tulip trees

Any place I hang my hat

The attic
The scary basement
The old pictures
Grandpa's old jigsaw puzzles

## Consider Your Audience

Essays would be pointless without an audience. Why write an essay if no one wants or needs to read it? Why add evidence, organize your ideas, or correct bad grammar? The reason to do any of these things is because someone out there needs to understand what you mean or say.

What does the audience need to know to believe you or to come over to your position? Imagine someone you know listening to you declare your position or opinion and then saying, "Oh, yeah? Prove it!" This is your audience—write to them. Ask yourself the following questions so that when you are confronted by a person who says "Prove it," you will have a well thought-out response.

- What evidence do I need to prove my idea to this skeptic?

- What would he or she disagree with me about?

- What does he or she share with me as common knowledge? What do I need to tell the reader?

## Writing for a Specific Audience, Purpose, and Occasion

For effective communication, a writer or speaker must consider three factors:

1. the audience addressed (for whom or to whom the message is being sent);

2. the purpose of the message; and

3. the occasion of the message.

Perhaps William Shakespeare best demonstrated the importance of these concepts when he created the speech that Marcus Antonius delivered to the aroused Roman populace. Previously, Marcus Brutus had delivered a funeral oration that assured the Romans that it was for their best interests and the welfare of the nation that Caesar was assassinated. When Marcus Antonius rose to speak, he addressed the crowd of Romans as "friends, Romans, countrymen," immediately appealing to their common spirit with him. Antonius then continued to gather support for the dead emperor by reciting the events of the political conspiracy, apparently not criticizing those involved in the assassination. Actually his words brought honor to Caesar, who always acted in a way that brought honor and support to the Roman people. By the end of his clever address, the crowd was ready to chase the conspirators from Rome.

Shakespeare realized that the audience listening to Marcus Antonius's speech could not be immediately and directly brought to support Caesar and, in turn, brought to attack Marcus Brutus and other assassins. First, they must be exposed to a list of supposed "faults" of the emperor and then be led to view his shortcomings as positive traits, functioning always to bring benefits to the Romans. Finally, the occasion of the speech, immediately after Marcus Brutus's funeral oration, involved a volatile gathering. The Romans' attitudes toward Caesar must be brought into alignment with Marcus Antonius's for the clever spokesman to convert the people.

Not so dramatic an occasion or so clever a style of expression affects the typical writer today. Awareness of the audience addressed, the purpose of one's words, and the occasion for the words are all important. A communicator must know the audience and the individual attitudes, opinions, fears, and concerns that motivate.

## Drill 1

**Directions:** Read the following short essay. Then answer the questions.

Mankind has always attempted to assess the time. Ancient man used the position of the sun to determine the time of day. During the night, a water clock was used, working much like an hour glass. The sundial today is primarily an attractive garden item, no longer used to tell time.

Probably the Chinese designed the first mechanical time pieces in the eighth century. Europeans did not begin using them until the twelfth or thirteenth century. Early clocks were created to get people to the church on time. Church bells rang each hour, but there were no numbers on the face of the clock for the hour. Hence, the name for the time device was the French word *cloche*, meaning "bell." People were not too concerned about the exact time. Today many people want to have an accurate time awareness.

When hands were added to the face of a clock, they did not move although the face of the clock did sometimes, circling for the 12-hour period. Hands, which move, often appear on the face of the clock although many modern clocks and watches have numerals displayed digitally.

Early clocks were only approximately accurate. Today's atomic clocks are accurate to within one second each 60,000 years. Check the various clocks and watches in your household. Are all showing the same time?

1. The purpose of this essay is to

    (A) convince the reader of the importance of exact time.

    (B) suggest that people not pay so much attention to exact timing.

    (C) explain some of the steps in the development of time pieces.

    (D) show how much more useful modern clocks are.

2. The intended audience of the essay is

    (A) historians.

    (B) a reasonably well-educated group of young adults and adults.

    (C) collectors of old clocks.

    (D) educators.

---

**Drill 1 Answers**

1. (C)        2. (B)

# WRITING YOUR ESSAY

Once you have considered your position on the topic and thought of several examples to support it, you are ready to begin writing.

## Organizing Your Essay

Decide how many paragraphs you will write. In a timed exercise, you will probably have time for no more than four or five paragraphs. In such a format, the first paragraph should be the introduction, the next two or three should develop your thesis with specific examples, and the final paragraph should be a strong conclusion.

## Introduction (Thesis Statement)

The focus of your introduction should be the thesis statement. This statement allows your reader to understand the point and direction of your essay. The statement identifies the central idea of your essay and should clearly state your attitude about the subject. It will also dictate the basic content and organization of your essay. If you do not state your thesis clearly, your essay will suffer.

The thesis is the heart of the essay. Without it, readers won't know what your major message or central idea is in the essay.

The thesis must be something that can be argued or needs to be proven, not just an accepted fact. For example, "Animals are used every day in cosmetic and medical testing" is a fact—it needs no proof. But if the writer says, "Using animals for cosmetic and medical testing is cruel and should be stopped," we have a point that must be supported and defended by the writer.

The thesis can be placed in any paragraph of the essay, but in a short essay, especially one written for evaluative exam purposes, the thesis is most effective when placed in the last sentence of the opening paragraph.

Consider the following sample question:

**ESSAY TOPIC:** "That government is best which governs least."

**ASSIGNMENT:** Do you agree or disagree with this statement? Choose a specific example from current events, personal experience, or your reading to support your position.

After reading the topic statement, decide if you agree or disagree. If you agree with this statement, your thesis statement could be the following:

> **"Government has the right to protect individuals from interference but no right to extend its powers and activities beyond this function."**

This statement clearly states the writer's opinion in a direct manner. It also serves as a blueprint for the essay. The remainder of the introduction should give two or three brief examples that support your thesis.

## Supporting Paragraphs

The next two or three paragraphs of your essay will elaborate on the supporting examples you gave in your introduction. Each paragraph should discuss only one idea. Like the introduction, each paragraph should be coherently organized with a topic sentence and supporting details.

The topic sentence is to each paragraph what the thesis statement is to the essay as a whole. It tells the reader what you plan to discuss in that paragraph. It has a specific subject and is neither too broad nor too narrow. It also establishes the author's attitude and gives the reader a sense of the direction in which the writer is going. An effective topic sentence also arouses the reader's interest.

Although it may occur in the middle or at the end of the paragraph, the topic sentence usually appears at the beginning of the paragraph. Placing it at the beginning is advantageous because it helps you stay focused on the main idea.

The remainder of each paragraph should support the topic sentence with examples and illustrations. Each sentence should progress logically from the previous one and be centrally connected to your topic sentence. Do not include any extraneous material that does not serve to develop your thesis.

## Organizing and Reviewing the Paragraphs

The unit of work for revising is the paragraph. After you have written what you wanted to say based on your prewriting list, spend some time revising your draft by looking to see if you need to indent for paragraphs anywhere. If you do, make a little proofreader's mark (¶) to indicate to the reader that you think a paragraph should start here. Check to see if you want to add anything that would make your point of view more convincing. Be sure to supply useful transitions to keep up the flow and maintain the focus of your ideas. If you don't have room on the paper, or if your new paragraph shows up out of order, add that paragraph and indicate with a number or some other mark where you want it to go. Check to *make sure* that you gave examples or illustrations for your statements. In the examples below, two paragraphs are offered: one without concrete evidence and one with evidence for its idea. Study each. Note the topic sentence and how that sentence is or is not supported with evidence.

## Paragraphing with No Evidence

Television is bad for people. *Watching television takes time away from other things.* Programs on television are often stupid and depict crimes that people later copy. Television takes time away from loved ones, and it often becomes addictive. So, television is bad for people because it is no good.

In this example, the author has not given any concrete evidence for any of the good ideas presented. He or she just declares them to be so. Any one of the sentences above might make a good opening sentence for a whole paragraph.

## Paragraphing with Evidence

*Watching television takes time away from other things.* For example, all those hours people spend sitting in front of the tube could be spent working on building a chair or fixing the roof. *(first piece of evidence)* Maybe the laundry needs to be done, but because people watch television, they may end up not having time to do it. Then Monday comes around again and they have no socks to wear to work—all because they couldn't stand to miss that episode of "The Simpsons." *(second piece of evidence)* Someone could be writing a letter to a friend in Boston who hasn't been heard from or written to for months. *(third piece of evidence)* Or maybe someone misses the opportunity to take in a beautiful day in the park because he or she had to see "The View." They'll repeat "The View," but this beautiful day only comes around once. Watching television definitely keeps people from getting things done.

The primary evidence the author uses here is that of probable illustrations taken from life experience, largely anecdotal. Always *supply evidence.* Three examples or illustrations of your idea per paragraph is a useful number. Four is OK, but stop there. Don't go on and on about a single point. You don't have time.

## Conclusion

Your conclusion should briefly restate your thesis and explain how you have shown it to be true. Because you want to end your essay on a strong note, your conclusion should be concise and effective.

Do not introduce any new topics that you cannot support. If you were watching a movie that suddenly shifted plot and characters at the end, you would be disappointed or even angry. Similarly, conclusions must not drift away from the major focus and message of the essay. Make sure your conclusion is clearly on the topic and represents your perspective without any confusion about what you really mean and believe. The reader will respect you for staying true to your intentions.

The conclusion is your last chance to grab and impress the reader. You can even use humor, if appropriate, but a dramatic close will remind the reader you are serious, even passionate, about what you believe.

## Effective Use of Language

Clear organization, while vitally important, is not the only factor the graders of your essay consider. You must also demonstrate that you can express your ideas clearly, using correct grammar, diction, usage, spelling, and punctuation.

## Point of View

An important way to maintain unity in writing is to maintain consistency in the point of view selected by the writer. The writer has three choices, each of which has a special role in the writing process. Once selected, the point of view may not be switched back and forth without adversely affecting the unity of the piece of writing.

### First-person point of view

The first-person point of view method used in most personal writing—autobiographical, memories of feelings or experiences, viewpoints that are the writer's own beliefs—is identified by the use of *I, me, we, us, my, mine, our,* and *ours.*

EXAMPLE   **I often wondered about my childhood friend, Freddy. Freddy was my shadow when I was eight years old. We played the same games, read the same books, hiked the same paths, and fished the same streams. Then suddenly, Freddy's parents moved. I never even said good-bye to him. Where is Freddy today?**

ANALYSIS:   **This childhood memory is told by a narrator, recalling when he was eight years of age. Now, older, he wonders about his constant companion in those days. The narrator may use the pronoun *him* to refer to Freddy without changing the point of view since the narrator still refers to himself as *I*.**

## Second-person point of view

The second-person point of view uses the pronouns *you* and *your*. They are correctly used when someone is addressing a person in direct dialogue.

> **EXAMPLE**　The judge addressed the witness, "Are you sure of the time you saw the accident?"

One of the most common errors in writing, however, is using *you* (or *your*) in the midst of a passage that is written in first- or third-person point of view. The corrected passage uses a noun naming the person(s) addressed to maintain a consistent point of view.

> **INCORRECT:**　The group of tourists entered the mosque, removing their shoes as requested. Several had difficulty finding their shoes later. How would *you* have left *your* shoes so that *you* could find them easily?

> **CORRECT:**　The group of tourists entered the mosque, removing their shoes as requested. Several had difficulty finding their shoes later. How can *visitors* leave *their* shoes so that *they* can find them easily?

## Third-person point of view

Most writing uses the third-person point of view. Fiction, explanatory writing, persuasive writing, journalistic expression, and similar forms use this point of view. The pronouns identifying third person are *he, him, she, her, his, hers, them, their, theirs,* and *they*.

> **EXAMPLE**　Many people believe that Christopher Columbus was the first to visit the land that became known as North America. Actually, over 500 years earlier than Columbus, a Norseman named Biarni Heriulfson sighted Labrador when he missed his intended destination, Greenland. A few years after Heriulfson's voyage, Leif Ericson bought Heriulfson's ship and made the return journey to the new land in 1002. He and his shipmates probably landed at Cape Cod. They also explored Labrador and Nova Scotia. Remains of other early Viking settlements have been discovered. Since this was a hostile area for settlement, however, the northern explorers gave up ideas of living there by 1025.

---

# Drill 2

*Directions:* Rewrite the following passage so that the point of view is consistent.

> The stranger walked into the room with obvious intent. Stopping in the center, he slowly looked around, his eyes moving from person to person. If you had been the one for whom he searched, you would have moved rapidly for the nearest exit.

---

## Drill 2 Answers

The answers may vary from the following. The last sentence must remove the second person pronouns, however.

> The stranger walked into the room with obvious intent. Stopping in the center, he slowly looked around, his eyes moving from person to person. Anyone fearing the stranger was searching for him would have moved rapidly for the nearest exit.

## Tone

A writer's tone results from his or her attitude toward the subject and the reader. If the essay question requires you to take a strong stand, the tone of your essay should reflect this.

Your tone should also be appropriate for the subject matter. A serious topic demands a serious tone. For a more light-hearted topic, you may wish to inject some humor into your essay. Whatever tone you choose, be consistent. Do not make any abrupt shifts in tone in the middle of your essay.

## Verb Tense

Make sure to remain in the same verb tense in which you began your essay. If you start in the past, make sure all verbs are past tense. Staying in the same verb tense improves the continuity and flow of ideas. Avoid phrases such as "now was," a confusing blend of present and past. Consistency of time is essential to the reader's understanding.

## Common Writing Errors

The four writing errors most often made by beginning writers are run-ons (also known as fused sentences), fragments, lack of subject-verb agreement, and incorrect use of the object:

1. **Run-ons**: "She swept the floor it was dirty" is a run-on. A period or semicolon is needed after "floor."

2. **Fragments**: "Before Jimmy learned how to play baseball" is a fragment. The word "before" fragmentizes the clause.

3. **Problems with subject-verb agreement**: A singular subject requires a singular verb; a plural subject or a compound subject requires a plural verb. If the separate parts of a subject are connected by *either—or*, *neither—nor*, or *or*, the verb agrees in number with the nearer part of the subject. "Either Maria or Robert are going to the game" is incorrect because one of them is going, but not both. The sentence should say, "Either Maria or Robert is going to the game."

4. **Incorrect object**: An objective case pronoun serves as the direct or indirect object of a verb, as the object of a preposition, and in apposition with an object of a verb or preposition; the nominative case serves as the subject of a verb, as a predicate pronoun, in apposition with the subject or with a predicate noun, in direct address, and in the nominative absolute construction. For example, "between you and I" sounds correct, but isn't. "Between" is a preposition that takes the objective case "me." The correct usage is "between you and me."

Other writing problems that may occur on the Communication and Literacy Skills Test are lack of thought and development, misspellings, and use of incorrect pronouns or antecedents. Keep in mind that clear, coherent handwriting always works to your advantage. Readers will appreciate an essay they can read with ease.

## Five Words Weak Writers Overuse

Weak and inexperienced writers overuse the vague pronouns *you*, *we*, *they*, *this*, and *it* often without telling exactly who or what is represented by the pronoun.

1. Beginning writers often shift to second person *you*, when the writer means "a person." This shift confuses readers and weakens the flow of the essay. Although *you* is commonly accepted in creative writing, journalism, and other arenas, in a short, formal essay it is best to avoid *you* altogether.

2. *We* is another pronoun that should be avoided. If by *we* the writer means "Americans," "society," or some other group, then he or she should say so.

3. *They* is often misused in essay writing because it is overused in conversation: "I went to the doctor, and they told me to take some medicine." Identify *they* for the reader.

4. *This* is usually used incorrectly without a referent: "She told me she received a present. This sounded good to me." This what? This idea? This news? This present? Be clear—don't make your readers guess what you mean. The word *this* should be followed by a noun or referent.

5. *It* is a common problem among weak writers. To what does *it* refer? Your readers don't appreciate vagueness; take the time to be clear and complete in your expression of ideas.

## Use Your Own Vocabulary

Is it a good idea to use big words that sound sophisticated in the dictionary or thesaurus, but that you don't really use or understand? No. So whose vocabulary should you use? Your own. You will be most comfortable with your own level of vocabulary.

This "comfort zone" doesn't give you license to be informal in a formal setting or to violate the rules of standard written English, but if you try to write in a style that is not yours, your writing will be awkward and lack a true voice.

You should certainly improve and build your vocabulary at every opportunity, but remember: you should not attempt to change your vocabulary level at this point.

## Avoid the Passive Voice

In much of your writing you will want to use the active voice in order to convey a sense of directness and immediacy. However, avoiding the passive voice completely is neither possible nor desirable. Both constructions have their proper uses: the active voice stresses the actor while the passive voice stresses the action. Use the passive voice when the action of the verb is more important than the doer or when the doer is unknown.

**ACTIVE:  She kicked the winning field goal.**

In this case, the active construction directly and clearly communicates to the reader. The passive construction (The winning field goal was kicked by her.) would be awkward and wordy.

**PASSIVE:  She was arraigned and sentenced to ten years hard labor.**

In this case, the passive construction is preferable because the actor (the court or the judge) is unimportant to the sense of the sentence.

## PROOFREADING

Make sure to leave yourself enough time at the end to read over your essay for errors such as misspellings, omitted words, or incorrect punctuation. You will not have enough time to make large-scale revisions, but take this chance to make any small changes that will make your essay stronger. Consider the following when proofreading your work:

- Are all your sentences really sentences? Have you written any fragments or run-on sentences?

- Are you using vocabulary correctly?

- Did you leave out any punctuation? Did you capitalize correctly?

- Are there any misspellings, especially of difficult words?

If you have time, read your essay backwards from end to beginning. By doing so, you may catch errors that you missed reading forward only.

## REVISING

*Revising* occurs each time a concept in the rough draft is changed, rearranged, or altered. Be sure to examine the *organization, paragraphing, scope and nature of the thesis*, and *format* (the appearance and layout of the paper). This is the step and time in the process when *transitions, flow*, and the *logic* of the paper are analyzed. Revise before editing, and remember to keep paragraphs short and concise. This may entail moving whole paragraphs from one place to another within the text, adding a transition, or cutting out whole paragraphs. Continue this process until the paper logically supports the thesis.

## EDITING

*Editing* is the stage after revising in which *correct grammar*, *sentence style*, *diction*, *punctuation*, and *spelling* are inspected. When editing a paper, focus attention not on the concepts, content, or logic but on the clarity of sentences and the correctness of the grammar. If problems of organization and logic still exist, *revise* the paper more before *editing*. Editing should be strictly for grammar and individual sentence structure.

## Drill 3

*Directions:* You have 30 minutes to plan and write an essay on the topic below. You may write only on the assigned topic.

**Make** sure to give specific examples to support your thesis. Proofread your essay carefully and take care to express your ideas clearly and effectively.

**ESSAY TOPIC:** In the last 20 years, the deterioration of the environment has become a growing concern among both scientists and ordinary citizens.

**ASSIGNMENT:** Choose one pressing environmental problem, explain its negative impact, and discuss possible solutions.

### Drill 3 Answer

This answer key provides three sample essays that represent possible responses to the essay topic. Compare your own response to those given on the next few pages. Allow the strengths and weaknesses of the sample essays to help you to critique your own essay and improve your writing skills.

## Essay I (good)

There are many pressing environmental problems facing both this country and the world today. Pollution, the misuse and squandering of resources, and the cavalier attitude many people express all contribute to the problem. But one of the most pressing problems this country faces is the apathetic attitude many Americans have toward recycling.

Why is recycling so imperative? There are two major reasons. First, recycling previously used materials conserves precious national resources. Many people never stop to think that reserves of metal ores are not unlimited. There is only so much gold, silver, tin, and other metals in the ground. Once it has all been mined, there will never be any more unless we recycle what has already been used.

Second, the United States generates more solid waste per day than any other country on earth. Our disposable consumer culture consumes fast food meals in paper or styrofoam containers, uses disposable diapers with plastic liners that do not biodegrade, receives pounds, if not tons, of unsolicited junk mail every year, and relies more and more on prepackaged rather than fresh food.

No matter how it is accomplished, increased recycling is essential. We have to stop covering our land with garbage, and the best ways to do this are to reduce our dependence on prepackaged goods and to minimize the amount of solid waste disposed of in landfills. The best way to reduce solid waste is to recycle it. Americans need to band together to recycle, to preserve our irreplaceable natural resources, reduce pollution, and preserve our precious environment.

## Analysis

This essay presents a clearly defined thesis, and the writer elaborates on this thesis in a thoughtful and sophisticated manner. Various aspects of the problem under consideration are presented and explored, along with possible solutions. The support provided for the writer's argument is convincing and logical. There are few usage or mechanical errors to interfere with the writer's ability to communicate effectively. This writer demonstrates a comprehensive understanding of the rules of written English.

## Essay II (Average)

A pressing environmental problem today is the way we are cutting down too many trees and not planting any replacements for them. Trees are beneficial in many ways, and without them, many environmental problems would be much worse.

One of the ways trees are beneficial is that, like all plants, they take in carbon dioxide and produce oxygen. They can actually help clean the air this way. When too many trees are cut down in a small area, the air in that area is not as good and can be unhealthy to breath.

Another way trees are beneficial is that they provide homes for many types of birds, insects, and animals. When all the trees in an area are cut down, these animals lose their homes and sometimes they can die out and become extinct that way. Like the spotted owls in Oregon, that the loggers wanted to cut down the trees they lived in. If the loggers did cut down all the old timber stands that the spotted owls lived in, the owls would have become extinct.

But the loggers say that if they can't cut the trees down then they will be out of work, and that peoples' jobs are more important than birds. The loggers can do two things—they can either get training so they can do other jobs, or they can do what they should have done all along, and start replanting trees. For every mature tree they cut down, they should have to plant at least one tree seedling.

Cutting down the trees that we need for life, and that lots of other species depend on, is a big environmental problem that has a lot of long term consaquences. Trees are too important for all of us to cut them down without thinking about the future.

## Analysis

This essay has a clear thesis, which the author supports with good examples. However, the writer shifts between the chosen topic, which is that indiscriminate tree-cutting is a pressing environmental problem, and a list of the ways in which trees are beneficial and a discussion about the logging profession. Also, while there are few mistakes in usage and mechanics, the writer has some problems with sentence structure. The writing is pedestrian and the writer does not elaborate on the topic as much as he or she could have. The writer failed to provide the kind of critical analysis that the topic required.

## Essay III (Poor)

The most pressing environmental problem today is that lots of people and companies don't care about the environment, and they do lots of things that hurt the environment.

People throw litter out car windows and don't use trash cans, even if their all over a park, soda cans and fast food wrappers are all over the place. Cigarette butts are the worst cause the filters never rot. Newspapers and junk mail get left to blow all over the neighborhood, and beer bottles too.

Companies pollute the air and the water. Sometimes the ground around a company has lots of toxins in it. Now companies can buy credits from other companies that let them pollute the air even more. They dump all kinds of chemicals into lakes and rivers that kill off the fish and causes acid rain and kills off more fish and some trees and small animals and insects and then noone can go swimming or fishing in the lake.

People need to respect the environment because we only have one planet, and if we keep polluting it pretty soon nothing will grow and then even the people will die.

## Analysis

The writer of this essay does not define his or her thesis. Because of this lack of a clear thesis, the reader is left to infer the topic from the body of the essay. It is possible to perceive the writer's intended thesis; however, the support for this thesis is very superficial. The writer presents a list of common complaints about polluters without any critical discussion of the problems and possible solutions. Many sentences are run-ons and the writer has made several spelling errors. While the author manages to communicate his or her position on the issue, he or she does so on such a superficial level and with so many errors in usage and mechanics that the writer fails to demonstrate an ability to communicate effectively.

# MTEL Communication and Literacy Skills

## PRACTICE TEST 1

# PRACTICE TEST 1
# READING SUBTEST

## Multiple-Choice Section

*Directions:* Read each passage and answer the questions that follow. Answer sheets appear in the back of this book.

## Something about Lying

Why is everybody here lying—every single man? I am convinced that I will be immediately stopped and that people will start shouting: "Oh, what nonsense, by no means everybody! You have no topic, and so you are inventing things in order to begin in a more imposing fashion." I have already been upbraided for the lack of themes. But the point is that now I am earnestly convinced of the universality of our lying. One lives 50 years with an idea, one perceives and feels it, and all of a sudden it appears in such an aspect as to make it seem that one had hitherto not known it at all.

Lately, I was suddenly struck by the thought that in Russia, among our educated classes, there cannot be even one man who wouldn't be addicted to lying. This is precisely because among us even quite honest people may be lying. I am certain that in other nations, in the overwhelming majority of them, only scoundrels are lying; they are lying for the sake of material gain, that is, with directly criminal intent.

Well, in our case, even the most esteemed people may be lying for no reason at all, and with most honorable aims. We are lying almost invariably for the sake of hospitality. One wishes to create in the listener an aesthetical impression, to give him pleasure, and so one lies even, so to speak, sacrificing oneself to the listener.

*From Fyodor Dostoyevsky, "Something about Lying," 1873*

1. The central idea of this passage is that

   (A) people all over the world lie for the sake of material gain.

   (B) only scoundrels lie; respectable people do not.

   (C) everybody in Russia is lying, almost always for the sake of the listener.

   (D) there can be nothing wrong with lying since everybody is doing it.

2. In developing the passage, the organizational pattern used by the author could be described as

   (A) definition.

   (B) statement and clarification.

   (C) cause and effect.

   (D) classification.

3. In this passage, what is the meaning of the word "upbraided" in the first paragraph?

   (A) Reprimanded          (C) Distinguished

   (B) Complimented          (D) Noticed

4. What is the relationship between the first two sentences of Paragraph 2?

   (A) Statement and clarification

   (B) Generalization and example

   (C) Comparison and contrast

   (D) Cause and effect

## London and the English

The stranger who wanders through the great streets of London, and does not chance right into the regular quarters of the multitude, sees little or nothing of the fearful misery existing there. Only here and there at the mouth of some dark alley stands a ragged woman with a suckling babe at her weak breast, and begs with her eyes.

Perhaps if those eyes are still beautiful, we glance into them, and are shocked at the world of wretchedness visible within. The common beggars are old people, generally blacks, who stand at the corners of the streets cleaning pathways—a very necessary thing in muddy London—and ask for "coppers" in reward.

It is in the dusky twilight that Poverty with her mates Vice and Crime glide forth from their lairs. They shun daylight the more anxiously since their wretchedness there contrasts more cruelly with the pride of wealth which glitters everywhere; only Hunger sometimes drives them at noonday from their dens, and then they stand with silent, speaking eyes, staring beseechingly at the rich merchant who hurries along, busy and jingling gold, or at the lazy lord who, like a surfeited god, rides by on his high horse, casting now and then an aristocratically indifferent glance at the mob below, as though they were swarming ants, or rather a mass of baser beings, whose joys and sorrows have nothing in common with his feelings.

*From Heinrich Heine, "London and the English," 1828*

5. The author of this passage has created a tone that could be described as

   (A) apathetic.          (C) bitter.

   (B) arrogant.           (D) sympathetic.

6. What is the relationship between the second sentence ("Only here and there…") and the first sentence ("The stranger who…")?

   (A) Contrast

   (B) Statement and clarification

   (C) Addition

   (D) Generalization and example

7. Which statement below most accurately describes the main idea of this passage?

(A) London is a marvelous city to visit if you avoid the shabby sections.

(B) The wretchedness of London's poor is not obvious to the casual visitor.

(C) In London the rich and the poor live side by side in harmony.

(D) London should do something to hide the poor from the public eye.

## History

The effect of historical reading is analogous, in many respects, to that produced by foreign travel. The student, like the tourist, is transported into a new state of society. He sees new fashions. He hears new modes of expression. His mind is enlarged by contemplating the wide diversities of laws, of morals, and of manners. But men may travel far, and return with minds as contracted as if they had never stirred from their own market-town. In the same manner, men may know the dates of many battles and the genealogies of many royal houses, and yet be no wiser. Most people look at past times as princes look at foreign countries.

More than one illustrious stranger has landed on our island amidst the shouts of a mob, has dined with the King, has hunted with the master of the stag-hounds, has seen the guards reviewed, and a knight of the garter installed, has cantered along Regent Street, has visited Saint Paul's, and noted down its dimensions; and has then departed, thinking that he has seen England. He has, in fact, seen a few public buildings, public men, and public ceremonies.

But of the vast and complex system of society, of the fine shades of national character, of the practical operation of government and laws, he knows nothing. He who would understand these things rightly must not confine his observations to palaces and solemn days. He must see ordinary men as they appear in their ordinary business and in their ordinary pleasures. He must mingle in the crowds of the exchange and the coffee-house.

He must obtain admittance to the convivial table and the domestic hearth. He must bear with vulgar expression. He must not shrink from exploring even the retreats of misery. He who wishes to understand the condition of mankind in former ages must proceed on the same principle. If he attends only to public transactions, to wars, congresses, and debates, his studies will be as unprofitable as the travels of those imperial, royal, and serene sovereigns who form their judgment of our island from having gone in state to a few fine sights, and from having held formal conferences with a few great officers.

*From Thomas B. Macaulay, "History," 1828*

8.  In developing the paragraph, the organizational pattern used by the author could be described as

    (A)  comparison.

    (B)  time order.

    (C)  cause and effect.

    (D)  classification.

9.  The sentence "But men may travel far, and return with minds as contracted as if they had never stirred from their own market-town" is a statement of

    (A)  fact.

    (B)  opinion.

    (C)  fact and opinion.

    (D)  neither fact nor opinion.

10.  This passage indicates that the author's purpose is to

    (A)  describe what the typical visitor to England sees.

    (B)  point out the differences between traveling and reading history.

    (C)  show how the study of history is similar to foreign travel.

    (D)  mock those who think they know England but do not.

## Democracy in America

In democratic armies the desire of advancement is almost universal: it is ardent, tenacious, perpetual; it is strengthened by all other desires and extinguished only with life itself. But it is easy to see that, of all armies in the world, those in which advancement must be slowest in time of peace are the armies of democratic countries. As the number of commissions is naturally limited while the number of competitors is almost unlimited, and as the strict law of equality is over all alike, none can make rapid progress; many can make no progress at all. Thus the desire of advancement is greater and the opportunities of advancement fewer than elsewhere. All the ambitious spirits of a democratic army are consequently ardently desirous of war, because war makes vacancies and warrants the violation of that law of seniority which is the sole privilege natural to democracy.

We thus arrive at this singular consequence, that, of all armies, those most ardently desirous of war are democratic armies, and of all nations, those most fond of peace are democratic nations; and what makes these facts still more extraordinary is that these contrary effects are produced at the same time by the principle of equality.

*From Alexis de Tocqueville, "Democracy in America," 1840*

11. The central idea of this passage is that

   (A) democratic armies desire war, whereas democratic nations desire peace.

   (B) no one can be promoted in a democratic army because all are equal.

   (C) war is the only means by which an army can justify its existence.

   (D) in a democracy, war is justified by the common will of the people.

12. The author of this passage has created a tone that could be described as

   (A) objective.                    (C) malicious.

   (B) impassioned.                  (D) depressed.

13. The author implies that

   (A) democracy is an inferior form of government.

   (B) the principle of equality has both good and bad effects.

   (C) armies everywhere should be abolished because they become corrupted.

   (D) democracy is the best form of government ever devised.

## Elements of Chemistry

Cold is a negative condition, and depends on the absence, or privation, of heat. Intense artificial cold may be produced by the rapid absorption of heat during the conversion of solids into liquids. Dr. Black long since discovered the principle, that when bodies pass from a denser to a rarer state, heat is absorbed and becomes latent in the body so transformed, and consequently cold is produced. And also that when bodies pass from a rarer to a denser state, their latent heat is evolved, and becomes sensible.

It is known to almost everyone, that dissolving common salt in water, particularly if the salt is fine, will render the water so cold, even in summer, as to be painful to the hand. The salt, as it passes from the solid to the liquid state, absorbs caloric from the water, and thus the heat that was before sensible, becomes latent, and cold is produced.

On the contrary, when a piece of lead, or iron, is beaten smartly with a hammer, it becomes hot, because the metal, in consequence of the hammering, has its capacity for caloric reduced, and thus the heat which was before latent, now becomes sensible. For the same reason, when air is compressed forcibly in a tube, or as it is sometimes called, in a *fire-pump*, the heat, which was before latent, becomes sensible, because the condensation lessens its capacity for caloric.

The principle on which all freezing mixtures act is therefore the change of state which one or more of the articles employed undergo, during the process, and this change consists in an enlarged capacity for caloric. The degree of cold will then depend on the quantity of caloric which passes from a free to a latent state, and this again will depend on the quantity of substance liquefied, and the rapidity of the liquefaction.

The substances most commonly employed for this purpose are those originally used by Fahrenheit, to produce the zero of his thermometric scale; viz. common salt and snow, or pounded ice. For this purpose the salt should be fine, and the ice, which must always be used in summer, is to be reduced to small particles in a cold mortar.

The vessel to contain the substance to be frozen may be made of tin. It is simply a tall vessel, holding a few pints, with a close cover, and a rim round the top, for the convenience of handling it. For common purposes, this may be set into any convenient wooden vessel (having first introduced the substance to be frozen) and then surrounded by the freezing mixture. The only care to be taken in this part of the process is to see that the freezing mixture in the outside vessel reaches as high as the contents of the internal one. With two or three pounds of fine common salt, and double this weight of pounded ice, three or four pints of iced cream may be made in this way, during the warmest days of summer. The process requires two or three hours, and while it is going on, the vessel should be set in a cellar, or covered with a flannel cloth, as a bad conductor of the external heat.

*From J.L. Comstock, "Elements of Chemistry, 1833"*

14. After reading the above passage, the reader could correctly infer that dissolving sugar in hot tea will

   (A) lower the temperature of the hot tea.

   (B) cause the temperature of the tea to become even warmer just as beating a piece of lead with a hammer will raise its temperature.

   (C) lower the temperature of hot tea so that if it were placed about cream in a tin container, the cream would freeze within two to three hours.

   (D) reduce the temperature of the hot tea to such a low temperature as to be painful to the hand.

15. The drop in temperature that occurs when sugar is added to coffee is the result of

   I.   sugar passing from a solid to a liquid state.

   II.  sugar absorbing caloric from the water.

   III. heat becoming latent when it was sensible.

   (A) I only.                  (C) I, II, and III.

   (B) I and II.                (D) I and III.

16. Which is the best example of Dr. Black's discovery as outlined in the article?

(A) To gargle with warm salt water, one should start with water cooler than one desires and then add the salt.

(B) To gargle with warm salt water, one should start with salt and then pour water which is cooler than that desired over the salt.

(C) To gargle with warm salt water, one should adjust the temperature of the tap water to the temperature desired and then add fine salt; the fineness of the salt will prevent any change in the water temperature.

(D) To gargle with warm salt water, one should start with water warmer than desired and then add the salt.

17. The narrator seems to base this article on

(A) a sociological study.        (C) scientific procedures.

(B) trial-and-error methods.     (D) historical research.

18. The word "mortar" (Paragraph 5) as used in this article can be best interpreted to mean

(A) that which can fix or hold together, as mortar holds bricks.

(B) a weapon, a piece of artillery, or a small cannon.

(C) a container used for grinding or mixing.

(D) a mixture.

19. The writer does not make use of

(A) descriptions.        (C) mathematics.

(B) interviews.          (D) experiments.

20. In pumping up a basketball, one can infer from this article that the metal needle going into the ball

    (A) will become warm.

    (B) will not be affected by the process since metal is strong.

    (C) will become cooler.

    (D) will quickly reach a freezing temperature.

21. The writer can be best described as

    (A) concerned with literary form and stylistic devices.

    (B) subjective in his writing.

    (C) objective.

    (D) presenting facts which are new to most scientists in the twenty-first century.

22. A positive condition depending on the absence of cold is

    (A) Fahrenheit.

    (B) intense artificial cold.

    (C) heat.

    (D) a rarer state, according to Black.

23. Black found that when bodies pass from a rarer to a denser state, their latent heat is evolved, and becomes sensible. "Sensible" can be interpreted to mean

    (A) knowledgeable, making sense.

    (B) logical.

    (C) evolving.

    (D) perceptible.

## My Kinsman, Major Molineux

"Good evening to you, honored sir," said he, making a low bow, and still retaining his hold of the skirt. "I pray you tell me whereabouts is the dwelling of my kinsman, Major Molineux."

The youth's question was uttered very loudly; and one of the barbers, whose razor was descending on a well-soaped chin, and another who was dressing a Ramillies wig, left their occupations, and came to the door. The citizen, in the meantime, turned a long-favored countenance upon Robin, and answered him in a tone of excessive anger and annoyance. His two sepulchral hems, however, broke into the very centre of his rebuke, with most singular effect, like a thought of the cold grave obtruding among wrathful passions.

"Let go my garment, fellow! I tell you, I know not the man you speak of. What! I have authority, I have—hem, hem—authority; and if this be the respect you show for your betters, your feet shall be brought acquainted with the stocks by daylight, to-morrow morning!"

Robin released the old man's skirt, and hastened away, pursued by an ill-mannered roar of laughter from the barber's shop. He was at first considerably surprised by the result of his question, but, being a shrewd youth, soon thought himself able to account for the mystery.

"This is some country representative," was his conclusion, "who has never seen the inside of my kinsman's door, and lacks the breeding to answer a stranger civilly. The man is old, or verily—I might be tempted to turn back and smite him on the nose. Ah, Robin, Robin! even the barber's boys laugh at you for choosing such a guide! You will be wiser in time, friend Robin."

He now became entangled in a succession of crooked and narrow streets, which crossed each other, and meandered at no great distance from the water-side. The smell of tar was obvious to his nostrils, the masts of vessels pierced the moonlight above the tops of the buildings, and the numerous signs, which Robin paused to read, informed him that he was near the centre of business. But the streets were empty, the shops were closed, and lights were visible only in the second stories of a few dwelling-houses. At length, on the corner of a narrow lane, through which he was passing, he beheld the broad countenance of a British hero swinging before the door of an inn, whence proceeded the voices of many guests. The casement of one of the lower windows was thrown back, and a very thin curtain permitted Robin to distinguish a party at supper, round a well-furnished table. The fragrance of the good cheer steamed forth into the outer air, and the youth could not fail to recollect that the last remnant of his travelling stock of provision had yielded to his morning appetite, and that noon had found and left him dinnerless.

"Oh, that a parchment three-penny might give me a right to sit down at yonder table!" said Robin, with a sigh. "But the Major will make me welcome to the best of his victuals; so I will even stop boldly in, and inquire my way to his dwelling."

He entered the tavern, and was guided by the murmur of voices and the fumes of tobacco in the public-room. It was a long and low apartment, with oaken walls, grown dark in the continual smoke, and a floor which was thickly sanded, but of no immaculate purity. A number of persons—the larger part of whom appeared to be mariners, or in some way connected with the sea—occupied the wooden benches, or leather-bottomed chairs, conversing on various matters, and occasionally lending their attention to some topic of general interest. Three or four little groups were draining as many bowls of punch, which the West India trade had long since made a familiar drink in the colony. Others, who had the appearance of men who lived by regular and laborious handicraft, preferred the insulated bliss of an unshared potation, and became more taciturn under its influence. Nearly all, in short, evinced a predilection for the Good Creature in some of its various shapes, for this is a vice to which, as Fast Day sermons of a hundred years ago will testify, we have a long hereditary claim. The only guests to whom Robin's sympathies inclined him were two or three sheepish countrymen, who were using the inn somewhat after the fashion of a Turkish caravansary; they had gotten themselves into the darkest corner of the room, and heedless of the Nicotian atmosphere, were supping on the bread of their own ovens, and the bacon cured in their own chimney-smoke. But though Robin felt a sort of brotherhood with these strangers, his eyes were attracted from them to a person who stood near the door, holding whispered conversation with a group of ill-dressed associates. His features were separately striking almost to grotesqueness, and the whole face left a deep impression on the memory. The forehead bulged out into a double prominence, with a vale between; the nose came boldly forth in an irregular curve, and its bridge was of more than a finger's breadth; the eyebrows were deep and shaggy, and the eyes glowed beneath them like fire in a cave.

While Robin deliberated of whom to inquire respecting his kinsman's dwelling, he was accosted by the innkeeper, a little man in a stained white apron, who had come to pay his professional welcome to the stranger. Being in the second generation from a French Protestant, he seemed to have inherited the courtesy of his parent nation; but no variety of circumstances was ever known to change his voice from the one shrill note in which he now addressed Robin.

"From the country, I presume, sir?" said he, with a profound bow. "Beg leave to congratulate you on your arrival, and trust you intend a long stay with us. Fine town here, sir, beautiful buildings, and much that may interest a stranger. May I hope for the honor of your commands in respect to supper?"

"The man sees a family likeness! the rogue has guessed that I am related to the Major!" thought Robin, who had hitherto experienced little superfluous civility.

All eyes were now turned on the country lad, standing at the door, in his worn three-cornered hat, gray coat, leather breeches, and blue yarn stockings, leaning on an oaken cudgel, and bearing a wallet on his back.

*From Nathaniel Hawthorne, "My Kinsman, Major Molineux," 1831*

24. Of all the people in the room, Robin would be most inclined to strike up a conversation with the

(A) mariners.

(C) countrymen.

(B) day laborers.

(D) persons standing near the door.

25. From all indications, which of the following is probably true of the men eating their home-cooked food?

    I.   They are from the countryside.

    II.  They are uncomfortable being in the tavern.

    III. They are resented by the rest of the men in the tavern.

    (A) I only.                      (C) III only.

    (B) II only.                     (D) I and II only.

26. Taken in context of the passage, the best interpretation of "Nearly all, in short, evinced a predilection for the Good Creature" (Paragraph 8) is that nearly all the

    (A) mariners are celebrating a successful voyage to the West Indies.

    (B) people in the tavern are drinking an alcoholic beverage.

    (C) people in the tavern had been reformed by turning to religion.

    (D) men in the tavern were known for seeking out the enjoyable things in life.

27. To what vice does the author say "we have a long hereditary claim"?

    (A) Seafaring                    (C) Smoking

    (B) Drinking                     (D) Gossiping

28. The tone of the citizen in the barber's shop who responded to Robin can best be described as

    (A) jovial and lighthearted.     (C) interested and helpful.

    (B) disdainful and aloof.        (D) passionate and gloomy.

29. The statements "your feet shall be brought acquainted with the stocks" can be interpreted as

    (A) first-hand contact with farm animals.

    (B) personal attention to investment.

(C) punishment that could result from the youth's behavior.

(D) a reference to a dance step familiar to the common people.

30. "As a result of drink, some of the tavern occupants became more taciturn"; this can be interpreted to mean that they were

(A) unreticent.

(C) boisterous.

(B) talkative.

(D) uncommunicative.

**Questions 31, 32, and 33 refer to the graph below.**

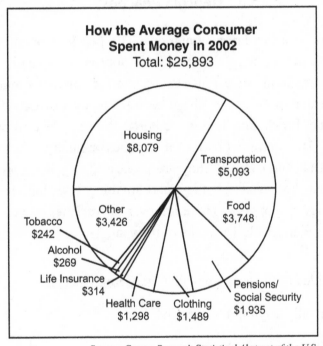

*Source: Census Bureau's Statistical Abstract of the U.S.*

31. According to the graph, the average consumer spent approximately 50 percent of her/his earnings on

(A) housing and health care costs.

(C) food.

(B) transportation and housing.

(D) transportation and pensions.

32. After transportation, the next greatest amount of money was spent on

    (A) clothing.                   (C) food.

    (B) other.                      (D) pensions/social security.

33. According to the graph, expenditure on health care was approximately equal to

    (A) clothing.                   (C) food.

    (B) pensions.                   (D) other.

## Georgia Peaches

Georgia and peaches are synonymous. The peach is practically a symbol of Georgia. The peach, being the state fruit, adorns all things in the state. The main growing area in the state consists of a band of counties running diagonally through the center of the state. These central counties of Crawford, Houston, Macon, Monroe, Peach, and Taylor are home to over 1 ½ million peach trees. They produce 100 million pounds of peaches annually. These peaches are sold as fresh fruit and canned. They are processed as jellies, preserves, peach cider, ice cream, hot sauce, chutney, and anything else that can benefit from the peach's tangy, sweet taste. There are over 40 varieties of peaches grown in Georgia. They are available 16 weeks of the year.

34. The central idea of the passage is that the Georgia peach

    (A) is practically a symbol of Georgia.

    (B) is available 16 weeks of the year.

    (C) is grown in 6 central counties of Georgia.

    (D) is processed in a variety of ways.

35. In the passage, the word *synonymous* is closest in meaning to

    (A) the same.

    (B) the opposite.

(C) equivalent in connotation.

(D) alike.

36. According to the passage, how many varieties of peaches are grown in Georgia?

(A) less than 30          (C) over 40

(B) more than 100          (D) a dozen

## Spa Water

1    Spa water quality is maintained through a filter to ensure cleanliness and clarity. Wastes such as perspiration, hairspray, and lotions, which cannot be removed by the spa filter, can be controlled by shock treatment or super chlorination every other week. Although the filter traps most of the solid material to control bacteria and algae and to oxidize any organic material, the addition of disinfectants such as bromine or chlorine is necessary.

2    As all water solutions have a pH that controls corrosion, proper pH balance is also necessary. A pH measurement determines if the water is acid or alkaline. Based on a 14-point scale, a pH reading of 7.0 is considered neutral while a lower reading is considered acidic, and a higher reading indicates alkalinity or basic. High pH (above 7.6) reduces sanitizer efficiency, clouds water, promotes scale formation on surfaces and equipment, and interferes with filter operation. When pH is high, add a pH decrease more rapidly. A weekly dose of a stain and scale fighter also will help to control this problem. Low pH (below 7.2) is equally damaging, causing equipment corrosion, water that is irritating, and rapid sanitizer dissipation. To increase pH, add sodium bicarbonate (e.g., *Spa Up*).

3    The recommended operating temperature of a spa (98°–104°) is a fertile environment for the growth of bacteria and viruses. This growth is prevented when appropriate sanitizer levels are continuously monitored. Bacteria can also be controlled by maintaining a proper bromine level of 3.0 to 5.0 parts per million (ppm) or a chlorine level of 1.0–2.0 ppm. As bromine tablets should not be added directly to the water, a bromine floater will properly dispense the tablets. Should chlorine be the chosen sanitizer, a granular form is recommended, as liquid chlorine or tablets are too harsh for the spa.

37. Although proper chemical and temperature maintenance of spa water is necessary, the most important condition to monitor is the

   (A) prevention of the growth of bacteria and viruses.

   (B) prevention of the corrosion of equipment.

   (C) prevention of the formation of scales.

   (D) prevention of cloudy water.

38. Of the chemical and temperature conditions in a spa, the condition most dangerous to one's health is

   (A) spa water temperature above 104°.

   (B) bromine level between 3.0 and 5.0.

   (C) pH level below 7.2.

   (D) spa water temperature between 90° and 104°.

39. The primary purpose of the passage is to

   (A) relate that maintenance of a spa can negate the full enjoyment of the spa experience.

   (B) convey that the maintenance of a spa is expensive and time consuming.

   (C) explain the importance of proper spa maintenance.

   (D) detail proper spa maintenance.

## Communication in Learning

1      There is an importance of learning communication and meaning in language. Yet the use of notions such as communication and meaning as the basic criteria for instruction, experiences, and materials in classrooms may misguide a child in several respects. Communication in the classroom is vital. The teacher should use communication to help students develop the capacity to make their private responses become public responses. Otherwise, one's use of language

would be in danger of being what the younger generation refers to as mere words, mere thoughts, and mere feelings.

2    Learning theorists emphasize specific components of learning; behaviorists stress behavior in learning; humanists stress the affective in learning; and cognitivists stress cognition in learning. All three of these components occur simultaneously and cannot be separated from each other in the learning process. In 1957, Festinger referred to dissonance as the lack of harmony between what one does (behavior) and what one believes (attitude). Attempts to separate the components of learning either knowingly or unknowingly create dissonances wherein language, thought, feeling, and behavior become diminished of authenticity. As a result, ideas and concepts lose their content and vitality, and the manipulation and politics of communication assume prominence.

40. Which of the following best describes the author's attitude toward the subject discussed?

   (A)  a flippant disregard          (C)  a passive resignation

   (B)  a mild frustration            (D)  an informed concern

41. The primary purpose of the passage is to

   (A)  discuss the relationships between learning and communication.

   (B)  assure teachers that communication and meaning are the basic criteria for learning in classrooms.

   (C)  stress the importance of providing authentic communication in classroom learning.

   (D)  address the role of communication and meaning in classrooms.

42. Which of the following is the most complete and accurate definition of the term *mere* as used in the passage?

   (A)  small                         (C)  little

   (B)  minor                         (D)  insignificant

# PRACTICE TEST 1
# WRITING SUBTEST

## Multiple-Choice Section

*Directions:* Read each passage and answer the questions that follow.

### Frederick Douglass

[1]Frederick Douglass wrote his autobiography in 1845, primarily to counter those who doubted his authentisity as a former slave. [2]His work became a <u>classic</u> in American literature and a primary source about slavery from the point of view of a slave. [3]Douglass went on a two-year speaking tour abroad to <u>avoid</u> recapture by his former owner and to win new friends for the Abolition movement. [4]He returned with funds to purchase his freedom, and to start his own anti-slavery newspaper. [5]He became a <u>consultent</u> to Abraham Lincoln and <u>throughout</u> Reconstruction fought doggedly for full civil rights for freedmen. [6]He was also an early supporter of the womens' rights movement.

1. Which of the following changes is needed in part 1?

    (A) Change spelling of authentisity.

    (B) Delete the comma.

    (C) Change "his" to "an."

    (D) Change spelling of primarily.

2. What word in the passage should not be capitalized?

    (A) American                    (C) Reconstruction

    (B) Abolition                    (D) Lincoln

3. What change is needed in the passage?

    (A) Part 1: Delete the comma after "1845."

    (B) Part 4: Place a comma after "funds."

    (C) Part 4: Delete the comma after "freedom."

    (D) Part 5: Place a comma after "Lincoln."

4. Which underlined word in the passage is misspelled?

    (A) classic          (C) consultent

    (B) avoid            (D) throughout

5. What change in the passage is needed to correct an error in punctuation?

    (A) Part 2: Add a comma after "slavery."

    (B) Part 3: Remove hyphen from two-year.

    (C) Part 5: Addd a comma after "Lincoln."

    (D) Part 6: Change "womens'" to "women's."

## Food Choices

[1]Each time a person opens his or her mouth to eat, he or she makes a nutritional decision. [2]These <u>selections</u>, make a definitive difference in how an individual <u>looks</u>, feels, and performs at work or play. [3]When a good assortment of food in appropriate amounts is selected and eaten, the consequences are likely to be desirable levels of health and energy to allow one to be as active as needed. [4]<u>Conversely</u>, when choices are less then desirable, the consequences can be poor health, limited <u>energy</u>, or both. [5]Studies of american diets, particularly the diets of the very young, reveal unsatisfactory dietary habits as evidenced by the numbers of overweight and out-of-shape young children. [6]Until these nutritional decisions change, avoiding obesity will remain a challenge faced by Americas young people.

6. Which comma needs to be removed?

   (A) The comma after "looks."

   (B) The comma after "selections."

   (C) The comma after "Conversely."

   (D) The comma after "energy."

7. Which part of the passage contains an incorrect spelling choice?

   (A) Part 2          (C) Part 5

   (B) Part 4          (D) Part 6

8. What part of the passage contains an error in capitalization?

   (A) Part 2          (C) Part 5

   (B) Part 4          (D) Part 6

9. Which part has a word that requires an apostrophe?

   (A) Part 2          (C) Part 5

   (B) Part 3          (D) Part 6

## Measuring Mass

[1]In a <u>labratory</u> setting, scientists can use the physical property of inertia to measure mass. [2]To determine mass in this way, a mass is placed on a frictionless horizontal surface. [3]When a known force is applied to it the <u>magnitude</u> of the mass is measured by the amount of <u>acceleration</u> produced upon it by the known force. [4]Mass measured in this way is said to be the Inertial Mass of the body in question. [5]This method is seldom used because it involves both a <u>frictionless</u> surface, and a difficult measurement of acceleration. [6]Measuring mass with a balance scale: where an unknown mass is measured against a known mass in increasing or decreasing units until balanced, is far easier.

10. Which underlined word in the passage is spelled incorrectly?

    (A) labratory

    (B) magnitude

    (C) acceleration

    (D) frictionless

11. Which sentence needs a comma after the introductory clause?

    (A) Part 1

    (B) Part 2

    (C) Part 3

    (D) Part 4

12. Which part of the passage contains an error in capitalization?

    (A) Part 1

    (B) Part 2

    (C) Part 3

    (D) Part 4

13. Which part of the passage contains a punctuation error?

    (A) Part 1

    (B) Part 2

    (C) Part 5

    (D) Part 6

## A Tragedy of the Civil War

[1]One of the many tragedies of the Civil war was the housing and care of prisoners. [2]The Andersonville prison, built by the Confederates in 1864 to accommodate 10,000 Union prisoners was not completed when prisoners started arriving. [3]Five months later, the total number of men incarcerated their had risen to 31,678. [4]Chances of survival for prisoners in Andersonville were not much better than in the throws of combat. [5]Next to overcrowding, inadequate shelter caused unimaginable suffering. [6]The confederates were not equipped with the manpower, tools, or supplies necessary to house such a population of captives; prisoners themselves gathered lumber, logs, anything they could find to construct some sort of protection from the elements.

14. Which of the following parts has a capitalization error?

    (A) Part 1

    (B) Part 2

    (C) Part 3

    (D) Part 4

15. What is the error in word usage in Part 3?

    (A) their                    (C) incarcerated

    (B) risen                    (D) number

16. Which word is misused in Part 4?

    (A) survival                 (C) chances

    (B) throws                   (D) combat

17. What word in the passage needs to be capitalized?

    (A) prisoners                (C) confederates

    (B) combat                   (D) population

## The Shakers

[1]Shaker furniture was created to exemplify specific characteristics: Simplicity of design, quality of craftsmanship, harmony of proportion, and usefulness. [2]The major emphasis was on function, and not on excessive or elaborate decorations that contributed nothing to the products usefulness. [3]There Society was founded in 1774 by Ann Lee, an Englishwoman from the working classes who brought eight followers to New York with her. [4]"Mother Ann" established her religious community on the belief that worldly interests were evil. [5]To gain entrance into the Society, believers had to remain celibate, have no private posessions, and avoid contact with outsiders. [6]The Order came to be called "Shakers" because of the feverish dance the group performed.

18. What is the error in part one?

    (A) too many commas

    (B) incorrect verb usage

    (C) incorrect capitalization of "simplicity"

    (D) misuse of colon

19. What change is needed in the passage?

   (A) Part 1: Change "was" to "were."

   (B) Part 2: Change "products" to "product's."

   (C) Part 3: Change "Society" to "society."

   (D) Part 4: Change "Mother Ann" to mother Ann

20. In what part of the passage is there an incorrect use of a homophone?

   (A) Part 3            (C) Part 5

   (B) Part 4            (D) Part 6

21. In what part of the passage is there a spelling error?

   (A) Part 2            (C) Part 4

   (B) Part 3            (D) Part 5

## Using Stucco

[1]Although most new homes across the United States are finished in brick, stucco is an old finish that is becoming increasingly popular. [2]Stucco finishes, applied with a trowel, <u>is</u> composed of sand, water, and a cementing mixture. [3]The first coat or two is thicker, about $3/8$ of an inch, with the final coat about $1/4$ to $1/8$ of an inch thick.

[4]Stucco has many advantages. [5]One of the most attractive selling features is that stucco is energy efficient. [6]In addition, a waterproof, low maintenance exterior is produced by coating the final application with a clear acrylic finish. [7]Since stucco finishes are mixed with color homeowners and designers can select from a wide range of shades. [8]Also, stucco is lightweight and quite inexpensive. [9]By substituting stucco for brick veneer, the typical home gains about 200 square feet of living space.

22. Which of the following, if added between Sentences 2 and 3, is most consistent with the writer's purpose and audience.

    (A) Personally, I know people who think stucco is an ugly finish for a home.

    (B) Sometimes, Spanish and Indian style homes in the Southwest are finished with stucco on the interior walls.

    (C) Indeed, stucco creates a California ambiance many wish to emulate.

    (D) The plaster-like stucco is applied in two or three thin coats.

23. Which of the following is needed in the second paragraph?

    (A) Sentence 5: Delete the second "is."

    (B) Sentence 6: Move "in addition" after "finish."

    (C) Sentence 7: Place a comma after "color."

    (D) Sentence 8: Move "quite" after "is."

24. Which of the following should be used in place of the underlined verb in Sentence 2?

    (A) are                    (C) being

    (B) will be                (D) should be

## Creative Recycling

[1]There are more things to recycle than tin, plastic, aluminum, and newsprint. [2]One type of recycling that is gaining in popularity is Christmas tree recycling. [3]Most of the 34 million Christmas trees that Americans buy every year end up in landfills. [4]This is an expensive waste of organic material and valuable space in the landfills. [5]Many communities have bought wood chippers so the trees can be turned into mulch for the garden. [6]Some areas dump the trees on the bottoms of lakes to supply habitat for fish and other organisms, and along the coastlines, states are tying Christmas trees into large bundles for use in coastline reclamation projects. [7]Eventually covered by sand and coastal vegetation, the trees become dunes which keep valuable beaches from being washed away.

[8]In Texas, along the Gulf Coast, there are people who recycle used oil rigs. [9]Following a master plan designed by a special advisory commission, this self-sustaining program encouraged the use of petroleum rigs for the development of underwater recreational areas. [10]Because it is cheaper to topple a rig rather than tow it back to shore, participating companies topple their tall offshore petroleum drilling platforms and give half the money saved to the Artificial Reef Fund. [11]The state has an Artificial Reef Fund, a program which does not use the taxpayers' money. [12]These offshore rigs have already become underwater fish habitats because the rig's barnacle-encrusted legs provide protection against larger predators. [13]Often, undersea sport fishers and divers already know the locations of these platforms and come there even while drilling is in progress. [14]Once the rig is toppled, new organisms will inhabit the structure, and new types of fish will find a home there. [15]The toppled rigs become an artificial reef.

25. Which of the following, if added between Sentences 4 and 5, is most consistent with the writer's purpose and audience?

   (A) It makes more sense to recycle the trees.

   (B) Some people think the trees provide a useful function in the landfill by adding organic material.

   (C) A big problem is that people often don't take off the tinsel and artificial icicles.

   (D) How could anyone get out in the cold of late December?

26. Which of the following makes the sequence of ideas clearer in the second paragraph?

   (A) Delete Sentence 8.

   (B) Delete Sentence 10.

   (C) Reverse the order of Sentences 8 and 15.

   (D) Place Sentence 11 before Sentence 9.

27. Which one of the following changes is needed?

    (A) Sentence 8: Change "who" to "which."

    (B) Sentence 9: Change "encouraged" to "encourages."

    (C) Sentence 10: Change "cheaper" to "cheapest."

    (D) Sentence 13: Add a comma after "platforms."

## Free the Orcas

[1]Dena may die soon. [2]For 21 years, all Dena has ever known is captivity. [3]How would you like to spend your entire life in captivity? [4]Even though Dena is not a human, but an orca, a killer whale, like in the movie *Orca,* don't you think Dena deserves to be released from her natural habitat? [5]Orcas are much too intelligent and too delicate to be confined in tanks. [6]Dena's owners claim, Sea Habitat, Inc., she is displaying geriatric signs normal for an orca 25 years old. [7]Orcas are not meant to be caged, no matter how kind the jailer who holds the keys.

[8]We don't know enough about orcas and how they interact. [9]Who are we to confine a species that may be as intelligent as humans? [10]True, Dena may be rejected by her original pod, members of which stayed together for life. [11]_____. [12]Maybe she is too old to live much longer. [13]However, we should at least allow Dena to die with dignity in her natural surroundings. [14]And, if Dena succeeds in surviving in the wild, maybe we can pressure other zoos and marine institutions around the world to release these beautiful animals back to the wild, where they can have longer, healthier lives. [15]I urge everyone to write a letter to their local senator and congressperson demanding the return of all orcas to the oceans of the Earth.

28. Which of the following, if added between Sentences 6 and 7, is most consistent with the writer's purpose and audience?

(A) Some say leave her where she is because there's no use in crying over spilled milk.

(B) People attempt to obfuscate the issue by ignoring the fact that orcas have no natural enemy other than man.

(C) Did you know that orcas have an average of 40–48 teeth?

(D) However, the high death rate of orcas in captivity clearly indicates that Dena may be sick from having been confined.

29. Which of the following displays nonstandard pronoun usage?

(A) Sentence 3                 (C) Sentence 14

(B) Sentence 7                 (D) Sentence 15

30. Which of the following phrases is unnecessary and should be eliminated?

(A) "For 21 years" in Sentence 2

(B) "like in the movie *Orca*" in Sentence 4

(C) "that may be as intelligent as humans" in Sentence 9

(D) "to the oceans of the Earth" in Sentence 15

31. Which of the following corrects the underlined portion of Sentence 4?

Even though Dena is not a human, but an orca, a killer whale, like in the movie *Orca*, don't you think Dena deserves to be released from her natural habitat?

(A) Dena deserved to be released from her natural habitat?

(B) Dena deserves from her natural habitat to be released?

(C) Dena deserves to be released under her natural habitat?

(D) Dena deserves to be released into her natural habitat?

32. Which of the following best corrects Sentence 6?

    (A) Dena's owners, Sea Habitat, Inc., claim she is displaying geriatric signs normal for an orca 25 years old.

    (B) Since they are Dena's owners, Sea Habitat, Inc. claim she is displaying geriatric signs normal for an orca 25 years old.

    (C) Sea Habitat, Inc., Dena's owners, claim she is displaying geriatric signs normal for an orca 25 years old.

    (D) Choices (A) and (C) only.

33. Which of the following, if used between Sentences 10 and 12, best develops the main idea of the second paragraph?

    (A) Another problem to be overcome is training Dena to hunt live fish, instead of depending on being fed dead fish by her human captors.

    (B) As a matter of fact, it is now against the law to capture orcas in the wild and sell them to zoos.

    (C) As we all know, the breeding of captive orcas has not been successful.

    (D) This issue was made famous by the movie *Free Willy*.

34. Which of the following verbs are used incorrectly?

    (A) "deserves" in Sentence 4

    (B) "holds" in Sentence 7

    (C) "stayed" in Sentence 10

    (D) Choices (B) and (C) only.

35. Which of the following best punctuates Sentence 8?

    (A) We don't know enough, about orcas, and how they interact.

    (B) We don't know enough, about orcas and how they interact!

    (C) We don't know enough: about orcas and how they interact.

    (D) Best as is.

## DIRECTIONS FOR THE SHORT-ANSWER SECTION OF THE WRITING SUBTEST

There are seven questions in the short-answer section of the writing subtest. Each question is phrased in exactly the same way. You will be told that each text has two errors and that the proper names of people and places are correctly spelled. You will look for errors in construction, grammar, usage, spelling, capitalization, and punctuation. Then, you will rewrite each text so that it is correct. You may change the syntax but must keep the essential elements of the piece. Of course, you may not introduce any new errors.

## SHORT-ANSWER ASSIGNMENTS AND RESPONSE SHEET

36. The following sentence contains two errors (e.g., in construction, grammar, usage, spelling, capitalization, punctuation). Rewrite the text so that errors are addressed and the original meaning is maintained.

    Each of the desserts I enjoy making require so much butter that my friends and myself don't eat them.

    _____

    _____

37. The following sentence contains two errors (e.g., in construction, grammar, usage, spelling, capitalization, punctuation). Rewrite the text so that errors are addressed and the original meaning is maintained.

    Are they really aiming to help the neighborhood people or are they interested in making a tidy profit from the work of others.

    _____

    _____

38. The following sentence contains two errors (e.g., in construction, grammar, usage, spelling, capitalization, punctuation). Rewrite the text so that errors are addressed and the original meaning is maintained.

A person who studies hard will find that there grades improve.

_____

_____

39. The following sentence contains two errors (e.g., in construction, grammar, usage, spelling, capitalization, punctuation). Rewrite the text so that errors are addressed and the original meaning is maintained.

Using a thesaurus is very difficult you have to know how to spell the word before you can find words that go to gether.

_____

_____

40. The following sentence contains two errors (e.g., in construction, grammar, usage, spelling, capitalization, punctuation). Rewrite the text so that errors are addressed and the original meaning is maintained.

My uncle get very tired when he shovels snow in the Winter.

_____

_____

41. The following sentence contains two errors (e.g., in construction, grammar, usage, spelling, capitalization, punctuation). Rewrite the text so that errors are addressed and the original meaning is maintained.

    Each fruit that I kneed to cut require special handling.

    _____

    _____

42. The following sentence contains two errors (e.g., in construction, grammar, usage, spelling, capitalization, punctuation). Rewrite the text so that errors are addressed and the original meaning is maintained.

    After the tornado both of us wants to move to someplace far away.

    _____

    _____

## DIRECTIONS FOR THE WRITING SUMMARY EXERCISE

For this part of the test, you will read the passage on the next page and summarize it in your own words. Your summary should be approximately 150 to 250 words and effectively communicate the main idea and essential points of the passage. You are to identify the relevant information and communicate it clearly and concisely.

Your summary will be evaluated based on the following criteria:

- **FIDELITY:** Your accuracy and clarity in using your own words to convey and maintain focus on the main ideas of the passage

- **CONCISENESS:** Your appropriate use of length, depth, and specificity to convey the writer's main ideas

- **ORGANIZATION:** The clarity of your writing and your use of logical sequencing of ideas

- **SENTENCE STRUCTURE:** The effectiveness of your sentence structure and the extent to which those sentences are free of structural errors

- **USAGE:** Your care and precision in word choice and avoidance of usage errors

- **MECHANICAL CONVENTIONS:** Your use of conventional spelling and use of the conventions of punctuation and capitalization

The final version of your summary should conform to the conventions of edited American English, should be written legibly, and should be your own original work.

On the actual test you will be directed to write or print your summary on the pages provided in the test booklet.

## WRITING SUMMARY EXERCISE

*Directions:* Use the passage below to prepare a summary of 100–150 words.

1    In 1975, Sinclair observed that it had often been supposed that the main factor in learning to talk is being able to imitate. Schlesinger (1975) noted that at certain stages of learning to speak, a child tends to imitate everything an adult says to him or her, and it therefore seems reasonable to accord to such imitation an important role in the acquisition of language.

2    Moreover, various investigators have attempted to explain the role of imitation in language. In his discussion of the development of imitation and cognition of adult speech sounds, Nakazema (1975) stated that although the parent's talking stimulates and accelerates the infant's articulatory activity, the parent's phoneme system does not influence the child's articulatory mechanisms. Slobin and Welsh (1973) suggested that imitation is the reconstruction of the adult's utterance and that the child does so by employing the grammatical rules that he has developed at a specific time. Schlesinger proposed that by imitating the adult the child practices new grammatical constructions. Brown and Bellugi (1964) noted that a child's imitations resemble spontaneous speech in that they drop inflections, most function words, and sometimes other words. However,

the word order of imitated sentences usually was preserved. Brown and Bellugi assumed that imitation is a function of what the child attended to or remembered. Shipley et al. (1969) suggested that repeating an adult's utterance assists the child's comprehension. Ervin (1964) and Braine (1971) found that a child's imitations do not contain more advanced structures than his or her spontaneous utterances; thus, imitation can no longer be regarded as the simple behavioristic act that scholars assumed it to be.

## DIRECTIONS FOR THE COMPOSITION EXERCISE

For this part of the writing subtest you are asked to write a multiple-paragraph composition of approximately 300 to 600 words on an assigned topic. Your assignment will be to effectively communicate a complete message for the specified audience and purpose. The assessment of your composition will be based on your ability to express, organize, and support opinions and ideas. The position you take will not be part of the evaluation.

### Criteria for Evaluation:

- **Appropriateness:** Your attention to the topic and use of the language and style appropriate to the stated audience, purpose, and occasion

- **Mechanical Conventions:** Your use of standard spelling and use of the conventions of punctuation and capitalization

- **Usage:** Your care and precision in word choice and avoidance of usage errors

- **Sentence Structure:** The effectiveness of your sentence structure and the extent to which those sentences are free of structural errors

- **Focus and Unity:** Your clarity in stating and maintaining focus on your main idea or point of view

- **Organization:** The clarity of your writing and your use of logical sequencing of ideas

- **Development:** Your statements are of appropriate depth, specificity, and/or accuracy

Your final version needs to conform to the conventions of edited American English, be written legibly, and be your own original work.

On the actual test you will be directed to write or print your response on the pages provided in the test booklet.

## COMPOSITION EXERCISE

Read the following classroom situation and then in a well-constructed essay describe the strengths and/or weaknesses of the solution to it. Your audience is other teachers.

One of the teachers in the school where you teach has a student who speaks English as a second language. The teacher has definite ideas about how to deal with that student.

Mrs. Jones has told her entire class that they may not speak any language other than English at any time. She has encouraged them to eat the food prepared in the cafeteria where they can eat "American" food. She has told them that this is a better practice than bringing ethnic food from home. She often tells them: "After all, you are in America now."

Mrs. Jones believes that English is the only language that should be spoken in the United States. She also believes that a prime purpose of the school is to teach that language.

What is your reaction to this teacher and her ideas?

## PRACTICE TEST 1
## ANSWER KEY

### READING SUBTEST – MULTIPLE-CHOICE SECTION

| | | | |
|---|---|---|---|
| 1. (C) | 12. (A) | 23. (D) | 34. (A) |
| 2. (B) | 13. (B) | 24. (C) | 35. (C) |
| 3. (A) | 14. (A) | 25. (D) | 36. (C) |
| 4. (A) | 15. (C) | 26. (B) | 37. (A) |
| 5. (D) | 16. (D) | 27. (B) | 38. (A) |
| 6. (A) | 17. (C) | 28. (D) | 39. (C) |
| 7. (B) | 18. (C) | 29. (C) | 40. (D) |
| 8. (A) | 19. (B) | 30. (D) | 41. (C) |
| 9. (B) | 20. (A) | 31. (B) | 42. (D) |
| 10. (C) | 21. (C) | 32. (C) | |
| 11. (A) | 22. (C) | 33. (A) | |

### WRITING SUBTEST – MULTIPLE-CHOICE SECTION

| | | | |
|---|---|---|---|
| 1. (A) | 10. (A) | 19. (B) | 28. (D) |
| 2. (B) | 11. (C) | 20. (A) | 29. (D) |
| 3. (C) | 12. (D) | 21. (D) | 30. (B) |
| 4. (C) | 13. (D) | 22. (D) | 31. (D) |
| 5. (D) | 14. (A) | 23. (C) | 32. (D) |
| 6. (B) | 15. (A) | 24. (A) | 33. (A) |
| 7. (B) | 16. (B) | 25. (A) | 34. (C) |
| 8. (C) | 17. (C) | 26. (D) | 35. (D) |
| 9. (D) | 18. (C) | 27. (B) | |

# DETAILED EXPLANATIONS OF ANSWERS READING SUBTEST

## Multiple-Choice Section

1. **(C)** (C) is correct because the passage is specifically about lying in Russia. (A) contradicts reasons for lying given in the third paragraph; (B) contradicts material in the second paragraph; (D) is not implied by the passage.

2. **(B)** (B) is correct because the passage explains more fully the author's statement that everybody is lying. The passage does not work to show what conditions led to universal lying (C), does not divide the subject into categories (D), and does not seek to define any particular word or term (A).

3. **(A)** (A) is correct because lines 1–4 suggest that the author expected a negative response to his topic and (A) has a negative connotation. (B) has a positive meaning; (C) and (D) are more neutral.

4. **(A)** (A) is the correct answer because the sentence beginning in line 13 seeks to explain the previous sentence more carefully. It does not provide a specific example of lying (B), show differences or similarities that relate to lies (C), or show a cause or effect of lying (D).

5. **(D)** (D) is correct because the author describes poor people with compassion; (C) is incorrect because while the author treats the rich people who ignore the poor with some bitterness, the general mood of the passage is sympathetic. The author shows no arrogance (B) towards anyone he describes, and his use of emotional language suggests that he is not at all apathetic (A).

6. **(A)** (A) is correct because the second sentence contrasts the reality of the ragged woman with the great streets that the stranger in the first sentence sees. The forcefulness of this contrast makes (C) incorrect because (C) suggests a weaker connection between the sentences. (B) is incorrect because the second sentence does not explain the first sentence more fully; (D) is incorrect because the second sentence doesn't provide a specific example of what the stranger does see.

7. **(B)** (B) is correct because the passage mentions both the wretchedness of the poor and the visitor who doesn't see this wretchedness. While the author may imply (A), it is

not the point he wants to make in this passage; (C) is incorrect because the author does not describe harmony between the rich and the poor; (D) contradicts the sympathetic tone of the passage.

8. **(A)** (A) is correct because the author is comparing traveling with reading history. Because there is no causal relationship suggested, (C) is incorrect. (D) is incorrect because the author does not seek to divide up one subject; (B) is incorrect because there is no narration of chronological events.

9. **(B)** This is a statement of opinion because it is not possible to check with any accuracy the contraction of minds as the author has described it.

10. **(C)** The correct response is (C) because throughout the passage the author compares history with foreign travel; (B) contradicts the author's first sentence. (A) and (D) are incorrect because the author uses travel in England as a detail supporting his main point about similarities between travel and reading history.

11. **(A)** (A) is correct because it contains important points made in each paragraph. While (B) is implied, it is not the central idea of the passage. (C) and (D) are incorrect because the author makes no statements justifying the existence of armies or of war itself.

12. **(A)** (A) is correct because the author's tone is very neutral. (B), (C), and (D) are incorrect because the author shows little evidence of any passion or emotion.

13. **(B)** (B) is correct because the passage describes both good and bad attributes of democracy, a political system based on equality. (A), (C), and (D) all take either an all-good or all-bad position; however, the author is careful to address both good and bad effects.

14. **(A)** (A) is the best answer since, as stated in the third sentence of the passage, changing the solid to liquid will lower the temperature of the hot tea. Because changing the sugar to liquid will not raise, but rather lower, the temperature of the tea, (B) should not be selected. The temperature of the hot tea will not be lowered to such an extent that it will freeze cream (C) or cause the hand to be painful from the cold (D).

15. **(C)** The best answer is (C) since it includes three correct statements. The sugar does pass from a solid to a liquid state, the sugar does absorb caloric from the water, and the heat does become latent when it is sensible. Since I, II, and III are all causes of the drop of temperature when sugar is added to coffee, all three must be included when choosing an answer. (A) states that sugar passes from a solid to a liquid state (I), but no other information

is given. (B) includes two true statements (I and II), but it does not include all the information since there is no mention of heat becoming latent when it was sensible (III). (D) is not a proper answer since it excludes statement II—that sugar absorbs caloric from the water. While (A), (B), and (D) each contain one or more of these statements, none contains all three; consequently, each of these choices is incorrect.

16. **(D)** The best answer is (D). Answer (D) states that one should take into consideration that dissolving the salt in the water will lower the temperature of the water and that one should start with water that is warmer than is desired. One should not start with water that is cooler than one desires; (A) is not the best answer. The order of adding the salt and the water will make little difference; the temperature will be lowered in both instances; (B) is not the best answer. The salt will lower the temperature of the water; (C) suggests that this will not happen if the salt is fine, so (C) is not an acceptable choice.

17. **(C)** The writing seems scientific since it refers to principles, causes and effects, and measures of heat and cold; (C) is the best answer. The writing is not sociological since there is no description of people and their relationships; consequently, (A) should not be chosen. Because the narrator reports scientific facts and there is no trial-and-error reporting, (B) is not the best answer. Since the information is not reported as historical research with references, footnotes, or dates of previous discoveries, (D) should not be chosen.

18. **(C)** The best choice is (C); paragraph 5 shows that in this case a mortar is a container used for pounding, pulverizing, and/or mixing. As employed in the last sentence of the fifth paragraph, the use of the mortar is not to fix or hold together; (A) should not be chosen. A mortar can be a weapon (B), but that would not be used to reduce ice to small particles; therefore, (B) is not an acceptable choice. The word does not fit into the sentence in this context; choice (D) would not be practical.

19. **(B)** The best choice is (B). The only device that the writer does not record is that of interviews. The other items—descriptions (A), mathematics (C), and experiments (D)—are used.

20. **(A)** One can infer that the metal needle will become warm when the basketball is being inflated by the air pump. The reason is that the article states, "…air is compressed forcibly in a tube…the heat, which was before latent, becomes sensible…"; (A) is the correct answer. Choice (B) states that the needle will not be affected; (B) should not be chosen since the quotation from the passage states that there will be an effect. (C) is also incorrect because it states that the needle will become cooler, not warmer. (D) is also an incorrect choice; it states that the needle will become freezing cold.

21. **(C)** The writer is objective in his writing and offers no opinions of his own; (C) is the best answer. The writer's main concern is not literary form or stylistic devices; (A) is not acceptable. The writer is objective and does not offer his own opinions; since he is not subjective, (B) is not the best answer. Since the facts presented in the article are not new, (D) is not the best answer.

22. **(C)** Since heat is a positive condition depending on the absence of cold, (C) is the best answer. Fahrenheit is a measure of temperature, not a condition; therefore, (A) is an incorrect choice. Heat is the opposite of intense artificial cold; (B) is not acceptable. Black states that it is "…when bodies pass from a rarer to a denser state that their latent heat is evolved…"; (D) is incorrect.

23. **(D)** In this case, the word "sensible" means perceptible; (D) is the best answer. "Sensible" can mean knowledgeable (A), but the definition does not make sense in this case. The meaning of "sensible" can be logical (B), but that particular meaning does not fit the sentence or passage here. "Evolving" (C) is not an acceptable answer because it does not seem to fit the context.

24. **(C)** The correct choice is (C) because the author states that the "two or three sheepish country men" are the "only guests to whom Robin's sympathies inclined him." The mariners (A) and the day laborers (B) would not interest Robin and they are incorrect. Although the man at the door does draw Robin's attention, he does not seem like the type of person to start a conversation with; choice (D) is incorrect.

25. **(D)** Statements I and II best describe the diners, so choice (D) is correct. The author states that they are "countrymen" who are eating in the "darkest corner of the room"; that indicates that they do not wish to bring attention to themselves. There is no sign of hostility from the other men in the tavern; therefore, Statement III is invalid and cannot be a part of the correct answer; choice (C) is incorrect. Choices (A) and (B) are incorrect as they are incomplete.

26. **(B)** Almost all the tavern's patrons are drinking an alcoholic beverage of some kind, making choice (B) the correct one. The "Good Creature" is the punch "long since made a familiar drink in the colony." Also, some men prefer the "insulated bliss of an unshared potation"; "potation" is an alcoholic beverage. Where the mariners have returned from is not mentioned, so choice (A) should not be selected. There is no reference to religion in the passage; choice (C) is incorrect. Although drinking alcohol was most likely considered an enjoyable activity for the patrons, it was not described as such within the text; choice (D) is also incorrect.

27. **(B)** Choice (B) should be selected because we have already determined that the Good Creature to which "we have a long hereditary claim" is alcohol. Seafaring is hardly a vice; choice (A) is incorrect. Although smoking [choice (C)] and gossiping [choice (D)] could be considered vices, the author does not describe them as such and therefore these are incorrect selections.

28. **(D)** Choice (D) is the best answer. The citizen was passionate in his response and threats to Robin. The citizen was also described as being "sepulchral"; passionate and gloomy best describe him. The citizen was not jovial and lighthearted but rather angry and annoyed; choice (A) is incorrect. The citizen, while disdainful, was not aloof; choice (B) should not be selected. The citizen was neither interested nor helpful, so choice (C) is also incorrect; he denied his knowledge of the kinsman.

29. **(C)** Choice (C) is the acceptable answer; this quote from the passage refers to feet being locked in a pillory for punishment—the threat issued when the youth clutches the citizen's clothing. Even though the word "stock" can refer to animals, that is not the meaning in this case, so choice (A) is not the best answer. While the dictionary offers "stocks" as one definition of investments, that meaning does not fit this passage; choice (B) should not be chosen. Although feet are mentioned, it is not in relation to a dance step; choice (D) is incorrect.

30. **(D)** "Taciturn" means quiet, silent, and uncommunicative, so choice (D) is correct. The tavern occupants were often reticent or reluctant to talk when they were under the influence of potation; therefore, they were not unreticent, and choice (A) should not be chosen. The occupants were less talkative; choice (B), which states that they were talkative after drinking, should not be selected. "Boisterous," choice (C), means rowdy and noisy, and is therefore incorrect.

31. **(B)** Transportation and housing total about half of the $25,892.

32. **(C)** According to the graph, food is next, after transportation, in the amount of money spent by the consumer.

33. **(A)** According to the graph, health care was closest to clothing in total amount spent.

34. **(A)** The central idea of the passage is that the Georgia peach is practically a symbol of Georgia. Choices B, C, and D do not reflect the central idea. They are details in the passage.

35. **(C)** *Synonymous* is closest in meaning to *equivalent* in connotation.

36. **(C)** This choice is clearly stated in the passage.

37. **(A)** Choices B, C, and D present minor problems in spa maintenance. If bacteria and viruses are allowed to grow, they can become a possible source of health problems. They are controlled by both temperature and chemicals.

38. **(A)** Choices B, C, and D are correct levels or degrees.

39. **(C)** Choices A and B represent an inference that goes beyond the scope of the passage and would indicate a bias on the part of the reader. Although the passage explains spa maintenance, in choice D, the information is not adequate to serve as a detailed guide.

40. **(D)** Choices A, B, and C all connote extreme or inappropriate attitudes not expressed in the passage. The author presents an informed concern—choice D.

41. **(C)** For the other choices, A, B, and D, the criteria, the role, the discussion, and the assurance for communication or learning are not provided in the passage. The passage stresses the importance of authenticity in communication—choice C.

42. **(D)** Each of the choices is a possible definition, but the passage overall suggests that communication needs to be developed so that students' responses may become more significant and authentic—choice D.

# WRITING SUBTEST

## Multiple-Choice Section

1. **(A)** The correct spelling is "authenticity."

2. **(B)** The term "Abolition" should not be capitalized.

3. **(C)** This sentence does not need a comma after the word "freedom."

4. **(C)** "Consultant" is the correct spelling.

5. **(D)** The apostrophe is incorrectly placed in this sentence. It should be "women's rights movement."

6. **(B)** This sentence does not need a comma after the word "selections."

7. **(B)** "Than" is the correct spelling.

8. **(C)** "American" should be capitalized.

9. **(D)** An apostrophe is needed in this sentence. "Americas" should be "America's."

10. **(A)** "Laboratory" is the correct spelling.

11. **(C)** This sentence needs a comma after the introductory clause, "When a known force is applied to it."

12. **(D)** The phrase "Intertial Mass" should not be capitalized. It should be written as "intertial mass."

13. **(D)** The sentence does not need a colon after the word "scale." The sentence would be correctly punctuated with a comma.

14. **(A)** The correct capitalization of the phrase "Civil war" is "Civil War."

15. **(A)** The word "their" is incorrect and should be "there."

16. **(B)** The word "throws" is incorrect in this context. The correct spelling for this word is "throes."

17. **(C)** "Confederates" should be capitalized.

18. **(C)** The word "simplicity" should not be capitalized in this sentence.

19. **(B)** "Products" should have an apostrophe—"product's."

20. **(A)** "There" is incorrect. The correct spelling in this context is "their."

21. **(D)** The correct spelling is "possessions."

22. **(D)** Choice (D) is the logical transition between Sentence 2, which describes the composition of stucco, and Sentence 3, which describes how the finish is applied. Choice (A) contradicts the thesis and breaks voice with "I." Choice (B) and choice (C), although true facts, introduce extraneous ideas.

23. **(C)** In choice (C), a comma is necessary to set off the introductory adverbial clause that begins with "Since." Choice (A) would create an incoherent sentence. Choice (B) is

incorrect because the transition "In addition" can be placed at the beginning or the middle of a sentence, but not at the end. Choice (D) changes the meaning of the sentence since the cheapness is the main emphasis, not the weight.

24. **(A)** Choice (A) is correct because the plural verb "are" agrees with the plural subject "finishes." An intervening phrase, "applied with a trowel," does not affect the choice of verb, even if the phrase ends with a singular word, "trowel." Choice (B) is incorrect because future tense is not needed. Choice (C) would create a fragment. Choice (D) is conditional tense and inappropriate because the composition for a stucco finish is clearly defined, not subject to condition.

25. **(A)** Choice (A) is correct because it introduces the idea of recycling the trees. Choice (B) detracts from the thesis. Choice (C) introduces extraneous information. Choice (D) changes tone and detracts from support for the thesis.

26. **(D)** Choice (D) would move Sentence 11, which names the Artificial Reef Fund, before Sentence 9, which makes reference to "this self-sustaining program." Choice (A) deletes the topic sentence. Choice (B) would delete a vital piece of information, how the program works. Choice (C) incorrectly reverses the topic sentence, which introduces the topic, with the concluding sentence, which summarizes the usefulness of the rigs.

27. **(B)** Choice (B) is correct because present tense is needed to show this program is still operational. Choice (A) is incorrect because "who" can be used only for people, and "which" is used only for objects. Choice (C) changes the correct comparative degree used for two options to the superlative degree used for more than two options. Choice (D) would include an unnecessary comma, needed to form a compound sentence only if there were a subject after "and." Sentence 13 has a compound verb: "sport fishers and divers already know…and come."

28. **(D)** Choice (D) contains the idea of Dena's failing health, mentioned in Sentence 6, and the idea of captivity, followed up in Sentence 7. Choice (A) contradicts the author's point made in Sentence 7. Choice (B) is too formal in tone and does not fit logically. Choice (C) introduces irrelevant information.

29. **(D)** Choice (D) is correct because Sentence 15 contains an error in pronoun and antecedent agreement. The indefinite pronoun "everyone" is always singular and should be followed by the singular pronouns "his or her," not the plural pronoun "their." Choices (A), (B), and (C) all contain correct pronoun usage.

30. **(B)** The phrase "like in the movie *Orca*" not only disrupts the rhythm of the sentence, but the allusion itself is gratuitous and is not necessary to the author's point in this sentence, which is to ask rhetorically whether this particular killer whale should be released from captivity.

31. **(D)** "From her natural habitat" is clearly an error, because what is being debated in this letter is the fact that Dena does *not* live in her natural habitat. Therefore, "into" is the best substitution for "from." "Under" in choice (C) makes no sense in this context. Choice (A) changes the verb to the past tense, which is clearly wrong, since what is being discussed is surely that Dena presently deserves to be released. Choice (B) makes a quasi-poetical inversion, which is unnecessarily stylized for such a letter, and more importantly, the sentence retains the incorrect preposition "from."

32. **(D)** In the original, the modifier "Sea Habitat, Inc." was in the wrong position to be modifying "owners." Both choices (A) and (C) correct this in acceptable ways. Only choice (B) is incorrect; "Since" emphasizes the incidental fact that "Sea Habitat, Inc." is Dena's owner and creates a misleading logical relation.

33. **(A)** Choice (A) best follows Sentence 10 because it continues the theme of obstacles toward Dena's release. Choices (B) and (C) set up misleading logical relations with the phrases "As a matter of fact" and "As we all know," and would not follow well from Sentence 10. Choice (D) is as gratuitous and unnecessary as the *Orca* allusion in Sentence 4.

34. **(C)** "Stayed" in Sentence 10 should be "stay" to agree with the present tense of the rest of the passage. (A) and (B) are correct as written and should not be changed. (D), which suggests errors in both (B) and (C), is also an incorrect choice.

35. **(D)** Sentence 8 is simple in structure and direct in meaning; it is best with no punctuation.

## Short-Answer Section Sample Responses

36. Each of the desserts I enjoy making require so much butter that my friends and myself don't eat them.

    ***Errors:*** 1. lack of subject-verb agreement (require)

    2. incorrect use of reflexive pronoun (myself)

*Sample Correct Responses:*

*Each of the desserts I enjoy making requires so much butter that my friends and I don't eat them.*

*The amount of butter I use keeps my friends and me from eating the desserts I enjoy making.*

37. Are they really aiming to help the neighborhood people or are they interested in making a tidy profit from the work of others.

    *Errors:*   1.   Comma needed before the word "or."

                2.   Punctuation incorrect: question mark needed.

    *Sample Correct Responses:*

    *Are they really aiming to help the neighborhood people, or are they interested in making a tidy profit from the work of others?*

    *Are they really neighborly, or are they just looking to profit from the work of others?*

38. A person who studies hard will find that there grades improve.

    *Errors:*   1.   lack of pronoun/antecedent agreement

                2.   incorrect use of there; should be their

    *Sample Correct Responses:*

    *A person who studies hard will find that his grades improve.*

    *Those who study hard will find that their grades improve.*

39. Using a thesaurus is very difficult you have to know how to spell the word before you can find words that go to gether.

    *Errors:*   1.   run-on sentence

                2.   *to* and *gether* are one word

*Sample Correct Response:*

*Using a thesaurus is very difficult. You first have to know how to spell the word, then you can find words that go together.*

40. My uncle get very tired when he shovels snow in the Winter.

   *Errors:*   1.   missing verb ending

   2.   incorrect use of capitalization

*Sample Correct Responses:*

*My uncle gets very tired when he shovels snow in the winter.*

*When he shovels snow in the winter, my uncle gets very tired.*

41. Each fruit that I kneed to cut require special handling.

   *Errors:*   1.   lack of subject-verb agreement *(require)*

   2.   misuse of *kneed* in place of *need*

*Sample Correct Response:*

*Each fruit that I need to cut requires special handling.*

42. After the tornado both of us wants to move to someplace far away.

   *Errors:*   1.   misuse of a singular verb *(wants)*

   2.   missing comma after an introductory clause

*Sample Correct Response:*

*After the tornado, both of us want to move to someplace far away.*

## SCORING RUBRIC FOR THE WRITTEN SUMMARY EXERCISE

### Scoring Scale:

### Score of 4:  A well-formed written response

- You have accurately conveyed the main ideas of the passage, maintaining focus and unity, while using your own words.

- Your response is concise, but you have provided sufficient depth and specificity to convey the main points of the passage.

- Your response shows control and organization.

- You have used correct and effective sentence structure.

- Your usage and choice of words are careful and precise.

- You have shown a mastery of mechanical conventions (i.e., spelling, punctuation, and capitalization).

### Score of 3:  An adequately formed written response

- Generally using your own words, you have accurately conveyed most of the writer's main ideas and in most cases maintained focus and unity.

- Your response may have been too long or too short, but you generally provided sufficient depth and specificity to convey most of the main points of the passage.

- Your organization of ideas might be ambiguous, incomplete, or partially ineffective.

- You use adequate sentence structure, but minor errors may be present.

- Your usage and choice of words display minor errors.

- You have made some errors in the use of mechanical conventions (i.e., spelling, punctuation, and capitalization).

## Score of 2: A partially formed written response

- You have conveyed only some of the main ideas of the passage and/or did not keep focus on the topic. You relied heavily on the writer's words.

- Your response is too long or too short and/or did not included sufficient depth to effectively develop your response.

- You made a generally unsuccessful attempt to organize and sequence ideas.

- Your sentence structure contains significant errors.

- You are imprecise in usage and word choice.

- You have made frequent errors in the use of mechanical conventions (i.e., spelling, punctuation, and capitalization).

## Score of 1: An inadequately formed written response

- You have not identified the main ideas of the passage.

- You have failed to effectively develop your response.

- You have very little organization and what is there is not sequential.

- Your sentence structure is poor and most sentences contain errors.

- Your usage is imprecise and your word choices are ill-advised.

- You have made serious and numerous errors in the use of mechanical conventions (i.e., spelling, punctuation, and capitalization).

## Score of U

The response is unrelated to the assigned topic, illegible, primarily in a language other than English, not of sufficient length to score, or merely a repetition of the assignment.

## Score of B

There is no response to the assignment.

# SCORING RUBRIC FOR THE WRITTEN COMPOSITION EXERCISE

## Scoring Scale:

### Score of 4:  A well-formed written response

- You have addressed the assignment fully and used appropriate language and style.

- You have shown a mastery of mechanical conventions (e.g., spelling, punctuation, and capitalization).

- Your usage and choice of words are careful and precise.

- Your sentence structure is effective and free of errors.

- You have clearly stated a main idea and/or point of view, and maintained focus and unity throughout your composition.

- You have shown excellent organizational skills.

- You have fully developed your composition, providing ample and appropriate depth, specificity, and accuracy.

### Score of 3:  An adequately formed written response

- You have addressed the assignment adequately and have generally used appropriate language and/or style.

- You have some errors in the use of mechanical conventions (e.g., spelling, punctuation, and capitalization).

- You have some minor errors in usage and word choice.

- Your sentence structure is adequate, but there are some minor errors in your writing.

- The presentation of your main idea and/or point of view is generally clear and focused and you generally maintain unity.

- Your organization of ideas is a bit ambiguous, incomplete, or partially ineffective.

- You have provided sufficient depth, specificity, and accuracy to adequately develop the response.

## Score of 2: A partially formed written response

- You have only partially addressed the assignment and may have used inappropriate language and/or style.

- You have made frequent errors in the use of mechanical conventions (e.g., spelling, punctuation, and capitalization).

- You have been imprecise in your usage and word choice.

- Your sentence structure is poor with a number of errors.

- Your main idea and/or point of view is inconsistently treated and/or you have not maintained the focus and unity of your discussion.

- You have made an effort to organize and sequence ideas, but your organization is largely unclear.

- Your response includes very few ideas that aid in its development.

## Score of 1: An inadequately formed written response

- You have attempted to address the assignment, but your language and style are generally inappropriate for the given audience, purpose, and/or occasion.

- You have made many serious errors in the use of mechanical conventions (e.g., spelling, punctuation, and capitalization).

- You have been imprecise in usage and word choice.

- Your sentence structure is ineffective and error-ridden.

- You have not identified your main idea and/or point of view.

- Your limited organization fails to follow a logical sequence of ideas.

- You have failed to include ideas that would aide in the development of your response.

## Score of U

The response is unrelated to the assigned topic, illegible, primarily in a language other than English, not of sufficient length to score, or merely a repetition of the assignment.

## Score of B

There is no response to the assignment.

## Sample Strong Response for Composition Exercise

*Expecting students and the family to give up their culture and their language entirely is an unreasonable thing to do. Most people are proud of their language, their culture, and their families; rejecting their language and their culture implies rejecting them and the people that they hold most dear.*

*Rather than asking a student and family to discard beliefs and traditions that are a part of their culture, the teacher might ask the students to share with the class some of the things that are most important to them. The teacher must be prepared to ensure a climate of acceptance and cooperation among those in the classroom; the teacher might even want the student(s) to present their presentations with other classrooms or even with parents on PTA/PTO night. Knowledge may increase acceptance of one another and may encourage the cooperation that will help the school and family and the students within the classroom to work together in harmony.*

## Analysis

This essay would receive a high score because it very clearly expresses the view that teachers should take in their classrooms. Teachers must accept the students and their families for who they are: unique individuals with worth. Disseminating knowledge can only improve the situation and not worsen it. The suggestion of having a presentation at the parent-teacher association or organization (PTA/PTO) meetings is one that has merit. Hopefully, as the writer stated, the result will be working "together in harmony." The writer makes a statement, supports it in the essay, and presents the ideas clearly in the writing.

## Sample Weak Response for Composition Exercise

*I would encourage the teacher to work with me on a cooperative project that would result in a compilation of research on various cultures. Each student could take a topic and gather information through interviews, accessing the Internet, and reading. These research projects would focus on ways that people are different and the end result should be the idea that we all have similarities and differences. The United States is like a "salad bowl" and not like the "melting pot" of past generations and this is something that may change but until it does it is something we must deal with in the classroom.*

## Analysis

This essay approaches the various cultures as having worth. The research is a good idea, but the sentence structure in the last part of the paragraph is not the best.

# MTEL Communication and Literacy Skills

## PRACTICE TEST 2

## Multiple-Choice Section

*Directions:* Read each passage and answer the questions that follow.

### The Profitable Reading of Fiction

If we speak of deriving good from a story, we usually mean something more than the gain of pleasure during the hours of its perusal. Nevertheless, to get pleasure out of a book is a beneficial and profitable thing, if the pleasure be of a kind which, while doing no moral injury, affords relaxation and relief when the mind is overstrained or sick of itself. The prime remedy in such cases is change of scene, by which change of the material scene is not necessarily implied. A sudden shifting of the mental perspective into a fictitious world, combined with rest, is well known to be often as efficacious for renovation as a corporeal journey afar.

In such a case the shifting of scene should manifestly be as complete as if the reader had taken the hind seat on a witch's broomstick. The town man finds what he seeks in novels of the country, the countryman in novels of society, the indoor class generally in outdoor novels, the villager in novels of the mansion, the aristocrat in novels of the cottage.

The narrative must be of a somewhat absorbing kind, if not absolutely fascinating. To discover a book or books which shall possess, in addition to the special scenery, the special action required, may be a matter of some difficulty, though not always of such difficulty as to be insuperable; and it may be asserted that after every variety of spiritual fatigue there is to be found refreshment, if not restoration, in some antithetic realm of ideas which lies waiting in the pages of romance.

*From Thomas Hardy, "The Profitable Reading of Fiction," 1888*

1. The first sentence of this passage indicates that the author's purpose is to

   (A) suggest that people read only for pleasure.

   (B) analyze the benefits of reading stories.

   (C) defend the view that reading is a waste of time.

   (D) entertain the reader by telling a story.

2. In this passage the author shows bias in favor of

   (A) reading nonfiction.          (C) reading for relaxation.

   (B) reading thrillers.           (D) city life over country life.

3. The image in Paragraph 2 of the reader taking a ride on a witch's broomstick is used to illustrate

   (A) the frivolousness of reading merely for pleasure.

   (B) the complete change of scenery that reading can provide.

   (C) the wickedness of trying to escape reality.

   (D) the dangerous power of storytellers.

4. From this passage you could infer that the author

   (A) is a novelist trying to promote the reading of novels.

   (B) disapproves of pleasure reading.

   (C) believes there are other benefits to reading stories.

   (D) leads an unhappy life.

## The Interpretation of Dreams

I have noticed in the course of my psychoanalytic work that the state of mind of a man in contemplation is entirely different from that of a man who is observing his psychic processes. In contemplation there is a greater play of psychic action than in the most attentive self-observation; this is also shown by the tense attitude and wrinkled brow of contemplation, in contrast with the restful features of self-observation. In both cases, there must be concentration of attention, but, besides this, in contemplation one exercises a critique, in consequence of which he rejects some of the ideas which he has perceived, and cuts short others, so that he does not follow the trains of thought which they would open; toward still other thoughts he may act in such a manner that they do not become conscious at all—that is to say, they are suppressed before they are perceived. In self-observation, on the other hand, one has only the task of suppressing the critique; if he succeeds in this, an unlimited number of ideas, which otherwise would have been impossible for him to grasp, come to his consciousness. With the aid of this material, newly secured for the purpose of self-observation, the interpretation of pathological ideas, as well as of dream images, can be accomplished. As may be seen, the point is to bring about a psychic state to some extent analogous as regards the apportionment of psychic energy (transferable attention) to the state prior to falling asleep (and indeed also to the hypnotic state). In falling asleep, the "undesired ideas" come into prominence on account of the slackening of a certain arbitrary (and certainly also critical) action, which we allow to exert an influence upon the trend of our ideas; we are accustomed to assign "fatigue" as the reason for this slackening; the emerging undesired ideas as the reason are changed into visual and acoustic images. In the condition which is used for the analysis of dreams and pathological ideas, this activity is purposely and arbitrarily dispensed with, and the psychic energy thus saved, or a part of it, is used for the attentive following of the undesired thoughts now coming to the surface, which retain their identity as ideas (this is the difference from the condition of falling asleep). "Undesired ideas" are thus changed into "desired" ones.

The suspension thus required of the critique for these apparently "freely rising" ideas, which is here demanded and which is usually exercised on them, is not easy for some persons. The "undesired ideas" are in the habit of starting the most violent resistance, which seeks to prevent them from coming to the surface. But if we may credit our great poet-philosopher Friedrich Schiller, a very similar tolerance must be the condition of poetic production. At a point in his correspondence with Koerner, for the noting of which we are indebted to Mr. Otto Rank, Schiller answers a friend who complains of his lack of creativeness in the following words: "The reason for your complaint lies, it seems to me, in the constraint which your intelligence imposes upon your imagination. I must here make an observation and illustrate it by an allegory. It does not seem beneficial, and it is harmful for the creative work of the mind, if the intelligence inspects too closely the ideas already pouring in, as it were, at the gates. Regarded by itself, an idea may be very trifling and very adventurous, but it perhaps becomes important on account of one which follows it; perhaps in a certain connection with others, which may seem equally absurd, it is capable of forming a very useful construction. The intelligence cannot judge all these things if it does not hold them steadily long enough to see them in connection with the others. In the case of a creative mind, however, the intelligence has withdrawn its watchers from the gates, the ideas rush in pell-mell, and it is only then that the great heap is looked over and critically examined. Messrs. Critics, or whatever else you may call yourselves, you are ashamed or afraid of the momentary and transitory madness which is found in all creators, and whose longer or shorter duration distinguishes the thinking artist from the dreamer. Hence your complaints about barrenness, for you reject too soon and discriminate too severely" (Letter of December 1, 1788).

And yet, "such a withdrawal of the watchers from the gates of intelligence," as Schiller calls it, such a shifting into the condition of uncritical self-observation, is in no way difficult.

Most of my patients accomplish it after the first instructions; I myself can do it very perfectly, if I assist the operation by writing down my notions. The amount, in terms of psychic energy, by which the critical activity is in this manner reduced, and by which the intensity of the self-observation may be increased, varies widely according to the subject matter upon which the attention is to be fixed.

*From Sigmund Freud, "The Interpretation of Dreams," trans. A. A. Brill*

5. Which are characteristics of contemplation, according to the author of this article?

I. A greater play of psychic action than in the most attentive self-observation.

II. A tense attitude, a wrinkled brow, and a concentration of attention.

III. A suppression of some thoughts before they are perceived.

IV. A critique in which one rejects some of the ideas and cuts short others.

(A) I only.

(C) I, II, and III only.

(B) I and II only.

(D) I, II, III, and IV.

6. Which are characteristics of self-observation?

I.  Restful features and a suppressing of the criticism.

II.  Less play of psychic action and a concentration of attention.

III.  An interpretation of pathological ideas and dream images.

(A) I only.

(C) I, II, and III.

(B) I and II only.

(D) I and III only.

7. In sleep,

(A) no psychic energy is available for the attentive following of undesired thoughts.

(B) fatigue causes the slackening of a certain arbitrary and often critical action, according to most people's way of thinking.

(C) undesired and desired ideas are not modified.

(D) the watchers of the gates of intelligence have not withdrawn.

8. The writer states that shifting into the condition of uncritical self-observation

(A) is impossible.

(B) can be done perfectly by the writer's patients.

(C) is difficult in many ways.

(D) is a feat the writer of the article maintains he can do perfectly.

9. The lack of creativeness lies in the constraints imposed upon the imagination by the intelligence, according to

(A) Freud.

(C) Schiller.

(B) Rank.

(D) Koerner.

10. A trifling and very adventurous idea

   (A) is usually important in itself.

   (B) should be considered in isolation.

   (C) should not be held long in the mind to make room for other ideas.

   (D) may become important because of an idea which follows.

11. Uncritical self-observation

   (A) is difficult to perform since we are all biased toward ourselves.

   (B) should not be encouraged if creative thinking is to result.

   (C) is inherent, not learned.

   (D) requires one to be unashamed or unafraid of the momentary and transitory madness.

12. In a creative mind

   (A) each idea is examined critically and individually as it is received.

   (B) ideas enter in a systematic manner.

   (C) a heap of ideas are examined critically at one time.

   (D) rejection comes soon and discrimination must be severe at all times.

13. According to Schiller

   (A) the tolerance of undesired ideas must be eliminated.

   (B) freely rising ideas must be critically examined as they occur.

   (C) the suspension of freely rising ideas is necessary.

   (D) a tolerance for undesired ideas is a necessary condition.

14. The author notes that psychic energy, by which the critical activity is reduced and by which the intensity of the self-observation may be increased, varies according to

   (A) the time of day at which the activity occurs.

   (B) the subject matter upon which the attention is fixed.

   (C) whether the intelligence has withdrawn its watchers from the gate.

   (D) whether the idea is trifling or constructive.

## Gothic Architecture in France, England, and Italy

Vaulting played a great part—perhaps the greatest, though certainly not the only part in developing Gothic architecture; but it will not do to define it as simply the expression of scientific vaulting. The Romans were masters of the art of vaulting long before; they used—probably invented—the cross-vault, and understood the concentration of thrusts on isolated points. It was from them, and from Eastern Rome as well, that the Romanesque builders learned how to make their stone roofs, and they in their turn passed the art on to their Gothic successors, who improved and developed it in their own way, making in the end almost a new art of it. But it must be remembered that most of the problems of scientific vaulting had presented themselves before their time, and had been partially at all events solved by their predecessors, though not so completely.

Nor is it correct to regard vaulting as an essential feature of the style, however great its influence may have been on the structure of great churches. In England except on a grand scale it is exceptional; and yet if Westminster Hall with its stupendous timber covering, and the Fen churches with their glorious wooden roofs, and the splendid ceiling of the nave at St. David's are not Gothic what are they? And what else can we call the countless village churches, gems of modest art, that stud our country far and wide, and constitute one of its greatest charms, though it is only here and there that they aspire to the dignity of a vaulted ceiling?

Again if the test of Gothic is to be the logical expression of a vaulted construction what becomes of domestic architecture both here and abroad, in which vaulting certainly does not play an important part? Are the townhalls of Brussels, Ypres, and Louvain not Gothic, nor the Broletto of Como, the pontifical palace at Viterbo, or that of the popes at Avignon, or the ducal palace at Venice?

Still less is Gothic architecture, as it has appeared to the ordinary layman, a matter of quatrefoils and trefoils, of cusps and traceries, of crockets and finials, pinnacles and flying buttresses. These are but the accidents of the style, though no doubt they resulted naturally from the application of certain principles behind them. But they might all fly away and yet leave a Gothic building behind them. Many an old tithe barn of rough timber framework is as truly a piece of Gothic architecture as York Minster or Salisbury Cathedral.

If then none of these attempted definitions are really coextensive with the Gothic style of architecture, for a building may be Gothic and yet have none of these characteristics, how are we to define it?

The true way of looking at Gothic art is to regard it not as a definite style bound by certain formulas—for it is infinitely various—but rather as the expression of a certain temper, sentiment, and spirit which inspired the whole method of doing things during the Middle Ages in sculpture and painting as well as in architecture. It cannot be defined by any of its outward features, for they are variable, differing at times and in different places. They are the outward expression of certain cardinal principles behind them, and though these principles are common to all good styles—Gothic among them—the result of applying them to the buildings of each age, country, and people will vary as the circumstances of that country, that age, and that people vary.

*From Sir Thomas Graham Jackson, "Gothic Architecture in France, England & Italy"*

15. Which statement is most accurate?

(A) The Gothic forms were predecessors to the Romanesque builders.

(B) The Romanesque builders were successors to the Gothic builders.

(C) The Romanesque builders had partially solved many of the problems of scientific vaulting before their Gothic successors.

(D) In developing Gothic architecture, vaulting played only a minor role.

16. The author believes that

    (A) vaulting is an essential feature of Gothic architecture.

    (B) Gothic architecture had no influence in churches because, "…it is only here and there that they [the village churches] aspire to the dignity of a vaulted ceiling."

    (C) Gothic architecture might still exist even without quatrefoils, trefoils, cusps, traceries, pinnacles, flying buttresses, and finials.

    (D) Gothic architecture is a definite style bound by certain formulas.

17. Gothic art

    I.   is to be regarded as a definite style bound by certain formulas.

    II.  is the expression of a certain temper, sentiment, and spirit that inspired sculpture and painting.

    III. cannot be defined by any one of its outward features since they are variable.

    (A) I only.                          (C) II and III only.

    (B) I and II only.                   (D) I, II, and III.

18. The writer believes that Gothic art

    (A) is a thing of the past.

    (B) will be applied to buildings of each age and country exactly as in the past.

    (C) will be applied with some variation to buildings of each age and country.

    (D) does not follow the principles common to all good styles.

19. The central purpose of the article is to

    (A) define Gothic architecture.

    (B) give the characteristics of Gothic architecture.

    (C) present "the true way of looking at Gothic."

    (D) disparage Gothic architecture.

20. "Vaulting" in this article refers to

    (A) a way of leaping high, as in popularity.

    (B) a way of styling similar to that of vaults, or places where bodies are interred.

    (C) a way of producing high ceilings without visible support.

    (D) a way of drawing and producing plans on paper.

21. A "pontifical palace" may be best interpreted as

    (A) a place of happiness and merriment.

    (B) a place of rest and relaxation.

    (C) a place that seems friendly.

    (D) a place that seems dignified.

22. Quatrefoils, according to the article, are

    (A) not accidents of style.

    (B) not results of applications of principles.

    (C) essential to Gothic buildings.

    (D) results of the natural application of certain principles.

23. The author regards Gothic art as

    (A) a definite style bound by certain formulas.

    (B) having styles that are similar in all expressions.

    (C) the expression of infinitely various temper, sentiment, and spirit.

    (D) defined by outward features.

24. The author says Gothic art is NOT

(A) a whole method of doing things during the Middle Ages.

(B) an influence on architecture, painting, and sculpture.

(C) defined by its features.

(D) an outward expression of certain cardinal principles.

## The Slave Trade

The most significant demographic shift in these decades was the movement of blacks from the Old South to the new Southwest. Traders shipped servants by the thousands to the newly opened cotton lands of the gulf states. A prime field hand fetched an average price of $800, as high as $1500 in peak years. Families were frequently split apart by this miserable traffic. Planters freely engaged in this trade, but assigned very low status to the traders who carried it out.

Although the importation of slaves from abroad had been outlawed by Congress since 1808, they continued to be smuggled in until the 1850s. The import ban kept the price up and encouraged the continuation of the internal trade.

Blacks in bondage suffered varying degrees of repression and deprivation. The harsh slave codes were comprehensive in their restrictions on individual freedom, but they were unevenly applied, and so there was considerable variety in the severity of life. The typical slave probably received a rough but adequate diet and enjoyed crude but sufficient housing and clothing.

But the loss of freedom and the injustice of the system produced a variety of responses. Many "soldiered" on the job, and refused to work hard, or they found ways to sabotage the machinery or the crops. There was an underground system of ridicule toward the masters which was nurtured, as reflected in such oral literature as the "Brer Rabbit" tales.

## BLACK SOCIAL STRUCTURE IN THE OLD SOUTH, 1860

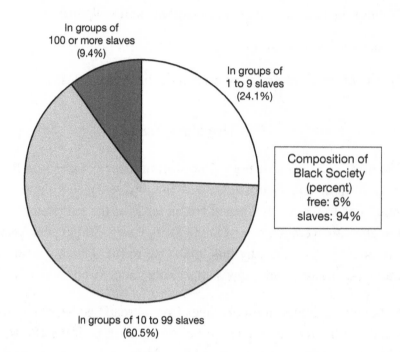

In groups of 100 or more slaves (9.4%)

In groups of 1 to 9 slaves (24.1%)

Composition of Black Society (percent)
free: 6%
slaves: 94%

In groups of 10 to 99 slaves (60.5%)

Violent reaction to repression was not uncommon. Gabriel Prosser in Richmond (1800), Denmark Vesey in Charleston (1822), and Nat Turner in coastal Virginia (1831) all plotted or led uprisings of blacks against their white masters. Rumors of such uprisings kept whites in a state of constant apprehension.

The ultimate rebellion was to simply leave, and many tried to run away, some successfully. Especially from the states bordering the North, an ever increasing number of slaves fled to freedom, many with the aid of the "underground railroad" and smugglers such as Harriet Tubman, who led over 300 of her family and friends to freedom after she herself had escaped.

Most of those in bondage, however, were forced simply to adapt, and they did. A rich culture was developed within the confines of the system, and included distinctive patterns of language, music, and religion. Kinship ties were probably strengthened in the face of the onslaughts of sale and separation of family members. In the face of incredible odds, the slaves developed a distinctive network of tradition and interdependence, and they survived.

25. The main idea portrayed in this passage is

    (A) Harriet Tubman and many slaves escaped bondage.

    (B) the oral literature of the underground ridiculed white slave-masters.

    (C) the slave market was run much the same way as other markets.

    (D) black society in the nineteenth century endured despite great hardship.

26. In what way is the word "soldiered" used in the second sentence of Paragraph 4?

    (A) Took up arms          (C) Undercut their labor

    (B) Labored               (D) Were uniformed

## Large and Small Towns, 1917

Great cities are levelling; they lift up the low and depress the high; they exalt mediocrity and abase superlativeness—the result of the action of the mass, as powerful in society life as in chemistry.

Soon after I came to this ancient city of Salamanca which has now become so dear to me, a city of some thirty thousand souls, I wrote to a friend and told him that if after two year's residence here he should be informed that I spent my time playing cards, taking siestas and strolling round the square for a couple of hours every day, he might give me up for lost; but if at the end of that time I should still be studying, meditating, writing, battling for culture in the public arena, he might take it that I was better off here than in Madrid. And so it has proved to be.

I remember that Guglielmo Ferrero's conclusion, based upon a review of ancient Greece, of the Italy of the Renaissance and of the Germany of a century ago, is that for the life of the spirit, small cities of a population like that of Salamanca are the best—better than very small towns or large ones of over a hundred thousand inhabitants.

This depends, of course, upon the quality of the spirit in question. I am convinced that the monastic cloister, which so often atrophies the soul and reduces the average intelligence to a lamentable slavery to routine, has in certain exceptional cases exalted the spirit by its arduous discipline.

Great cities are essentially democratic, and I must confess that I feel an invincible platonic mistrust of democracies. In great cities culture is diffused but vulgarized. People abandon the quiet reading of books to go to the theatre, that school of vulgarity; they feel the need of being together; the gregarious instinct enslaves them; they must be seeing one another.

*From Miguel de Unamuno, "Large and Small Towns," 1917*

27. From this passage, you could infer that

   (A) the author believes that great cities are essentially democratic.

   (B) given a choice, the author would prefer to live in a small city.

   (C) the author has never lived in a small town or out in the country.

   (D) the author believes that democracy is the best form of government.

28. Identify the statement below that gives the most accurate statement of the central idea of this passage.

   (A) Great cities tend to reduce everyone to the same level and are therefore not conducive to the life of the spirit.

   (B) The cloistered life of monks and nuns is perhaps the best way of life for the person interested in spiritual growth.

   (C) Smaller cities are not conducive to spiritual and intellectual growth because they are too sleepy and inactive.

   (D) As far as the spiritual life is concerned, great cities are superior both to small cities and to life in the country.

## Impressions of America

The first thing that struck me on landing in America was that if the Americans are not the most well-dressed people in the world, they are the most comfortably dressed. Men are seen there with the dreadful chimney-pot hat, but there are very few hatless men; men wear the shocking shallow-tail coat, but few are to be seen with no coat at all. There is an air of comfort in the appearance of the people which is a marked contrast to that seen in this country, where, too often, people are seen in close contact with rags.

The next thing particularly noticeable is that everybody seems in a hurry to catch a train. This is a state of things which is not favorable to poetry or romance. Had Romeo or Juliet been in a constant state of anxiety about trains, or had their minds been agitated by the question of return-tickets, Shakespeare could not have given us those lovely balcony scenes which are so full of poetry and pathos.

America is the noisiest country that ever existed. One is waked up in the morning not by the singing of the nightingale, but by the steam whistle. It is surprising that the sound practical sense of the Americans does not reduce this intolerable noise. All art depends upon exquisite and delicate sensibility, and such continual turmoil must ultimately be destructive of the musical faculty.

*From Oscar Wilde, "Impressions of America," 1882*

29. The example of Romeo and Juliet in the second paragraph is introduced in order to

   (A) criticize Americans for their ignorance of Shakespeare.

   (B) suggest humorously that their poetic and romantic world would be impossible in America.

   (C) underscore the need for silence if art is to thrive.

   (D) contrast the drabness of American dress with Romeo and Juliet's exquisite dress.

30. The word "faculty," as used in the last sentence of the passage, means

   (A) professors.                    (C) instrument.

   (B) a power of the mind.           (D) ease.

**Questions 31, 32, and 33 refer to the graph below.**

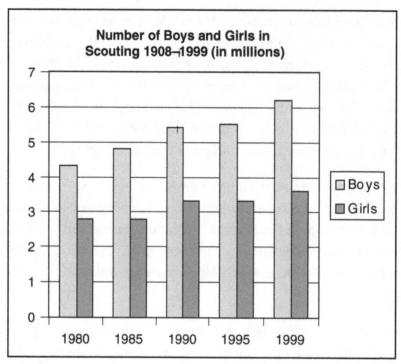

**Number of Boys and Girls in Scouting 1908–1999 (in millions)**

☐ Boys
◼ Girls

1980  1985  1990  1995  1999

*Source: United States Census Bureau*

31. In what year was the involvement in scouting closest to being equal between girls and boys?

    (A) 1980              (C) 1990

    (B) 1985              (D) 1995

32. What was the difference (in millions) between the number of boys and the number of girls involved in scouting in 1999?

    (A) 1.6 million        (C) 2.6 million

    (B) .9 million         (D) 2.0 million

33. What year had the greatest discrepancy between the involvement of boys and the involvement of girls in scouting?

    (A) 1980              (C) 1990

    (B) 1985              (D) 1999

### Frederick Douglass

1    Frederick Douglass was born Frederick Augustus Washington Bailey in 1817 to a white father and a slave mother. Frederick was raised by his grandmother on a Maryland plantation until he was eight. It was then that he was sent to Baltimore by his owner to be a servant to the Auld family. Mrs. Auld recognized Frederick's intellectual acumen and defied the law of the state by teaching him to read and write. When Mr. Auld warned that education would make the boy unfit for slavery, Frederick sought to continue his education in the streets. When his master died, Frederick was returned to the plantation to work in the fields at age 16. Later, he was hired out to work in the shipyards in Baltimore as a ship caulker. He plotted an escape but was discovered before he could get away. Five years later he was able to his way to New York City and then to New Bedford, Massachusetts. He eluded slave hunters by changing his name to Douglass.

2    At an 1841 anti-slavery meeting in Massachusetts, Douglass was invited to give a talk about his experiences under slavery. His impromptu speech was so powerful and so eloquent that it thrust him into a career as an agent for the Massachusetts Anti-Slavery Society.

3    Douglass wrote his autobiography in 1845 primarily to counter those who doubted his authenticity as a former slave. This work became a classic in American literature and a primary source about slavery from the point of view of a slave. Douglass went on a two-year speaking tour abroad to avoid recapture by his former owner and to win new friends for the abolition movement. He returned with funds to purchase his freedom and to start his own anti-slavery newspaper. He became a consultant to Abraham Lincoln and throughout Reconstruction fought doggedly for full civil rights for freedmen. He also supported the women's rights movement.

34. According to the passage, Douglass's autobiography was motivated by

   (A) the desire to make money for his anti-slavery movement.

   (B) the desire to start a newspaper.

   (C) his interest in authenticating his life as a slave.

   (D) His desire to educate people about slavery.

35. The central idea of the passage is that Frederick Douglass

    (A) was influential in changing the laws regarding the education of slaves.

    (B) was one of the most eminent human rights leaders of the century.

    (C) was a personal friend and confidant to a president.

    (D) wrote a classic in American literature.

36. According to the author of this passage, Mrs. Auld taught Frederick to read because

    (A) Frederick wanted to learn like the other boys.

    (B) she recognized his natural ability.

    (C) he needed to read to work in the home.

    (D) she obeyed her husband's wishes in the matter.

37. The title that best expresses the ideas of this passage is

    (A) The History of the Anti-Slavery Movement.

    (B) The Dogged Determination of Frederick Douglass.

    (C) Frederick Douglass's Contributions to Freedom.

    (D) The Oratorical and Literary Brilliance of Frederick Douglass.

38. In the context of the passage, *impromptu* is closest in meaning to

    (A) unprepared.            (C) forceful.

    (B) in a quiet manner.     (D) elaborate.

39. This passage is most likely written for an audience of

    (A) textbook publishers.   (C) biographers.

    (B) general readers.       (D) feminists.

## Literature-based Reading

In view of the current emphasis on literature-based reading instruction, a greater understanding by teachers of variance in cultural, language, and story components should assist in narrowing the gap between reader and text and improve reading comprehension. Classroom teachers should begin with students' meaning and intentions about stories before moving students to the commonalities of story meaning based on common background and culture. With teacher guidance, students should develop a fuller understanding of how complex narratives are when they are writing stories as well as when they are reading stories.

40. Which of the following is the intended audience for the passage?

    (A) teachers using literature-based curriculum

    (B) professors teaching a literature course

    (C) parents concerned about their child's comprehension of books

    (D) teacher educators teaching reading methods course

41. Which of the following is the most complete and accurate definition of the term *variance* as used in the passage?

    (A) change                    (C) diversity

    (B) fluctuations               (D) deviation

42. The passage supports a concept of meaning primarily residing in

    (A) culture, language and story components.

    (B) comprehension.

    (C) students' stories only.

    (D) students and narratives.

## PRACTICE TEST 2
## WRITING SUBTEST

## Multiple-Choice Section

**Directions:** Read each passage and answer the questions that follow.

### Benjamin Franklin

[1]Benjamin Franklin began writing his autobiography in 1771, but he set it aside to assist the Colonies in gaining independence from England. [2]After a hiatus of 13 years, he returned to chronicle his life, addressing his massage to the younger generation. [3]In this significant literary work of the early United States, Franklin portrays himself as benign, kindhearted, practical, and hardworking. [4]He established a list of ethical conduct and recorded his transgressions when he was unsuccessful in overcoming temptation. [5]Franklin wrote, that he was unable to arrive at perfection. [6]Still, he found value in the effort, writing, "yet I was, by the endeavor, a better and happier man than I otherwise should have been if I had not attempted it".

1. Which part of the passage has an error in capitalization?

   (A) Part 1          (C) Part 3

   (B) Part 2          (D) Part 4

2. Which part of the passage has a spelling error?

   (A) Part 2          (C) Part 4

   (B) Part 3          (D) Part 5

3. What punctuation correction is needed in Part 5?

   (A) Place comma after the word "arrive."

   (B) Remove comma after the word "wrote."

(C) Remove comma after the word "benign."

(D) Remove comma after the word "kindhearted."

4. In which part of the passage is there an incorrect placement of a period?

(A) Part 3

(C) Part 5

(B) Part 4

(D) Part 6

## The Scarlet Flamingo

[1]The scarlet flamingo is practically a symbol of Florida. [2]Once the west Indian flamingo population wintered in Florida Bay and as far north as St. John's River and Tampa Bay, but the brilliantly colored birds abandoned these grounds around 1885 due to the decimation of their numbers by feather hunters. [3]The flock at Hialeah Race Track is decended from a handful of birds imported from Cuba in the 1930s. [4]It took seven years before the first flamingo was born in captivity but several thousand have since been hatched.

[5]Flamingo raisers found that the birds require a highly specialized diet of shrimp and mollusks to maintain there attractive coloring. [6]It is speculated that hunters as well as the birds' selective breeding habits caused the disappearance of these beautiful birds from the wild in north America.

5. What is the capitalization error in Part 2?

(A) Indian

(C) population

(B) west

(D) River

6. What part of the passage contains a spelling error?

(A) Part 1

(C) Part 3

(B) Part 2

(D) Part 4

7. In which part of the passage is there an error in punctuation?

   (A) Part 2          (C) Part 4

   (B) Part 3          (D) Part 5

8. What word in Part 5 is used incorrectly?

   (A) found           (C) there

   (B) diet            (D) to

9. What is the error in Part 6?

   (A) birds'          (C) north

   (B) no comma after hunters    (D) these

## Free Speech

[1]Teachers should be cognizant of the responsibility they have for the development of children's competencies in basic concepts and principals of free speech. [2]Freedom of Speech is not merely the utterance of sounds into the air; rather, it is couched in a set of values and legislative processes that have developed over time. [3]These values and processes are a part of our political conscience as Americans. [4]Teachers must provide ample opportunities for children to express themselves effectively, in an environment where their opinions are valued. [5]Children should have ownership in the decision-making process in the classroom; and should be engaged in activities where alternative resolutions to problems can be explored. [6]If we want children to develop their own voices in a free society, then teachers must support participatory democratic experiences in the daily workings of the classroom.

10. What word is used incorrectly in Part 1?

    (A) cognizant       (C) development

    (B) responsibility  (D) principals

11. What change is needed in Part 2?

   (A) The word "speech" should be lowercased.

   (B) The semi-colon should be deleted.

   (C) The word "legislative" should be capitalized.

   (D) The word "have" should be eliminated.

12. In what part of the passage is there an incorrect use of a comma?

   (A) Part 1          (C) Part 3

   (B) Part 2          (D) Part 4

13. In what part of the passage is there an incorrect use of a semi-colon?

   (A) Part 3          (C) Part 5

   (B) Part 4          (D) Part 6

14. Which word is misspelled in Part 6?

   (A) develope        (C) participatory

   (B) society         (D) experiences

## The Contribution of Story Elements

[1]The relationship of story elements found in children-generated stories to reading achievement was analysed. [2]Correlations ranged from .61101 (p = .64) at the beginning of first grade to .83546 (p = .24) at the end of first grade. [3]Multiple Regression equation analyses dealt with the relative contribution of the story elements to reading achievement. [4]The contribution of certain story elements were substantial. [5]At the beginning of first grade story conventions added 40 percent to the total variance while the other increments were not significant. [6]At the end of first grade, story plot contributed 44 percent to the total variance, story conventions contributed 20 percent, and story sources contributed 17 percent.

15. What word is misspelled in Part 1?

(A) relationship

(C) achievement

(B) elements

(D) analysed

16. In what part of the passage is there a capitalization error?

(A) Part 2

(C) Part 4

(B) Part 3

(D) Part 5

17. Which change is needed in the passage?

(A) Part 3: Change "with" to "by."

(B) Part 4: Change "were" to "was."

(C) Part 5: Change "variance" to "variation."

(D) Part 6: Change "At" to "From."

18. What punctuation needs to be added to part 5?

(A) Place a comma after the word "grade."

(B) Place a semi-colon after the word "conventions."

(C) Place a comma after the word "increments."

(D) Place a semi-colon after the word "grade."

## Early American Peoples

[1]Actually, the term "Native American" is incorrect. [2]Indians migrated to the North American continent from other areas, just earlier than Europeans did. [3]The ancestors of the Anasazi—Indians of the four-state area of Colorado, New Mexico, Utah, and Arizona—probably crossed from Asia into Alaska. [4]About 25,000 years ago, while the continental land bridge still existed. [5]This land bridge arched across the Bering Strait in the last Ice Age. [6]About 500 CE the ancestors of the Anasazi moved onto the Mesa Verde, a high plateau in the

desert country of Colorado. [7]The Wetherills, five brothers who ranched in the area, are general given credit for the first exploration of the ruins in the 1870s and 1880s. [8]There were some 50,000 Anasazi thriving successfully in the four-corners area by the 1200s CE. [9] At their zenith, 700 to 1300 CE, the Anasazi had established widespread communities and built thousands of sophisticated structures—cliff dwellings, pueblos, and kivas. [10]They even engaged in trade with Indians in surrounding regions by exporting pottery and other goods.

19. Which of the following number parts is a sentence fragment?

    (A) Part 1              (C) Part 4

    (B) Part 2              (D) Part 5

20. Which of the following draws attention away from the main idea of the paragraph?

    (A) Part 3              (C) Part 7

    (B) Part 4              (D) Part 8

21. Which of the following changes is needed to make the passage conform to the conventions of Standard American English?

    (A) Part 2: Change "earlier" to "more early."

    (B) Part 3: Change "probably" to "more probably."

    (C) Part 7: Change "general" to "generally."

    (D) Part 8: Change "successfully" to "most successful."

## Lincoln

[1]The Lincoln Cent was first struck in 1909 to celebrate the 100th Anniversary of the birth of Abraham Lincoln, our 16th President. [2]Designed by Victor D. Brenner, the coin carried the motto "In God We Trust"—the first time it appeared on this denomination coin. [3]It is interesting that the law for the motto was passed during Lincoln's administration as president. [4]Though we might not think so at first glance, the lowly Cent is a fitting memorial for the great man

whose profile graces this most common coin of the realm and is a tolerable symbol for the nation whose commerce it serves.

[5]The obverse has the profile of Lincoln as he looked during the trying years of the War Between the States. [6]Faced with the immense problems of a divided nation, the prevention of the split between North and South was difficult. [7]"A house divided against itself cannot stand," he warned the nation. [8]With the outbreak of war at Fort Sumter. [9]Lincoln was saddened to see his beloved country caught up in the senseless war in which father fought against son, brother against brother. [10]Throughout America, war captured the attention of people: the woman who saved the lives of the wounded, the soldier waiting to go into battle, the bewildered child trying hard to understand the sound of guns. [11]Lincoln stood on the broad, silent battlefield at Gettysburg in 1863 to dedicate the site as a national cemetery. [12]Gettysburg had been the scene of some of the most bitter fighting of the war and had ended in a Union victory. [13]In his special address at Gettysburg, he called upon the American people to end the war. [14]His words boomed out over the large audience before him:

[15]It is rather for us [the living] to be here dedicated to the great task remaining before us—that from these honored dead we take increased devotion to that cause for which they gave the last full measure of devotion; that we here highly resolve that these dead shall not have died in vain; that this nation under God, shall have a new birth of freedom; and that government of the people, by the people and for the people, shall not perish from the earth."

[16]Barely a month before the end of the war, Lincoln took the oath of office a secondly time as President. [17]With the war still raging, his inaugural address took on added meaning:

[18]With malice toward none, with charity for all, with firmness in the right as God gives us to see the right, let us strive on to finish the work we are in, to bind up the nation's wounds, to care for him who shall have borne the battle and for his widow and his orphan, to do all which may achieve and cherish a just and lasting peace among ourselves and with all nations.

22. Which of the following changes is needed in the fourth paragraph?

    (A) Sentence 16: Change "end" to "climax."

    (B) Sentence 16: Change "secondly" to "second."

    (C) Sentence 17: Change "With" to "Of."

    (D) Sentence 17: Change "on" to "in."

23. Which of the following changes is needed in the second paragraph?

    (A) Sentence 5: Change "has" to "had."

    (B) Sentence 6: Change "the prevention of the split between North and South was difficult" to "Lincoln found it difficult to prevent the split between North and South."

    (C) Sentence 10: Change "waiting" to "waited."

    (D) Sentence 11: Change "site" to "sight."

24. Which of the following sentences is a nonstandard sentence?

    (A) Sentence 2          (C) Sentence 8

    (B) Sentence 4          (D) Sentence 12

## Ransom Eli Olds

[1]Many people think of Ransom Eli Olds as the actual founder of the automobile industry. [2]He built the first automobile factory and was the first to mass produce cars with an assembly-line method. [3]In the late 1800s he experimented with steam engines; the first steam-powered four-wheeled vehicle came out in 1883. [4]This car was sold to a company in India. [5]In 1896 he built his first gasoline-powered car. [6]He helped found the Olds Motor Works in 1899, which produced gasoline-engine automobiles.

[7]However, it was in 1901 that he introduced the method that turned out the "curved dash" Oldsmobile in an <u>assembly-line</u> or "stage" production. [8]Assem-

bled in a <u>process</u> using jigs and machine tools, the vehicle was a light-weight, one-cylinder model. [9]This car sold for $650, <u>about one-half</u> the price of similar vehicles from competitors. [10]<u>Many</u> were sold by 1906. [11]In 1904, for example, 5,000 cars, more than three times that of its larger competitor, Peugeot.

[12]Later, in 1914, Henry Ford revolutionized the automotive industry at the Ford Motor Co. plant. [13]This plant used the first moving assembly production line and could turn out a complete vehicle in 90 minutes.

25. Which of the following underlined words in the second paragraph should be replaced by more precise wording?

   (A) assembly-line

   (B) process

   (C) about one-half

   (D) Many

26. Which of the following is a nonstandard sentence?

   (A) Sentence 3

   (B) Sentence 7

   (C) Sentence 11

   (D) Sentence 12

27. Which of the following is least relevant to the main idea of the first paragraph?

   (A) Sentence 1

   (B) Sentence 2

   (C) Sentence 3

   (D) Sentence 4

## Child Poverty in America

[1]Sandra Davis and her two children are finding out just how cold life can be when you're poor. [2]It's the beginning of fall, and a chill wind briskly tosses red and gold leaves into a pile by the front door of the Davis home on Rand Street. [3]But, the inside of the house is cold, too, because the gas has just been turned off for non-payment of the bill. [4]Sandra is out of a job. [5]She suffers, but her children will suffer as much or more.

[6]In fact poor children across America are suffering. [7]According to the stereotype, we believe that poor children are born into large families in big cities,

and these families are headed by minority, welfare mothers. [8]Nothing could be further from the truth. [9]More poor children live outside cities. [10]Nearly two-thirds of all poor families have only one or two children. [11]Most poor families' income comes from the wages of one or more workers. [12]Most shocking of all is that even if every single-parent family was to disappear, the United States would still have one of the highest child poverty rates among industrialized nations. [13]This problem is a disgrace in a country as great as ours, but the government cannot legislate a solution. [14]The people of the United States must become concerned about child poverty and commit to a personal involvement before there can be an effective solution.

28. Which of the following, if added between Sentences 6 and 7, is most consistent with the writer's purpose and audience?

    (A) Who can blame Sandra for being angry about being laid off her job?

    (B) However, many of the stereotypes about poor children to which most Americans subscribe are not on target.

    (C) A study on child poverty made newspaper headlines on the front pages of American newspapers.

    (D) Frankly, I am shocked by the poverty that still exists in the United States.

29. Which of the following is needed?

    (A) Sentence 1: Delete the word "out."

    (B) Sentence 3: Change the comma after "too" to a semicolon.

    (C) Sentence 6: Place a comma after the phrase "In fact."

    (D) Sentence 7: Place a colon after the word "stereotype."

30. Which of the following uses a nonstandard verb form?

    (A) Sentence 11          (C) Sentence 13

    (B) Sentence 12          (D) Sentence 14

## The Bolero

[1]A French composer, the bolero inspired Maurice Ravel to create the ballet *Bolero*. [2]The sister of the legendary Russian dancer Vaslav Nijinsky choreographed the ballet created by Ravel. [3]A popular and well-known folk dance in Spain, the bolero as we know it is credited to Maurice Bolsche and Sebastian Cerezo around the mid 1700s. [4]Although almost no one has seen the ballet, the music from *Bolero* has retained immense popularity and is performed on a regular basis around the world.

[5]The center and driving force of it is a snare drum. [6]The percussionist begins by playing a rhythmic pattern lasting two measures and six beats, the rhythm of the bolero dance, as quietly as possible. [7]At the beginning, other instruments pick up the rhythm as the frenzy builds. [8]The first flute then introduces the melody, the second important part of *Bolero*; different instruments play individual parts, such as the clarinet, bassoon, and piccolo. [9]The buildup of the music occurs in two ways: the individual musicians play their instrument louder and louder, and more and more instruments beginning to play together. [10]For most of the 15 to 17 minutes of the performance, *Bolero* is played in a relentless harmony of C Major. [11]The end is signaled by a brief shift to E Major and then a strong return to C Major.

31. Which of the following is least relevant to the main idea of the first paragraph?

    (A) Part 1

    (B) Part 2

    (C) Part 3

    (D) Part 4

32. Which of the following, if added between Sentences 6 and 7 of the second paragraph, is most consistent with the writer's purpose and audience?

    (A) Doesn't that sound kind of boring?

    (B) It's pretty obvious why this piece is not currently popular.

    (C) It would be helpful to see the ballet, as bolero dancers use facial expressions and wave their arms to express emotions.

    (D) This rhythm does not change during the entire performance, but the music becomes gradually louder until the final crescendo.

33. Which of the following contains a misplaced modifier?

    (A) Part 1          (C) Part 6

    (B) Part 3          (D) Part 10

34. Which of the following revisions would best improve Sentence 1?

    (A) The bolero inspired Maurice Ravel to create the ballet *Bolero*, a French composer.

    (B) The bolero, a French composer, inspired Maurice Ravel to create the ballet *Bolero*.

    (C) The bolero inspired Maurice Ravel, a French composer, to create the ballet *Bolero*.

    (D) The bolero inspired Maurice Ravel to create the ballet, a French composer, *Bolero*.

35. Which of the following would best replace "it" in Sentence 5?

    (A) this musical composition

    (B) the folk dance

    (C) them

    (D) Maurice Bolsche and Sebastian Cerezo

## DIRECTIONS FOR THE SHORT-ANSWER SECTION OF THE WRITING SUBTEST

There are seven questions in the short-answer section of the writing subtest. Each question is phrased in exactly the same way. You will be told that each text has two errors and that the proper names of people and places are correctly spelled. You will look for errors in construction, grammar, usage, spelling, capitalization, and punctuation. Then, you will rewrite each text so that it is correct. You may change the syntax but must keep the essential elements of the piece. Of course, you may not introduce any new errors.

## SHORT-ANSWER ASSIGNMENTS AND RESPONSE SHEET

36. The following sentence contains two errors (e.g., in construction, grammar, usage, spelling, capitalization, punctuation). Rewrite the text so that errors are addressed and the original meaning is maintained.

    The new rule prohibits smoking of the employee's inside the building.

    _____

    _____

37. The following sentence contains two errors (e.g., in construction, grammar, usage, spelling, capitalization, punctuation). Rewrite the text so that errors are addressed and the original meaning is maintained.

    Australia is noted for their unique animals: koalas, platypus, kangaroo, and emu.

    _____

    _____

38. The following sentence contains two errors (e.g., in construction, grammar, usage, spelling, capitalization, punctuation). Rewrite the text so that errors are addressed and the original meaning is maintained.

    Economics can teach a person to effectively manage their own affairs and be a contributing member of society.

    _____

    _____

39. The following sentence contains two errors (e.g., in construction, grammar, usage, spelling, capitalization, punctuation). Rewrite the text so that errors are addressed and the original meaning is maintained.

When someone thinks they can do everything they want to do they will almost invariably be disappointed.

_____

_____

40. The following sentence contains two errors (e.g., in construction, grammar, usage, spelling, capitalization, punctuation). Rewrite the text so that errors are addressed and the original meaning is maintained.

In the summer I usually like swimming and to water-ski.

_____

_____

41. The following sentence contains two errors (e.g., in construction, grammar, usage, spelling, capitalization, punctuation). Rewrite the text so that errors are addressed and the original meaning is maintained.

I found five dollars eating lunch in the park.

_____

_____

42. The following sentence contains two errors (e.g., in construction, grammar, usage, spelling, capitalization, punctuation). Rewrite the text so that errors are addressed and the original meaning is maintained.

Janet is one of those people who you can't really describe with words.

_____

_____

## DIRECTIONS FOR THE WRITING SUMMARY EXERCISE

For this part of the test, you will read the passage on the next page and summarize it in your own words. Your summary should be approximately 150 to 250 words and effectively communicate the main idea and essential points of the passage. You are to identify the relevant information and communicate it clearly and concisely.

Your summary will be evaluated based on the following criteria:

- **FIDELITY:** Your accuracy and clarity in using your own words to convey and maintain focus on the main ideas of the passage

- **CONCISENESS:** Your appropriate use of length, depth, and specificity to convey the writer's main ideas

- **ORGANIZATION:** The clarity of your writing and your use of logical sequencing of ideas

- **SENTENCE STRUCTURE:** The effectiveness of your sentence structure and the extent to which those sentences are free of structural errors

- **USAGE:** Your care and precision in word choice and avoidance of usage errors

- **MECHANICAL CONVENTIONS:** Your use of conventional spelling and use of the conventions of punctuation and capitalization

The final version of your summary should conform to the conventions of edited American English, should be written legibly, and should be your own original work.

On the actual test you will be directed to write or print your summary on the pages provided in the test booklet.

## WRITING SUMMARY EXERCISE

*Directions:* Use the passage below to prepare a summary of 100–150 words.

Throughout its history, the American school system has often been the target of demands that it change to meet the social priorities of the times. This theme has been traced the following significant occurrences in education: Benjamin Franklin's advocacy in 1749 for a more useful type of education; Horace Mann's zealous proposals in the 1830s espousing the tax supported public school; John Dewey's early twentieth-century attack on traditional schools for not developing the child effectively for his or her role in society; the post-Sputnik pressure for academic rigor; the prolific criticism and accountability pressures of the 1970s; and the ensuing disillusionment and continued criticism of schools through the last decade of the twentieth century and into the current century. Indeed, the waves of criticism about American education have reflected currents of social dissatisfaction for any given period of this country's history.

As dynamics of change in the social order result in demands for change in the American educational system, so in turn insistence has developed for revision of teacher education (witness the more recent Holmes report (1986)). Historically, the education of American teachers has reflected evolving attitudes about public education. With slight modifications, the teacher's education pattern established following the demise of the normal school during the early 1900s has persisted in most teacher preparation programs. The pattern has been one requiring certain academic and professional (educational) courses often resulting in teachers prone to teach as they had been taught.

# DIRECTIONS FOR THE COMPOSITION EXERCISE

For this part of the writing subtest you are asked to write a multiple-paragraph composition of approximately 300 to 600 words on an assigned topic. Your assignment will be to effectively communicate a complete message for the specified audience and purpose. The assessment of your composition will be based on your ability to express, organize, and support opinions and ideas. The position you take will not be part of the evaluation.

## Criteria for Evaluation:

- **Appropriateness:** Your attention to the topic and use of the language and style appropriate to the stated audience, purpose, and occasion

- **Mechanical Conventions:** Your use of standard spelling and use of the conventions of punctuation and capitalization

- **Usage:** Your care and precision in word choice and avoidance of usage errors

- **Sentence Structure:** The effectiveness of your sentence structure and the extent to which those sentences are free of structural errors

- **Focus and Unity:** Your clarity in stating and maintaining focus on your main idea or point of view

- **Organization:** The clarity of your writing and your use of logical sequencing of ideas

- **Development:** Your statements are of appropriate depth, specificity, and/or accuracy

Your final version needs to conform to the conventions of edited American English, be written legibly, and be your own original work.

On the actual test you will be directed to write or print your response on the pages provided in the test booklet.

# COMPOSITION EXERCISE

Many scholars note the decline in the use of research resources that are only available in print form. With the onset of the availability of many resources such as journal articles, encyclopedias and other sources such as public records and almanacs online, the use of libraries by individuals who are seeking information has also declined.

In an essay written to a local school board, argue whether you feel the trend of accessing research resources online versus physically visiting a library is commendable or contemptible. Reflect on modern research techniques and the effects of a strictly online environment on the culture of academic investigation. Discuss the advantages and or disadvantages of researching a topic that excludes or minimizes the need to physically search for resources. Finally, draw upon your own exposure to and attitude toward online resources and print copy resources, respectively.

## PRACTICE TEST 2
## ANSWER KEY

### READING SUBTEST – MULTIPLE-CHOICE SECTION

| | | | | | | | |
|---|---|---|---|---|---|---|---|
| 1. | (B) | 12. | (C) | 23. | (C) | 34. | (C) |
| 2. | (C) | 13. | (D) | 24. | (C) | 35. | (B) |
| 3. | (B) | 14. | (B) | 25. | (D) | 36. | (B) |
| 4. | (C) | 15. | (C) | 26. | (C) | 37. | (C) |
| 5. | (D) | 16. | (C) | 27. | (B) | 38. | (A) |
| 6. | (C) | 17. | (C) | 28. | (A) | 39. | (B) |
| 7. | (B) | 18. | (C) | 29. | (B) | 40. | (A) |
| 8. | (D) | 19. | (A) | 30. | (B) | 41. | (C) |
| 9. | (C) | 20. | (C) | 31. | (A) | 42. | (D) |
| 10. | (D) | 21. | (D) | 32. | (C) | | |
| 11. | (D) | 22. | (D) | 33. | (D) | | |

### WRITING SUBTEST – MULTIPLE-CHOICE SECTION

| | | | | | | | |
|---|---|---|---|---|---|---|---|
| 1. | (A) | 10. | (D) | 19. | (C) | 28. | (B) |
| 2. | (A) | 11. | (A) | 20. | (C) | 29. | (C) |
| 3. | (B) | 12. | (D) | 21. | (C) | 30. | (B) |
| 4. | (D) | 13. | (C) | 22. | (B) | 31. | (C) |
| 5. | (B) | 14. | (A) | 23. | (B) | 32. | (D) |
| 6. | (C) | 15. | (D) | 24. | (C) | 33. | (A) |
| 7. | (C) | 16. | (B) | 25. | (D) | 34. | (C) |
| 8. | (C) | 17. | (B) | 26. | (C) | 35. | (A) |
| 9. | (C) | 18. | (A) | 27. | (D) | | |

# DETAILED EXPLANATIONS OF ANSWERS
# READING SUBTEST

## Multiple-Choice Section

1. **(B)** (B) is correct because the author refers to gaining pleasure from reading stories without himself telling a story (D). Because the author clearly indicates that he does not believe reading is a waste of time, (C) is incorrect; he also suggests the possibility of benefits beyond reading only for pleasure, so (A) is incorrect.

2. **(C)** (C) is correct because the author describes reading as a pleasant means of relieving spiritual fatigue. (B) is more specific than the author is. (A) is incorrect because the author specifically refers to reading stories, a form of fiction. (D) refers only to one particular example used to illustrate the relaxing effect reading can have.

3. **(B)** (B) is correct because the following sentence clearly describes examples of scenery changes. (A) contradicts the main point of the passage; (C) and (D) have more negative meanings than the author intended.

4. **(C)** (C) is correct because although the author advocates the relaxing effects of reading, he refers to the possibility of "something more than the gain of pleasure..." (B) contradicts the main point of the passage. There is no evidence that the author is himself a novelist or that he leads an unhappy life, so (A) and (D) are incorrect.

5. **(D)** All the statements given in the question are true and are taken from the passage, but only (D) allows one to select I, II, III, and IV; therefore, it is the correct answer. The passage states that in contemplation there is a greater play of psychic action than in the most attentive self-observation (I), a tense attitude, a wrinkled brow, and a concentration of attention (II), a suppression of some thoughts before they are perceived (III), and a critique in which one rejects some of the ideas and cuts short others (IV).

6. **(C)** (C) is the best answer since it includes three correct statements. The passage includes the statements that self-observation involves restful features and a suppressing of the criticism (I), less play of psychic action and a concentration of attention (II), and an interpretation of pathological ideas and dream images (III). Answers (A), (B), and (D) do not allow the reader to include all the correct choices.

7. **(B)** The best answer is (B); according to the passage, most people believe that fatigue causes the slackening of a certain arbitrary and often critical action. According to the reading passage, even in sleep there is psychic energy available for the attentive following of undesired thoughts; (A) is false and should not be chosen. At the end of the first paragraph of the reading passage, Freud refers to undesired ideas being changed into desired ones during sleep; therefore, (C) is incorrect. Since in sleep the watcher of the gates of intelligence may be withdrawn, (D) is not correct.

8. **(D)** The feat the writer, Freud, mentions is that he can perform self-observation perfectly; therefore, (D) is the correct answer. Because the writer states that self-observation is possible, (A) is incorrect. The writer maintains that he, not the patients, can perform self-observation perfectly; hence, (B) should not be chosen. The writer believes that self-observation can be taught; he does not make the statement that self-observation is difficult in many ways, so (C) should not be selected.

9. **(C)** The passage states that the lack of creativeness lies in the constraints imposed upon the imagination by the intelligence, according to Schiller; therefore, (C) is the best answer choice. It is neither Freud (A), Rank (B), nor Koerner (D) who is directly quoted in the reading passage and credited with this statement.

10. **(D)** (D) is the best choice because, according to Schiller's correspondence, a trifling, very adventurous idea may become important because of another idea which follows it. The trifling idea is not usually important in itself; it is when the idea is followed by another that it may become important; hence, (A) should not be chosen. The trifling idea should not be considered in isolation in most cases, but rather it should be considered in connection with others; (B) is not the best selection. The trifling, adventurous idea should be held in the mind for a while; (C) suggests the opposite and is not acceptable.

11. **(D)** Uncritical self-observation requires one to be unashamed or unafraid of the momentary madness; (D) is the best answer. The writer tells the reader that uncritical self-observation is in no way difficult. Since (A) states that such self-observation is difficult, (A) should not be chosen. (B) states that self-observation should *not* be encouraged; (B) is an incorrect choice. The author of the passage states that uncritical self-observation can be learned; (C), which suggests the opposite, should not be selected.

12. **(C)** In a creative mind, a heap of ideas will be collected and examined critically at a later time; (C) is the best choice. A creative mind collects the ideas; it does not try to examine each critically and individually at the time they are collected; therefore, (A) is an incorrect answer. Because ideas enter in random order at times, there may not be a systematic way of

collecting the ideas; (B) is not a good choice. According to Schiller's letter, it is the withdrawal of the watchers (i.e., rejection and discrimination) from the gates of intelligence which identifies the creative mind; since (D) suggests the opposite, it is another incorrect choice.

13. **(D)**  Schiller suggests that in order to be creative, one must learn to accept even undesired ideas as a possibility; (D) suggests this very idea and is, therefore, the best answer. (A) suggests that the tolerance must be eliminated, which is the opposite of what Schiller states, and, thereby, causes (A) to be incorrect. According to Schiller's letter in the reading passage, one should not critically examine freely rising ideas as they occur; (B) should be rejected. Schiller states that one must allow freely rising ideas to occur and the suspension of these ideas is not acceptable; therefore, (C) should not be selected.

14. **(B)**  In the last sentence, the author suggests that the subject matter upon which the attention is fixed can affect psychic energy and intensity; (B) is the best answer. Neither time of day (A), watchers from the gate (C), nor the idea being trifling or constructive (D) can be the answer since none of these choices is supported in the passage as being the cause of variation in psychic energy. While (C) and (D) are mentioned in the passage, it is in reference to the creative mind, rather than psychic energy.

15. **(C)**  Since the Romanesque builders had partially solved many of the problems of scientific vaulting before their Gothic successors, (C) is the best answer. Since the Romanesque builders were predecessors to the Gothic forms (not the other way around), (A) is false. The Romanesque builders were predecessors (not successors) to the Gothic builders; therefore, (B) should not be chosen. In the first sentence, it is stated that vaulting played a great part in Gothic architecture; (D) is false.

16. **(C)**  Gothic architecture might still exist even without quatrefoils, trefoils, cusps, traceries, pinnacles, flying buttresses, crockets, and finials; therefore, (C) is the best answer. Since vaulting is not essential to Gothic architecture, (A) is false. Gothic architecture had an influence in churches even if only here and there the village churches "…aspire to the dignity of a vaulted ceiling." (B) should not be chosen. Gothic architecture cannot be described as a definite style with certain formulas; (D) is incorrect.

17. **(C)**  (C) is the best answer since it includes both II (Gothic art is the expression of a certain temper, sentiment, and spirit which inspired sculpture and painting) and III (Gothic art cannot be defined by any of its outward features since they are variable). Both II and III are correct, but I, which states that Gothic art is bound by certain formulas, is not true. Since (A), (B), and (D) all include I, only (C) is correct.

18. **(C)** The best answer is (C); it states that the writer believes Gothic art will be applied with some variation to buildings of each age and country. (A), which states that Gothic art is a thing of the past, is false. Choice (B) states that Gothic art will be applied to buildings of each age and country exactly as in the past; (B) is inaccurate due to the inclusion of the words "exactly as in the past." Gothic art follows the principles common to all good styles; (D) states that Gothic art does not follow the principles common to all good styles. Since (D) is refuted by the last sentence of the passage, it is incorrect as an answer.

19. **(A)** The best choice is (A); it states that the central purpose of the article is to define Gothic architecture, which is an accurate statement. Since the characteristics of Gothic architecture vary so much, (B) should not be chosen since a comprehensive analysis of the article does not give characteristics of Gothic architecture. (C) is incorrect since there is no true way of viewing Gothic architecture. (D) is inaccurate since the writer seems to value Gothic architecture and this answer suggests the opposite.

20. **(C)** Vaulting is a way of producing high ceilings without visible support; (C) can be inferred from reading the passage. (A) is incorrect since no mention of leaping is made in the passage. (B) is also incorrect since vaulting is part of a style rather than a style. (D) is incorrect since neither drawing nor producing plans on paper is mentioned or alluded to in the reading passage.

21. **(D)** (D) is the best answer since "pontifical" is used to describe palaces in this reading passage; "pontifical" means dignified. Such a place is not necessarily a happy, merry place; (A) should not be chosen. A "pontifical palace" is not necessarily a place of rest and relaxation; (B) should not be selected. (C) should not be chosen since it suggests that a "pontifical palace" necessarily involves a place which is friendly.

22. **(D)** Quatrefoils are the result of the natural application of certain principles; (D) is the best answer. By referring to the passage, it can be ascertained that (A), (B), and (C) are all opposites of what the author writes; therefore, all are incorrect.

23. **(C)** Gothic art is the expression of infinitely various temper, sentiment, and spirit; (C) is the best choice. It is perhaps easier to define, first of all, what Gothic architecture is not. It is not bound by formulas (A); it is not characterized by similar styles (B); and it is not defined by outward features (D).

24. **(C)** Choice (C)—Gothic art is not defined by its features—is stated in the last paragraph of the passage. Since the reader is searching for a statement which is not true, (C) should be selected. In perusing the passage, statements (A), (B), and (D) will be found;

the author says that Gothic art is a whole method of doing things during the Middle Ages (A), an influence on architecture, painting, and sculpture (B), and an outward expression of certain cardinal principles (D). None of these answers should be chosen.

25. **(D)** This message either underlies or is explicitly stated in every part of the passage. Though the statements regarding Harriet Tubman (A), the oral literature (B), and the slave market (C) are all true, they are only important in the respective paragraphs in which they appear.

26. **(C)** This is evident from the results of "soldiering" in the rest of the sentence (i.e., refusing to work hard, sabotaging the machinery and crops). It could not mean "labored" (B), because this is incompatible with the remainder of the sentence. The sentence does not imply armed resistance to oppression (A), nor certainly does it mention anything to do with uniforms (D).

27. **(B)** (B) is correct because the author in lines 14–16 praises small cities, and throughout the passage is critical of great cities. (A) is incorrect because the author directly states this point. (D) is incorrect because the author clearly indicates that he mistrusts democracies. There is no evidence in the passage indicating (C).

28. **(A)** (A) summarizes points the author makes in the first and last paragraphs. Because the author refers to cloisters but doesn't consider them best for spiritual growth, (B) is incorrect. (C) contradicts the point he makes in lines 8–11; (D) contradicts the main point of the passage.

29. **(B)** (B) is correct. The author does not mention either ignorant Americans or Romeo and Juliet's dress, so (A) and (D) are incorrect. (C) is incorrect because the example of Romeo and Juliet is introduced to highlight the American people's anxiety to catch the trains, not to advocate the need for silence.

30. **(B)** (B) is correct; the third paragraph describes noise and hearing and uses the word "sensibility," all of which are abstract ideas related to the power of people's minds to perceive things. (D) is incorrect because while "ease" is an abstract idea, it does not relate to how people perceive things; (A) and (C) are not abstract ideas.

31. **(A)** In 1980, the difference between the numbers of boys and girls involved in scouting was 1.5 million. This represents the closest margin.

32. **(C)** In 1999, the difference between the number of boys and girls involved in scouting was 2.6 million.

33. **(D)** The greatest difference between the number of boys and the number of girls involved in scouting was in 1999, at 2.6 million. There were almost twice as many boys as there were girls.

34. **(C)** Douglass was interested in raising social consciousness about slavery. The passage stresses his interest in refuting those who doubted his claim to have been a slave.

35. **(B)** Choice A is not supported by the text. All other choices, while true, are irrelevant to the question.

36. **(B)** This choice is supported by the statement, "Mrs. Auld recognized Frederick's intellectual acumen. . . ." Choice D contradicts information in the passage. The passage does not support choices A and C.

37. **(C)** Choices A and B are either too broad or too general. Choice D is too specific and limited to cover the information in the passage

38. **(A)** An *impromptu* speech is one given suddenly without preparation.

39. **(B)** The writer's accessible style, use of easy-to-understand supporting details and examples, and avoidance of technical language indicate that the passage was most likely written for an audience of general readers.

40. **(A)** Although audiences in choices B, C, and D may benefit from the information provided in the passage, the passage explicitly states that a greater understanding of the information in the passage should assist teachers—choice A.

41. **(C)** Each of the choices is a definition of variance. However, for this passage, choice C is the most appropriate.

42. **(D)** Although meaning is found in the components of each choice, the passage states that we should begin with students' meaning before moving to the commonalities of story meaning—choice D.

# WRITING SUBTEST

## Multiple-Choice Section

1. **(A)** The word "colonies" should not be capitalized in this sentence.

2. **(A)** The correct spelling is "message."

3. **(B)** There should not be a comma after the word "wrote."

4. **(D)** This sentence would be correctly punctuated with the period inside the final quotation mark.

5. **(B)** "West" should be capitalized.

6. **(C)** The correct spelling is "descended."

7. **(C)** A comma is needed after the word "captivity."

8. **(C)** The word "there" is incorrect in this context, and should be spelled "their."

9. **(C)** The word "north" should be capitalized.

10. **(D)** The word "principals" is incorrect in this context. It should be "principles."

11. **(A)** The word "speech" should not be capitalized.

12. **(D)** A comma is not needed after the word "effectively."

13. **(C)** A semicolon is not needed in sentence 5.

14. **(A)** The correct spelling is "develop."

15. **(D)** The correct spelling is "analyzed."

16. **(B)** The word "regression" should not be capitalized.

17. **(B)** The correct verb is "was" to match the singular subject, "contribution."

18. **(A)** There should be a comma after the word "grade."

19. **(C)** Choice (C) is a prepositional phrase, "About 25,000 years ago," which is followed by a subordinate clause. This part should be linked to the previous sentence as it is integral to the migration of the Anasazi. Choices (A), (B), and (D) are all complete sentences.

20. **(C)** Choice (C) has to do with the later history of the Mesa Verde area, after the Anasazi had abandoned it. Since this is so far removed chronologically, Part 7 should be deleted or further developed in a third paragraph. Choices (A) and (B) discuss the very early history of the Indians. Choice (D) follows the chronological time order from 500 CE and leads into a discussion of the height of the Anasazi civilization.

21. **(C)** Choice (C) indicates the change of the incorrect word "general" to an adverb form "generally" to modify the verb phrase "are given." Choice (A), (B), and (D) would all change a correct comparison phrase to an incorrect one.

22. **(B)** The adjectival form "second," not the adverbial form "secondly," is appropriate here, since it modifies a noun, not a verb.

23. **(B)** The opening verbal phrase is a dangling modifier. "Prevention" is not "faced" with anything; Lincoln is. All the other choices are standard English sentences.

24. **(C)** "With the outbreak…" is a prepositional phrase that is stopped with a period[.]. It has no subject or verb and is not a standard English sentence. All the rest are correct English.

25. **(D)** Choice (D) should be made more precise. It would add a needed specific, concrete detail to bolster the interest of the passage. Choice (A) is readily understood as it is. Choice (B) does not really need clarification because it can be inferred that the "process" is an assembly-line method. Choice (C) is a common and simple concept.

26. **(C)** Choice (C) is a fragment lacking a verb for the apparent subject, "5,000 cars." Sentence 11 should probably be combined with Sentence 10. Choices (A), (B), and (D) are all standard sentences.

27. **(D)** In choice (D), although it is interesting to note that India bought steam-powered vehicles from Ransom Eli Olds, the information is really not essential and is the least relevant. Choice (A) is the topic sentence. Choice (B) and choice (C) are proof to substantiate what the pioneering Olds did in the automobile industry.

28. **(B)** Choice (B) contains the continuation of the topic "poor children" with the addition of "stereotype." Therefore, choice (B) would be the logical sentence to tie together

Sentences 6 and 7. Choice (A) is a question best asked in the first paragraph. Choice (C) might be a logical choice, but there is no transition included to tie together Sentences 6 and 7. Choice (D) shifts voice with "I."

29. **(C)**  In choice (C), a comma is indicated for the introductory phrase "In fact." Choice (A) creates no difference. Choice (B) would create a fragment in the second half of the sentence by isolating the subordinate clause beginning with "because." Choice (D) is incorrect because no colon should be used after the introductory phrase.

30. **(B)**  Choice (B) has an incorrect verb form. The subjunctive mood "were" is needed in conditions contrary to fact. Thus, the sentence should read, "even if every single-parent family were to disappear" because the clause beginning with "if" signals a condition contrary to fact. Choices (A), (C), and (D) are all correct.

31. **(C)**  Choice (C) indicates that information about the originators of the folk dance is not necessary in a paragraph about the ballet. Choice (A) introduces the topic of the ballet and its composer. Choice (B) tells who choreographed the ballet. Choice (D) gives further information on the ballet and its music.

32. **(D)**  Choice (D) is the only choice containing information about the rhythm discussed in Sentences 6 and 7. Choice (A) and choice (B) both break the formal tone and use contractions. Choice (C), although a possible choice, has nothing to do with rhythm and introduces new information on the folk dance.

33. **(A)**  Choice (A) contains the phrase, "A French composer," which does not modify "the bolero." The phrase should be placed after "Maurice Ravel" to correct the error. Choices (B), (C), and (D) are all correct sentences.

34. **(C)**  The clause "a French composer" modifies Maurice Ravel. In the original, it would appear to modify "the bolero." Choice (C) best corrects this ambiguity. Each of the other choices places the modifier in an incorrect place.

35. **(A)**  "This musical composition" should replace "it" in Sentence 5 because the paragraph should not start off with a pronoun that lacks a clear antecedent. Choice (B) ("the folk dance") may look right, but since the rest of the passage concerns the music and not the dance, it would be inappropriate. Choices (C) and (D) are clearly the wrong antecedents for "it" in this sentence.

## Short-Answer Section Sample Responses

36. The new rule prohibits smoking by the employee's inside the building.

    ***Errors:*** 1. misplaced apostrophe

    2. misplaced modifier

    ***Sample Correct Responses:***

    *The new rule prohibits employees' smoking inside the building.*

    *The new rule prohibits employee smoking inside the building.*

37. Australia is noted for their unique animals: koalas, platypus, kangaroo, and emu.

    ***Errors:*** 1. lack of subject – verb agreement

    2. plural needed for object nouns

    ***Sample Correct Response:***

    *Australia is noted for its unique animals: kolas, platypuses, kangaroos, and emus.*

38. Economics can teach a person to effectively manage their own affairs and be a contributing member of society.

    ***Errors:*** 1. misplaced adverb

    2. preposition needed (to)

    ***Sample Correct Response:***

    *Economics can effectively teach people to manage their own affairs and to be contributing members of society.*

39. When someone thinks they can do everything they want to do they will almost invariably be disappointed.

    ***Errors:*** 1. lack of pronoun/antecedent agreement

    2. missing comma after an introductory clause

*Sample Correct Response:*

*When people think they can do everything they want to do, they will almost invariably be disappointed.*

40. In the summer I usually like swimming and to water-ski.

    *Errors:* 1. noun "swimming" doesn't balance with prepositional phrase "to water-ski."

    2. "swim" and "water-sky" need to both be objects of the preposition: "to."

    *Sample Correct Responses:*

    *In the summer I usually like to swim and water-ski.*

    *I usually like to swim and water-ski in the summer.*

    *I usually like swimming and water-skiing in the summer.*

41. I found five dollars eating lunch in the park.

    *Errors:* 1. Misplaced predicate

    2. Five dollars would not be eating in the park.

    *Sample Correct Response:*

    *I found five dollars while I was eating lunch in the park.*

42. Janet is one of those people who you can't really describe with words.

    *Errors:* 1. misplaced object

    2. unnecessary additional phrasing

    *Sample Correct Responses:*

    *You cannot describe Janet with words.*

    *Janet cannot be described with words.*

## SCORING RUBRIC FOR THE WRITTEN SUMMARY EXERCISE

### Scoring Scale:

### Score of 4: A well-formed written response

- You have accurately conveyed the main ideas of the passage, maintaining focus and unity, while using your own words.

- Your response is concise, but you have provided sufficient depth and specificity to convey the main points of the passage.

- Your response shows control and organization.

- You have used correct and effective sentence structure.

- Your usage and choice of words are careful and precise.

- You have shown a mastery of mechanical conventions (i.e., spelling, punctuation, and capitalization).

### Score of 3: An adequately formed written response

- Generally using your own words, you have accurately conveyed most of the writer's main ideas and in most cases maintained focus and unity.

- Your response may have been too long or too short, but you generally provided sufficient depth and specificity to convey most of the main points of the passage.

- Your organization of ideas might be ambiguous, incomplete, or partially ineffective.

- You use adequate sentence structure, but minor errors may be present.

- Your usage and choice of words display minor errors.

- You have made some errors in the use of mechanical conventions (i.e., spelling, punctuation, and capitalization).

## Score of 2:  A partially formed written response

- You have conveyed only some of the main ideas of the passage and/or did not keep focus on the topic. You relied heavily on the writer's words.

- Your response is too long or too short and/or did not included sufficient depth to effectively develop your response.

- You made a generally unsuccessful attempt to organize and sequence ideas.

- Your sentence structure contains significant errors.

- You are imprecise in usage and word choice.

- You have made frequent errors in the use of mechanical conventions (i.e., spelling, punctuation, and capitalization).

## Score of 1:  An inadequately formed written response

- You have not identified the main ideas of the passage.

- You have failed to effectively develop your the response.

- You have very little organization and what is there is not sequential.

- Your sentence structure is poor and most sentences contain errors.

- Your usage is imprecise and your word choices are ill-advised.

- You have made serious and numerous errors in the use of mechanical conventions (i.e., spelling, punctuation, and capitalization).

## Score of U

The response is unrelated to the assigned topic, illegible, primarily in a language other than English, not of sufficient length to score, or merely a repetition of the assignment.

## Score of B

There is no response to the assignment.

# SCORING RUBRIC FOR THE WRITTEN COMPOSITION EXERCISE

## Scoring Scale:

### Score of 4:  A well-formed written response

- You have addressed the assignment fully and used appropriate language and style.

- You have shown a mastery of mechanical conventions (e.g., spelling, punctuation, and capitalization).

- Your usage and choice of words are careful and precise.

- Your sentence structure is effective and free of errors.

- You have clearly stated a main idea and/or point of view, and maintained focus and unity throughout your composition.

- You have shown excellent organizational skills.

- You have fully developed your composition, providing ample and appropriate depth, specificity, and accuracy.

### Score of 3:  An adequately formed written response

- You have addressed the assignment adequately and have generally used appropriate language and/or style.

- You have some errors in the use of mechanical conventions (e.g., spelling, punctuation, and capitalization).

- You have some minor errors in usage and word choice.

- Your sentence structure is adequate, but there are some minor errors in your writing.

- The presentation of your main idea and/or point of view is generally clear and focused and you generally maintain unity.

- Your organization of ideas is a bit ambiguous, incomplete, or partially ineffective.

- You have provided sufficient depth, specificity, and accuracy to adequately develop the response.

## Score of 2: A partially formed written response

- You have only partially addressed the assignment and may have used inappropriate language and/or style.

- You have made frequent errors in the use of mechanical conventions (e.g., spelling, punctuation, and capitalization).

- You have been imprecise in your usage and word choice.

- Your sentence structure is poor with a number of errors.

- Your main idea and/or point of view is inconsistently treated and/or you have not maintained the focus and unity of your discussion

- You have made an effort to organize and sequence ideas, but your organization is largely unclear.

- Your response includes very few ideas that aid in its development.

## Score of 1: An inadequately formed written response

- You have attempted to address the assignment, but your language and style are generally inappropriate for the given audience, purpose, and/or occasion.

- You have made many serious errors in the use of mechanical conventions (e.g., spelling, punctuation, and capitalization).

- You have been imprecise in usage and word choice.

- Your sentence structure is ineffective and error ridden.

- You have not identified your main idea and/or point of view .

- Your limited organization fails to follow a logical sequence of ideas.

- You have failed to include ideas that would aide in the development of your response.

## Score of U

The response is unrelated to the assigned topic, illegible, primarily in a language other than English, not of sufficient length to score, or merely a repetition of the assignment.

## Score of B

There is no response to the assignment.

## Sample Strong Response for Composition Exercise

*The ability to search for resources for research papers at any time of the day or night makes the online environment very appealing. Not having to be restricted by library hours or reserving computer time in the labs means that an individual can complete assignments that require research whenever he or she feels like it. Being able to search for appropriate supporting documentation whether in one's pajamas or dressed for work is a very liberating idea and also provides the opportunity to more quickly locate needed citations through a variety of helpful search engines.*

*Unfortunately, much can be lost through this ease-of-use research modality. Libraries themselves in many ways promote a sense of academic integrity that cannot be experienced by simply searching for a topic online. When unsure of a topic or thesis, roaming through the stacks of journals contained within a library's research section often provide inspiration that cannot be found with the electronic version of a journal. Many times the topic selection and all supporting details can be located within a relatively short period of time if the existing catalogs are used. The librarians are real people who are familiar with the available resources and can point the would-be researcher in the right direction. This human touch can often provide clarification on topic selection as well as provide insight into resources that the researcher might not have considered.*

*Research in many ways is meant to be excavated, discovered, and illuminated through the skill of the researcher, not masticated, reconstituted and regurgitated through the wonders of modern technology. A research topic that allows the researcher to use only resources available online reduces input from other sources that may support or refute whatever the topic is that has been selected. While this essay does not support the abandonment of the use of the internet to search for supporting documentation, it is more important to search all possible resources rather than just those available online.*

*Considering this practice of using online sources exclusively for research purposes brings to mind the question of whether libraries may eventually be abandoned. The peculiar experience afforded by going to a library to study or to conduct research cannot be replaced by sitting in front of a computer. The ease of skimming through a wide range of printed resources versus reading from a computer screen means that the individual can quickly decide if the resource is viable or not and move on without having to click one's way back to a list. Unfortunately, the library and librarian many indeed be a thing of the past. With the onset of strictly online coursework and degrees, more and more journals may be transposed to online availability and the days of searching through the stacks of journals in the library for a particular issue may be over.*

## Analysis of the Strong Response to the Composition Exercise

**Appropriateness**—The essay addressed the topic of whether it was better to use online sources exclusively or if going to the library to do a thorough search of all sources was more appropriate. While the topic paragraph did promote the idea that there were advantages to using online resources, the remainder of the essay was focused on how going to the library to search a find print sources added to the total research experience.

**Focus and Organization**—The essay followed the prompts as given and the opinion of the writer, that the sources found in print were important, was the evident focus of the essay. The organization went from refuting the advantages of using online sources to the less tangible advantages of studying and researching in a library.

**Support**—The writer provides a strong argument that all possible resources should be investigated and utilized, and not just those that may be found online. The writer also puts forward the point that by searching through the connections available in printed text, the researcher strengthens his or her own researching techniques, something that cannot be done as easily by using search engines.

**Grammar, Sentence Structure, and Usage**—The sentences contain appropriate grammar and are standardized and vary in form with the use of different phrases to begin sentences ("While this essay . . . ," "With the onset") to add interest. The use of vivid imagery (working in pajamas, roaming through journal stacks) also adds to the readability of the essay. The comparison of researching using the printed word as a discovery as compared to researching using the computer and simply eating is easy to follow.

**Conventions**—Spelling and punctuation are mostly standard throughout the essay. There are some lengthy sentences throughout the essay, but for the most part all sentences and transitions can be easily followed.

## Sample Weak Response to Composition Exercise

*It is obvious to nearly everyone that nobody uses the library to do research papers any more and that most people prefer to just search for the topic online. The time it takes to gather up paper and pencil and drive to the library is a waste of time and most people end up just searching for stuff on the computer when they get to the library. Almost everything you need can be found through online sources and those journals that aren't online don't have to be used.*

*Using the research online makes it easier and quicker to do assignments. Having to find information in journals and magazines can be hard to do if you don't know how to use the card catalog and who wants to ask the librarian? Not me. It makes more sense to use the computer to find the research that is out there and put that in your paper. Using online resources helps the writer use your time more efficiently and finish more quicker. Most topics have already been completely researched, so the technique of doing research is to find what has already been done and paraphrase it. There is plenty of research out there to support whatever topic you want to write about, so going to the library to try and find more just doesn't make any sense to me.*

*Using online sources esclusively from here on out to write about whatever topic is assigned is the way of the future and soon everything will be online so there's no real need to figure out how to use the library and the Dewey decimal system and all that other stuff anyway. There's no reason to ever bother to go to the library to write a research paper again.*

## Analysis of the Weak Response to the Composition Exercise

**Appropriateness**—The writer uses only one argument, that everything necessary to write a research paper is online, and that argument is not inclusive of the topic, which is the advantages and disadvantages of the process of online research versus using printed text. The language used is also not appropriate for the audience, an English instructor, as it is too informal. There are also examples of colloquialisms ("from here on out," "all that stuff") that are not appropriate for a formal paper.

**Focus and Organization**—The thesis statement is that all resources to complete research are easily found online, but there is no clarity about what that means or how that comes about. The paragraphs and sentences within the paragraphs do restate this single thesis, but the thesis itself is unclear and unfounded.

**Support**—There is no reasoned support or specific examples given to develop the thesis. The support that is given, that the existing information about any given topic can be taken and paraphrased and so there is no need for any input from the researcher, is nonsensical and doesn't portray a mature attitude toward the process of conducting research.

**Grammar, Sentence Structure, and Usage**—Sentence 5 in the second paragraph has an incorrect use of comparison ("more quicker" instead of "more quickly") and Sentence 3, which answers the question at the end of Sentence 2, is a fragment. The first sentence of the third paragraph is a run-on sentence even with the use of "and." There are several instances of switching point of view (Sentence 5 switches from the third person "the writer" to second person "your.") and the use of first and second person throughout the essays adds to the informal tone.

**Conventions**—The words are spelled correctly with the exception of "esclusively" which should be spelled "exclusively."

# MTEL Communication and Literacy Skills

## PRACTICE TEST 3

## PRACTICE TEST 3
## READING SUBTEST

### Multiple-Choice Section

*Directions:* Read each passage and answer the questions that follow.

### The Ambassador of Political Reason

An ancient Sage boasted, that, tho' he could not fiddle, he knew how to make a *great city* of a *little one*. The science that I, a modern simpleton, am about to communicate, is the very reverse.

I address myself to all ministers who have the management of extensive dominions, which from their very greatness are become troublesome to govern, because the multiplicity of their affairs leaves no time for *fiddling*.

In the first place, gentlemen, you are to consider, that a great empire, like a great cake, is most easily diminished at the edges. Turn your attention, therefore, first to your *remotest* provinces; that, as you get rid of them, the next may follow in order.

That the possibility of this separation may always exist, take special care the provinces are never incorporated with the mother country; that they do not enjoy the same common rights, the same privileges in commerce; and that they are governed by *severer* laws, all of *your enacting*, without allowing them any share in the choice of the legislators. By carefully making and preserving such distinctions, you will (to keep to my simile of the cake) act like a wise ginger-bread-baker, who, to facilitate a division, cuts his dough half through in those places where, when baked, he would have it *broken to pieces*.

Those remote provinces have perhaps been acquired, purchased, or conquered, at the *sole expence* of the settlers, or their ancestors, without the aid of the mother country. If this should happen to increase her *strength*, by their growing numbers, ready to join in her wars; her *commerce*, by their growing demand for her manufactures; or her *naval power*, by greater employment for her ships and seamen, they may probably suppose some merit in this, and that it entitles them to some favour; you are therefore to *forget it all, or resent it*, as if they had done you injury. If they happen to be zealous Whigs, friends of liberty, nurtured in revolution principles, *remember all that* to their prejudice, and resolve to punish it; for such principles, after a revolution is thoroughly established, are of *no more use*; they are even *odious* and *abominable*.

However peaceably your colonies have submitted to your government, shewn their affection to your interests, and patiently borne their grievances; you are to *suppose* them always inclined to revolt, and treat them accordingly. Quarter troops among them, who by their insolence may *provoke* the rising of mobs, and by their bullets and bayonets *suppress* them. By this means, like the husband who uses his wife ill *from suspicion*, you may in time convert your *suspicions* into *realities*...

If, when you are engaged in war, your colonies should vie in liberal aids of men and money against the common enemy, upon your simple requisition, and give far beyond their abilities, reflect that a penny taken from them by your power is more honourable to you than a pound presented by their benevolence; despise therefore their voluntary grants, and resolve to harass them with novel taxes. They will probably complain to your parliaments, that they are taxed by a body in which they have no representative, and that this is contrary to common right. They will petition for redress. Let the Parliaments flout their claims, reject their petitions, refuse even to suffer the reading of them, and treat the petitioners with the utmost contempt. Nothing can have a better effect in producing the alienation proposed; for though many can forgive injuries, *none ever forgave contempt*...

Lastly, invest the General of your army in the provinces, with great and unconstitutional powers, and free him from the controul of even your own Civil Governors. Let him have troops enow under his command, with all the fortresses in his possession; and who knows but (like some provincial Generals in the Roman empire, and encouraged by the universal discontent you have produced) he may take it into his head to set up for himself? If he should, and you have carefully practised these few *excellent rules* of mine, take my word for it, all the provinces will immediately join him; and you will that day (if you have not done it sooner) get rid of the trouble of governing them, and all the *plagues* attending their *commerce* and connection from henceforth and for ever.

*From Benjamin Franklin, "The Ambassador of Political Reason"*

1. The author's purpose is

    (A) to communicate the wisdom of an ancient sage.

    (B) to advise ministers of churches who do not take time for fun and fiddling.

    (C) to describe how a little country can make itself a great one.

    (D) to tell how a great city may be reduced to a small one.

2. The author compares

    (A) an empire to a cake.

    (B) a country to a gingerbread baker.

    (C) a minister to a cake.

    (D) a religious minister to a gingerbread baker.

3. The passage was

    (A) to give advice to all rulers of small countries.

    (B) a tongue-in-cheek article.

    (C) from the viewpoint of a religious minister.

    (D) to inspire ministers to take time to "fiddle," or smell the roses.

4. The best interpretation of the clause, "Let him [the General] have troops enow under his command..." is

    (A) let the General keep the troops in tow.

    (B) let the General have enough soldiers to command.

    (C) let the General have troops endowed with skill under his control.

    (D) let the General have captured troops to control.

5. The author's reason for writing this passage is that he

(A) hopes to help the ministers rid themselves of the trouble of governing the provinces.

(B) hopes to help the ministers build their powers and increase the provinces.

(C) is proposing new ideas on increasing the provinces of a country since this article was written only a few years ago.

(D) is presenting the viewpoint of the colonies and the provinces to the mother country.

6. Which of the following actions is least advisable in order to keep a large country intact?

(A) Limit the General of the army of the large country to constitutional powers.

(B) Give the citizens of the provinces the same rights as the citizens of the mother country.

(C) Suppose the provinces to be always ready to revolt and treat them as if you expect revolt.

(D) Do not require taxation without representation.

## Engineering Thermodynamics

Though it is generally recognized from philosophic investigations extending over many years that heat is one manifestation of energy capable of being transformed into other forms such as mechanical work, electricity, or molecular arrangement, and derivable from them through transformations, measurements of quantities of heat can be made without such knowledge, and were made even when heat was regarded as a substance. It was early recognized that equivalence of heat effects proved effects proportional to quantity; thus, the melting of one pound of ice can cool a pound of hot water through a definite range of temperature, and can cool two pounds through half as many degrees, and so on. The condensation of a pound of steam can warm a definite weight of water a definite number of degrees, or perform a certain number of pound-degrees heating effect in water. So that taking the pound-degree of water as a basis the ratio of the heat liberated by steam condensation to that absorbed by ice melting can be found. Other substances such as iron or oil may suffer a certain number of pound-degree changes and affect water by another number of pound-degrees. The unit of heat quantity might be taken as that which is liberated by the condensation of a pound of steam, that absorbed by the freezing of a pound of water, that to raise a pound of iron any number of degrees or any other quantity of heat effect. The heat unit generally accepted is, in metric measure, the calorie, or the amount to raise one kilogram of pure water one degree centigrade, or the B.T.U., that is necessary to raise one pound of water one degree Fahrenheit.

All the heat measurements are, therefore, made in terms of equivalent water heating effects in pound-degrees, but it must be understood that a water pound-degree is not quite constant. Careful observation will show that the melting of a pound of ice will not cool the same weight of water from 200° F to 180° F, as it will from 60° F to 40° F, which indicates that the heat capacity of water or the B.T.U. per pound-degree is not constant. It is, therefore, necessary to further limit the definition of the heat unit, by fixing on some water temperature and temperature change, as the standard, in addition to the selection of water as the substance, and the pound and degree as units of capacity. Here there has not been as good an agreement as is desirable, some using 4° C = 39.4° F as the standard temperature and the range one-half degree both sides; this is the point of maximum water density. Others have used one degree rise from the freezing point 0° C or 32° F. There are good reasons, however, for the most common present-day practice which will probably become universal, for taking as the range and temperatures, freezing-point to boiling-point and dividing by the number of degrees. The heat unit so defined is properly named the mean calorie or mean British thermal unit; therefore,

Mean calorie = (amount of heat to raise 1 Kg. water from 0° C to 100° C)

Mean B.T.U. = (amount of heat to raise 1 lb. water from 32° F to 212° F)

*From Charles Edward Lucke, "Engineering Thermodynamics," 1912*

7. According to the author, which of the following is NOT true?

(A) Heat is capable of being transformed into mechanical work.

(B) Heat is derivable from molecular arrangement.

(C) Heat should be regarded as a substance.

(D) Measurements of quantities of heat can be made without knowledge of heat being derivable from mechanical work, electricity, or molecular arrangement.

8. The calorie and the B.T.U. are similar in that they both relate to

(A) one pound of water.

(B) the amount of heat necessary to raise the temperature one degree.

(C) the metric system.

(D) a pound of iron.

9. The author denies which of the following?

(A) The equivalence of heat effects proves proportional to quantity.

(B) The melting of one pound of ice can cool a pound of hot water through a definite range of temperature and can cool two pounds through twice as many degrees.

(C) The melting of one pound of ice can cool a pound of hot water through a definite range of temperature and can cool two pounds through half as many degrees.

(D) The condensation of a pound of steam can warm a definite weight of water a definite number of degrees.

10. The author states that

(A) a water pound-degree is constant.

(B) the melting of ice will cool the same weight of water from 60° to 40° Fahrenheit as it will from 200° to 180° Fahrenheit.

(C) the heat capacity of water or the B.T.U. per pound-degree is constant.

(D) the heat capacity of water or the B.T.U. per pound-degree is not constant.

11. The author indicates a point of disagreement among scientists; this point of contention is

(A) whether the melting point of ice will not cool the same amount of water from 200° to 180° Fahrenheit as it will from 60° to 40° Fahrenheit.

(B) whether the heat capacity of water is constant.

(C) whether the equivalence of heat effects proved effects proportional to quantity.

(D) how to best limit the definitions of the heat unit.

12. The author appears to

    (A) be a proponent of the metric system.

    (B) be a proponent of the customary system.

    (C) be an opponent of the use of the mean calorie.

    (D) suggest that there are good reasons for taking the freezing-point to boiling-point as the range.

13. The purpose of the passage is to

    (A) advocate mean calories.

    (B) advocate mean British thermal units (B.T.U.).

    (C) oppose mean calories and B.T.U.

    (D) advocate both mean calories and mean B.T.U.

14. The author predicts

    (A) the universal adoption of the B.T.U.

    (B) the universal adoption of the calorie.

    (C) the universal acceptance of the mean B.T.U. and the mean calorie.

    (D) the demise of the calorie and the universal adoption of the mean B.T.U.

## Three Essays on Oriental Painting

What, then, is the cause of the difference between Japanese painting and that of the Occident? Some say that the difference in the colouring matter and the brushes used has caused a wide divergence in the tone of Oriental and of Occidental painting. This opinion is, however, far from conclusive. For, looking deeper into the matter, the question arises, "What has brought about all these differences in the pigments and the brushes, as well as in the technique adopted by artist of the East and of the West?" In my opinion here lies the key to the whole problem. In the first place, Eastern and Western painters hold somewhat different views concerning the primary object of art, and from these results their disagreement in technique and other details. In order to understand the real source of the differences between Eastern and Western painting it is therefore requisite to study closely their contents, which differ to some extent in essentials.

Painting should have for its object the expression of ideas, and as such "it is invaluable, being by itself nothing." In art an idea may be expressed in ways which differ, principally according to the two modes, the subjective and the objective. To state the matter more explicitly, a painter may use the object he delineates chiefly for expressing his own thought, instead of revealing the idea inherent in the object itself. On the contrary, another painter strives to bring out the spirit of the object he portrays, rather than to express ideas of his own that may arise in association with the object. In general, Western painters belong to the latter class, while those of Japan to the former; the one laying stress on objective, and the other on subjective ideas. This distinction discloses the fundamental differences between Eastern and Western painting, which causes wide dissimilarities in conception and execution.

Take for instance their subjects. Here one cannot fail to notice a marked contrast between Japanese and European pictures. In Western painting, where special importance is attached to objective qualities, the portraiture of human figures naturally receives the foremost attention, as though it were nobler and grander than other themes. Is it not because in man, unlike the lower creations, there exists a spirit, the interpretation of which, in its different manifestations, affords a rare scope for the artist's talent? Accordingly, in Occidental painting in which the expression of the spirit externally manifest in the object is made the chief point, human portraiture necessarily claims the first consideration. The same holds true not only of painting, but almost every other art. Conversely in Japanese pictures, flowers, birds, landscapes, even withered trees and lifeless rocks, are esteemed as highly as God's highest creation—human being. The reason is not far to seek; it is simply this: landscapes, birds, flowers, and similar things may be devoid of soul, but the artist may turn them into nobler objects, as his fancy imparts to them the lofty spiritual attributes of man.

Anyone with an extensive knowledge of our pictures cannot fail to discern this common characteristic of composition, namely, that the centre of a picture is not found in any single individual object, for the guiding principle of the synthesis is expressed in the mutual relations of all the objects treated. In other words, in Japanese painting no serious attempt is made to give all-exclusive prominence to any one particular object, but, instead, the effect of the whole is considered the point of prime importance. Hence in the minds of our painters, not each and every portion of a picture need be accurate, but the picture as a whole should be microcosmically complete. Such is but the inevitable outcome of stress laid almost exclusively on subjective ideas.

*From Sei-ichi Taki, "Three Essays on Oriental Painting," 1910*

15. The term "Occidental art" refers to

   (A) accidental, or unintentional, art.

   (B) Western art.

   (C) non-Western art.

   (D) Oriental art.

16. The purpose of the article is to

   (A) contrast the paintings of the Japanese and the Occident.

   (B) compare the paintings of the Japanese and the Occident.

   (C) compare the contents of the paintings of the Occident and of the Japanese.

   (D) compare the composition of the paintings of the Japanese and the Occident.

17. A main difference between the Occidental and the Japanese paintings is

   (A) differing views concerning the primary object of art.

   (B) differing views on technique.

   (C) differing views of details.

   (D) differences in pigments and brushes.

18. The author's area of expertise appears to be primarily

   (A) Occidental painting.       (C) Oriental painting.

   (B) Japanese painting.        (D) Asian painting.

19. The Japanese painter can be said to

    (A) use the object he delineates to express his own thoughts.

    (B) express ideas of his own that may arise in association with the object.

    (C) stress objective ideas.

    (D) stress the spirit of the object being portrayed.

20. The painters of the pictures in Western art

    (A) give foremost attention to the human figure.

    (B) do not believe the human figure is grander than other themes.

    (C) accept the expression of the spirit.

    (D) esteem God's creations highly.

## Religion without Dogma

Professor Hostead, in his article "Modern Agnosticism Justified," argues that a) religion is basically belief in God and immortality, b) most religions consist of "accretions of dogma and mythology" that science has disproven, c) it would be desirable, if it were possible, to keep the basic religious belief without those accumulations of religious notions and legends, but that d) science has rendered even the basic elements of religion almost as incredible as the "accretions." For the doctrine of immortality involves the view that man is a composite creature, a soul in a state of symbiosis with a physical organism. But science can successfully regard man only monastically, as a single organism whose psychological characteristics all arise from his physical nature; the soul then becomes indefensible. In conclusion, Professor Hostead asserts that our only hope rests in empirical, observable evidence for the existence of the soul; in fact, in the findings of psychical research.

My disagreement with Professor Hostead starts at the beginning. I do not consider the essence of religion as simply the belief in God and immortality. Early Judaism, for example, didn't accept immortality. The human soul in Sheol (the afterworld) took no account of Jehovah, and God in turn took no account of the soul. In Sheol all things are forgotten. The religion revolved around the ritual and ethical demands of God and on the blessings people received from him. During earthly life these blessings were usually material in nature: happy life, many children, good health, and such. But we do see a more religious note also. The Jew hungers for the living God; he obeys God's laws devoutly; he considers himself as impure and sinful in Jehovah's presence. God is the sole object of worship. Buddhism makes the doctrine of immortality vital, while we find little in the way of that which is religious. The existence of the gods is not denied, but it has no religious significance. In Stoicism again both the practice of religion and the belief in immortality are variables, not absolute traits of religion. Even within Christianity itself we find, as in Stoicism, the subordinate position of immortality.

*From C. S. Lewis, "Religion without Dogma"*

21. Which of the following best defines the phrase "accretions of dogma and mythology" as it is used in the first paragraph?

(A) Combinations of fact and fiction

(B) Conflicts of sound principles and unsound theories

(C) Implications and ideas of religion

(D) Religious ideas and fables that have gradually accumulated to form accepted religious belief

22. What is the main idea of the entire passage?

(A) Belief in God is scientifically valid.

(B) Professor Hostead's assumption that the essence of religion is the belief in God and immortality is incorrect.

(C) Neither Judaism, Buddhism, Stoicism, nor Christianity fit into Hostead's definition of religion.

(D) Judaism, Buddhism, Stoicism, and Christianity are all valid ideologies in their regard for immortality and belief in God.

23. The writer's purpose in this passage is to

    (A) outline basic tenets of Judaism, Buddhism, Stoicism, and Christianity.

    (B) establish scientific credibility of four ideologies so as to undermine Hostead's positions.

    (C) attack Hostead's views by establishing the vulnerability of Hostead's first position.

    (D) define the essence of religion.

## The Aims of Education

Intelligence and will support a man. Man relies not merely on physical existence, for something beyond the physical resides within him. This "something" transcends the physical; it is a more rewarding existence. Through knowledge and love, man has a "spiritual superexistence" which creates him more than a part of a whole but instead creates a microcosm, containing within himself the elements of the entire universe through knowledge. And the characteristic of love enables him to give freely to others whom he regards as other selves. Nowhere in the physical environment can we find such a unique relationship as this.

At the root of this phenomenon is the concept of the soul, which Aristotle described as the first principle of life in any organism and which he thought contained a superior intellect in man. Christianity maintains that the soul is the dwelling place of God and is therefore created for eternity. The human soul exists within our physical framework, amidst all the bones and tissue and internal organs, and has greater value than the entire universe. Though a man is subject to the slightest material accidents, his soul dominates time and death. The soul is the root of personality.

*From Jacques Maritain, "The Aims of Education"*

24. According to this selection, how could we best define the term "spiritual super-existence"?

    (A) That quality that makes man more than simply another part of the universe

    (B) That quality that lives forever

(C) Supreme intelligence

(D) Knowledge and love

25. Which of the following statements best sums up the central idea of this selection?

    (A) Man's knowledge and love separate him from the lower animals.

    (B) The human soul is the key factor that makes man a microcosm instead of simply another part of our universe.

    (C) Both Aristotle and Christianity have placed tremendous importance on the human soul.

    (D) The value of the soul is greater than that of the physical universe.

26. Which of the following statements represents an opinion of the writer rather than a fact?

    (A) Christians maintain that the soul is the dwelling place of God.

    (B) Aristotle dismissed the idea of the soul.

    (C) Intelligence and will support a man.

    (D) Man is subject to accidents.

## The Human Environment

A rock-solid consensus of opinion exists in urban-industrial society regarding the correct means of measuring our progress beyond the primal, the period when human civilization was in its infancy. The prevailing conclusion is that we measure progress by examining how artificial our environment becomes, either by ridding ourselves of nature's presence or by controlling natural forces. Without much doubt, human environment must always maintain an artificial flair about it. In fact, we might almost say that the human space is destined to possess an "artificial naturalness" in that people spontaneously fill their universe with artifacts and man-made, non-natural institutions.

Humans invent and scheme, devise and intricately thread a finished product: culture, a buffer zone conceived by and intended for man where man may live legitimately as plant and animal inhabit their environment of instinct, reflex, and roteness. But as we acknowledge human culture, we must also acknowledge natural environment—the mountain and the shore, the fox and its flora, the heavenly bodies—and the close relationship primitives had with this natural habitat for millennia.

These people used as their clocks the seasonal rhythms, timing their own activities to these smooth organic cycles. They learned from the plants and animals that surrounded them, spoke with them, worshipped them. Primitives considered their destiny tied inherently to the non-humans, allies and foes alike, and created places of honor for them in their culture.

We cannot possibly exaggerate the importance of this intimacy between human and nature to the growth of human awareness. This inadequate, sterile term "nature" that we use to categorize the non-human world has regretfully lost its impact through the simple connotation we give it today: a designated area of random physical things and events outside and other than ourselves.

We may think of "nature poetry" as poems that touch on daisies and sunsets, one possible topic out of myriad possibilities, many of which are irrelevant to polluted city streets and the asphalt aura of modern life. We overlook the universal view of nature, which includes us. Nature, however, has brought us into existence and will outdistance us; from it we have learned of our destiny. It mirrors who we are.

Whatever our culture produces that severs humans from a vibrant tie with nature, that removes us from or alienates nature is—strictly speaking—a sick delusion. What culture produces unmindful of the natural world doesn't merely lack ecological soundness; more alarmingly it lacks psychological completeness. It remains devoid of a truth our primitive counterparts learned from an infant world of nature: the reality of spiritual being.

*From Theodore Roszak, "The Human Environment"*

27. Which of the following best defines "culture" as the writer uses the term?

    (A)  The result of mankind changing his otherwise natural environment to an artificial one

    (B)  The condition of being destructive to the forces of nature

    (C)  The condition of being literate and articulate in the ways of human life

    (D)  Man's recognition of nature's elements

28. For what purpose does the writer use the phrase "artificial naturalness"?

    (A)  To show how man should treat nature

    (B)  To suggest an insincere attitude on man's part

    (C)  To suggest man's integral tie to nature

    (D)  To demonstrate man's natural tendency to create an artificial environment

29. According to this passage, what caused primitive peoples to place importance on elements of nature?

    (A)  The belief that their fates were intricately entwined with the natural world

    (B)  Simply their primitive, superstitious ignorance

    (C)  Their lack of an artificial environment

    (D)  Their ecological concerns

30. The first means used to tell time, according to the passage, was

    (A)  plants and animals.

    (B)  human instinct, reflex, and roteness.

    (C)  the awareness of spiritual being, which man derived from his awareness of nature.

    (D)  seasonal rhythms.

## The Study of Children's Stories

**1**     As noted by Favat in 1977, the study of children's stories has been an on-going concern of linguists, anthropologists, and psychologists. The past decade has witnessed a surge of interest in children's stories from researchers in these and other disciplines. The use of narratives for reading and reading instruction has been commonly accepted by the educational community. The notion that narrative is highly structured and that children's sense of narrative structure is more highly developed than expository structure has been proposed by some researchers.

**2**     Early studies of children's stories followed two approaches for story analysis: The analysis of story content or the analysis of story structure. Story content analysis has centered primarily on examining motivational and psychodynamic aspects of story characters as noted in the works of Erikson and Pitcher and Prelinger in 1963 and Ames in 1966. These studies have noted that themes or topics predominate and the themes change with age.

**3**     Early research on story structure focused on formal models of structure, such as story grammar and story schemata. These models specified basic story elements and formed sets of rules similar to sentences grammar for ordering the elements.

**4**     The importance or centrality of narrative in a child's development of communicative ability has been proposed by Halliday (1976) and Hymes (1975). Thus, the importance of narrative for language communicative ability and for reading and reading instruction has been well documented. However, the question still remains about how these literacy abilities interest and lead to conventional reading.

31. This passage is most probably directed at which of the following audiences?

   (A)  reading educators           (C)  psychologists

   (B)  linguists                    (D)  reading researchers

32. According to the passage, future research should address

    (A) how story structure and story schema interact with comprehension.

    (B) how children's use and understanding of narrative interacts and leads to conventional reading.

    (C) how story content interacts with story comprehension.

    (D) how narrative text structure differs from expository text structure.

33. The major distinction between story content and story structure is that

    (A) story content focuses on motivational aspects whereas story structure focuses on rules similar to sentence grammar.

    (B) story content focuses on psychodynamic aspects whereas story structure focuses on formal structural models.

    (C) story content and story structure essentially refer to the same concepts.

    (D) story content focuses primarily on characters whereas story structure focuses on story grammar and schemata.

34. Which of the following is the most complete and accurate definition of the term *surge* as used in the following sentence? The past decade has witnessed a surge of interest in children's stories from researchers in these and other disciplines.

    (A) a heavy swell          (C) a sudden increase

    (B) a sudden rise          (D) a sudden rush

## Tainted Water

A toxic spill took place on the upper Sacramento River in California when a slow moving Southern Pacific train derailed north of the town of Dansmuir. A tank car containing 19,500 gallons of pesticide broke open and spilled into the river. This pesticide is used to kill soil pests. Since the spill, thousands of trout and other fish were poisoned along a 45-mile stretch of river. In addition, 190 people were treated at a local hospital for respiratory and related illnesses. Residents along the river were warned to stay away from the tainted water. Once this water reached Lake Shasta, a source of water for millions of Californians, samples were taken to assess the quality of the water.

35. Which of the following statements conveys the message in the passage?

(A) Pesticides intended to kill pests can be dangerous to all living things.

(B) Water uncontaminated by pesticides is safe to drink.

(C) Take every precaution not to come in contact with pesticide-infected water.

(D) Pesticides that killed thousands of trout and other fist would not necessarily kill human beings.

36. The Southern Pacific train that derailed was

(A) a passenger train.         (C) a cargo and passenger train.

(B) a cargo train.             (D) a special train.

37. The most serious problem that could have come about as a result of the toxic spill was

(A) possible movement of residents in Dansmuir to another place of residence.

(B) the negative effects on those whose livelihood depended on the fishing industry.

(C) when the tainted water reached Lake Shasta, which is a source of water supply for millions of Californians.

(D) the uncertain length of time it would take to make the tainted water safe and healthy again.

38. This unfortunate incident of toxic spill resulting from train derailment implies

(A) that there is the need for more environmental protection.

(B) that other means for transporting pesticides need to be considered.

(C) that there should be an investigation as to the cause of the train derailment and that effective measures to prevent its occurrence again should be applied.

(D) that there should be research on how to expedite making infected water safe and healthy again.

## Lead Poisoning

Lead poisoning is considered by health authorities to be the most common and devastating environmental disease of young children. According to studies made, it affects 15% to 20% of urban children and from 50% to 75% of inner-city, poor children. As a result of a legal settlement, all of California's Medi-Cal-eligible children, ages one through five, will now be routinely screened annually for lead poisoning. Experts estimate that more than 50,000 cases will be detected in California because of the newly mandated tests. This will halt at an early stage a disease that leads to learning disabilities and life-threatening disorders.

39. Lead poisoning among young children, if not detected early, can lead to

(A) physical disabilities.

(C) learning disabilities.

(B) mental disabilities.

(D) death.

40. The mandate to screen all young children for lead poisoning is required of

(A) all young children in California.

(B) all children with learning disabilities.

(C) all Medi-Cal-eligible children, ages one through five, in California.

(D) all school-age children in California.

41. According to findings, more cases of lead poisoning are found among

(A) urban children.

(C) immigrant children.

(B) inner-city, poor children.

(D) children in rural areas.

42. The implication of this mandate in California regarding lead poisoning is that

   (A) non-eligible children will not be screened.

   (B) children older than five years will not be screened.

   (C) middle-class children will not be screened.

   (D) thousands of young children in California will remain at risk for lead poisoning.

## PRACTICE TEST 2
## WRITING SUBTEST

### Multiple-Choice Section

*Directions:* Read each passage and answer the questions that follow.

### Components of Learning

[1]Learning Theorists emphasize specific components of learning: behaviorists stress behavior in learning; humanists stress the affective in learning; and cognitivists stress cognition in learning. [2]All three of these <u>components</u> occur <u>simultaneously</u> and cannot be <u>separated</u> from each other in the learning process. [3]In 1957, Festinger referred to dissonance as the lack of harmony between what one does (behavior) and what one believes (attitude). [4]Attempts to separate the components of learning, either knowingly or unknowingly, create dissonances wherein language thought, feeling, and behavior become diminished of authenticity. [5]As a result, ideas and concepts <u>loose</u> their content and vitality, and the manipulation and politics of communication assume prominence. [6]In such cases, ones use of language would be in danger of being what the younger generation refers to as mere words, mere thoughts, and mere feelings.

1. What correction should be made in Part 1?

   (A) delete colon after learning

   (B) change Theorists to lower-case

(C) change semi-colon after learning to a comma

(D) change "cognitivists" to uppercase

2. Which underlined word is spelled incorrectly in the passage?

(A) components

(B) simultaneously

((C) separated

((D) loose

3. Which part has a punctuation error?

(A) Part 3

(B) Part 4

(C) Part 5

(D) Part 6

4. What part of the passage contains an incorrect homonym?

(A) Part 2

(B) Part 3

(C) Part 4

(D) Part 5

5. Which of the following revisions is needed to correct an error in the use of apostrophes?

(A) Part 3: Change "Festinger" to "Festinger's"

(B) Part 4: Change "dissonances" to "dissonances'"

(C) Part 5: Change "ideas" to "idea's"

(D) Part 6: Change "ones" to "one's"

## Learning to Talk

[1]In 1975, Sinclair observed that it had often been supposed that the main factor in learning to talk is being able to imitate. [2]Schlesinger (1975) noted that at certain stages of learning to speak, a child tends to imitate everything an adult says to him or her, and it therefor seems reasonable to accord to such imitation an important role in the acquisition of language.

[3]Moreover various investigators have attempted to explain the role of imitation in language. [4]In his discussion of the development of imitation and cognition of adult speech sounds, nakazema (1975) stated that although the parent's talking stimulates and accelerates the infant's articulatory activity, the parent's phoneme system does not influence the child's articulatory mechanisms. [5]Slobin and Welsh (1973) suggested that imitation is the reconstruction of the adult's utterence and that the child does so by employing the grammatical rules that he has developed at a specific time. [6]Schlesinger proposed that by imitating the adult the child practices new grammatical constructions.

6. What word is spelled incorrectly in Part 2?

   (A) noted

   (B) therefor

   (C) reasonable

   (D) accord

7. What part of the passage contains an error in punctuation?

   (A) Part 1

   (B) Part 2

   (C) Part 3

   (D) Part 4

8. What needs to be changed in Part 4?

   (A) Place a comma after the word "discussion.

   (B) Remove the comma after the word "sounds"

   (C) Capitalize the first letter of nakazema.

   (D) Capitalize the first letter of phoneme.

9. Which part of the passage has a spelling error?

   (A) Part 1

   (B) Part 3

   (C) Part 4

   (D) Part 5

10. What punctuation needs to be placed after the word "adult" in Part 6?

(A) a period

(C) a semi-colon

(B) a comma

(D) a colon

## Studies of Children's Stories

[1]Early studies of childrens' stories followed two approaches for story analysis: the analysis of story content or the analysis of story structure. [2]Story content analysis has centered primarily on examining motivational and <u>psychodynamic</u> aspects of story character's as noted in the works of Erikson and Pitcher and Prelinger in 1963 and Ames in 1966. [3]These studies have noted that themes or topics <u>predominate</u> and that themes change with age.

[4]Early research on story structure focused on formal models of structure, such as story <u>grammer</u> and story schemata. [5]These Models specified basic story elements and formed sets of rules similar to sentence grammar for ordering the elements. [6]The importance or centrality of narrative in a child's <u>development</u> of communicative ability has been proposed by Halliday (1976) and Hymes (1975).

11. What punctuation mark is incorrectly used in the passage?

(A) the colon

(C) the period

(B) the apostrophe

(D) the semi-colon

12. Which underlined word in the passage is spelled incorrectly?

(A) psychodynamic

(C) grammer

(B) predominate

(D) development

13. What part of the passage contains a word that should not be capitalized?

(A) Part 2

(C) Part 5

(B) Part 4

(D) Part 6

## Change in America's Schools

[1]Seldom, has the American school system not been the target of demands for change to meet the social priorities of the times. [2]This theme has been traced through the following significant occurrences in education: Benjamin Franklin's advocacy in 1749 for a more useful type of education; Horace Mann's zealous proposals in the 1830s espousing the tax-supported public school; John Dewey's early twentieth-century attack on traditional schools for not developing the child effectively for his or her role in society; the Post-Sputnik pressure for academic rigor; the prolific criticism and accountability pressures of the 1970s, and the ensuing disillusionment and continued criticism of schools into the twenty-first century. [3]Indeed, the waves of criticism about American education have reflected currants of social dissatisfaction for any given period of this country's history.

[4]As dynamics for change in the social order result in demands for change in the American educational system, so, in turn, has insistence developed for revision of teacher education. [5]Historically, the education of american teachers has reflected evolving attitudes about public education. [6]With slight modifications, the teacher education pattern established following the demise of the normal school during the early 1900s has persisted in most teacher preparation programs.

14. Which part has a comma that is not needed?

    (A) Part 1                 (C) Part 3

    (B) Part 2                 (D) Part 4

15. What correction is needed in part 2?

    (A) Place a comma after 1749.

    (B) Change the semi-colon after the word "education" to a comma.

    (C) Change Post-Sputnik to post-Sputnik.

    (D) Delete the comma after 1970s.

16. What is the spelling error in part 3?

    (A) criticism

    (B) reflected

    (C) currants

    (D) dissatisfaction

17. Which part of the passage contains a word that needs to be capitalized?

    (A) Part 1

    (B) Part 3

    (C) Part 4

    (D) Part 5

## The Child's Acquisition of Regime Norms: Political Efficacy

[1]Reduced to its simplest form, a political system is really no more than a devise enabling groups of people to live together in a more or less orderly society. [2]As they have developed, political systems generally have fallen into the broad categories of those which do not offer direct subject participation in the decision-making process, and those which allow citizen participation—in form, if not in actual effectiveness.

[3]Let us consider, however the type of political system that is classified as the modern democracy in a complex society. [4]Such a Democracy is defined by Lipset (1963) as "a political system which supplies regular constitutional opportunities for changing the governing officials, and a social mechanism which permits the largest possible part of the population to influence major decisions by choosing among alternative contenders for political office." [5]Proceeding from another concept (that of Easton and Dennis), a political system is one of inputs, conversion, and outputs by which the wants of a society are transformed into binding decisions? [6]As a rule, this interaction evolves around the settling of differences (satisfying wants or demands) involving the elements of a "political regime", which consists of minimal general goal constraints, norms governing behavior, and structures of authority for the input-output function.

*Adapted from Easton, B. and J. Dennis, "The Child's Acquisition of Regime Norms: Political Efficacy," American Political Science Review, March 1967.*

18. Which part of the passage has a spelling error?

    (A) Part 1

    (C) Part 3

    (B) Part 2

    (D) Part 4

19. Where should there be an additional comma in the second paragraph?

    (A) after the word "however"

    (C) after the word " system"

    (B) after the word "defined"

    (D) after the word " opportunities"

20. What punctuation needs to be corrected in part 5?

    (A) Move the comma from after the parenthesis to after the word "Dennis."

    (B) Remove the comma from after the word inputs."

    (C) Change the comma after the word "conversion" to a semi-colon.

    (D) Change the question mark after the word "decisions" to a period.

21. Which part of the passage has an incorrect placement of a comma?

    (A) Part 2

    (C) Part 5

    (B) Part 4

    (D) Part 6

## Sun Protection

[1]Summer is upon us, and many students are going out to "catch some rays." [2]In order to keep themselves beautiful and healthy, these sun worshipers should show respect for the power of old Sol. [3]Frequent or prolonged exposure to the sun can cause skin cancer, the deadliest form of which is malignant melanoma, and incidences of this disease are rising faster than any cancer. [4]Ninety percent of skin cancer is caused by overexposure to the sun.

[5]While most Americans believe application of sun screen helps prevent cancer, less than ten percent of us use it when we go out. [6]Also, we tend to go out during the most dangerous part of the day, between 10 a.m. and 2 p.m. in the summer. [7]This is the time when the sun emits peak ultraviolet radiation in the

Northern Hemisphere. [8]Even hiding under an umbrella near a pool or beach is insufficient to protect us from the damaging effects of the sun because the UV rays are reflected off the surface of sand and water.

[9]Wearing sunscreen may protect us a little, but sweat or swimming washes the lotion off, so the sunscreen really doesn't help protect us very much. [10]It's hard to use self-control in a nation that worships the rich, the thin, and the tan, but the burning rays of the sun can give cancer to anyone who wants a dark tan every summer. [11]We'd be better off just trying to get rich and thin.

22. Which of the following is needed?

    (A) Part 3: Add "other" between "any" and "cancer."

    (B) Part 5: Change "application" to "applying."

    (C) Part 8: Change "to protect us" to "in protecting us."

    (D) Part 9: Delete "off."

23. Which of the following requires revision for unnecessary repetition?

    (A) Part 2    (C) Part 8

    (B) Part 3    (D) Part 9

## Home Mortgage Advice

[1]When interest rates decrease, home mortgage rates also drop. [2]Homeowners who bought a house when rates were high seek to refinance their mortgage loans in order to take advantage of the cheaper rates. [3]Lower interest rates <u>results</u> in lower monthly payments.

[4]A person who owns a $100,000 home with a fixed interest rate of 11 percent for 30 years pays almost $1,000 in monthly principal and interest. [5]However, there is a fee of $1,800 to $2,400 for refinancing. [6]The same home with a 30 year loan, but with a 9 percent loan, pays about $850 a month. [7]Obviously, it is to the consumer's advantage to refinance his home. [8]The "rule of thumb" in the mortgage industry is that the homeowner is wise to refinance if he or she can get a loan at two or more percentage points lower than his or her current

rate. [9]Therefore, if the homeowner is planning to move within a year or two, re-financing is not considered a wise choice of action.

24. Which of the following should be used to replace the underlined word in Sentence 3?

    (A) result                    (C) is resulting

    (B) resulted                  (D) had resulted

25. Which of the following makes the sequence of ideas clearer in the second paragraph?

    (A) Place Sentence 5 between Sentences 8 and 9.

    (B) Reverse the order of Sentences 4 and 5.

    (C) Reverse the order of Sentences 7 and 9.

    (D) Delete Sentence 6.

26. Which of the following is a nonstandard sentence?

    (A) Sentence 4                 (C) Sentence 8

    (B) Sentence 6                 (D) Sentence 9

### Pearls

[1]One of the world's most valuable gems, pearls are valued for their luminous beauty. [2]Pearls are formed when an irritant, like a few grains of sand or a parasite, enters a mollusk. [3]Nacre-forming cells begin to cover the intruder with smooth layers of calcium carbonate until the irritant assumes the same appearance as the inside of the mollusk. [4]Only rarely, and after many years, do the layers of nacre form a pearl.

[5]When a cut pearl is examined under a microscope, concentric layers of nacre are revealed. [6]Tiny crystals of the mineral aragonite, held in place by a cartilage-like substance called conchiolin, reflects light in an iridescent rainbow effect. [7]Jewelers call this iridescence *orient*. [8]Most mollusks do not make iridescent pearls because their aragonite crystals are too large. [9]Perfectly round pearls

are quite rare in natural occurrence. ¹⁰Most pearls now are cultured. ¹¹A young oyster receives both a piece of mantle from a donor oyster and a seeding bead of mussel shell. ¹²These are tucked into a carefully-made incision in an oyster. ¹³Which is then lowered into the ocean in a wire cage so it can be cleaned and periodically x-rayed to check on progress. ¹⁴Because the oyster is a living organism and not a machine in a factory, the oyster may choose to spit out the introduced nucleus or the resulting pearl may be full of lumps and stains. ¹⁵Minor stains and imperfections, however, may be eliminated by carefully grinding down the surface of the pearl in order to produce a smaller, but more valuable, perfect pearl.

27. Which of the following is needed in the first paragraph?

    (A) Sentence 1: Delete "One of."

    (B) Sentence 2: Change "like" to "such as."

    (C) Sentence 3: Change "until" to "because."

    (D) Sentence 4: Change "and after" to "and then."

28. Which of the following is needed in the second paragraph?

    (A) Hyphenate "Perfectly round" in Sentence 9.

    (B) Combine Sentences 12 and 13 by changing the period after "oyster" to a comma.

    (C) Delete Sentence 14.

    (D) Add a sentence between Sentences 14 and 15 to give examples of defects.

29. What change needs to be made to paragraph 2?

    (A) Sentence 6: Change "reflects" to "reflect."

    (B) Sentence 8: Change "too" to "to."

    (C) Sentence 12: Delete the hyphen in "carefully-made."

    (D) Sentence 15: Change "minor stains and imperfections" to "minor stains or imperfections."

## Clearing Up the Columbus Story

[1]One thing is certain: Christopher Columbus was a real person who left real logs of his journey from Spain on August 3, 1492, to the Bahamas and back. [2]_____. [3]To the Spanish he is Cristobal Colon, but the Italians call him Cristoforo Colombo. [4]The Italians insist he is a native of Genoa, but some claim he was a Jew born in Spain, or born in Spain but not a Jew. [5]One version has touted Columbus as a Norwegian.

[6]Contrary to the popular myth, most educated people of the 1400s believed the world was round. [7]Columbus didn't have to sell almost anyone on that idea. [8]What he was trying to sell was a faster route to India. [9]Trade with India went by the centuries-old overland routes or the newer route by ship around the southern tip of Africa. [10]Also, another common myth is that Isabella had to sell her jewels in order to provide financing; actually, her husband had to approve all expenses, and funding was taken from the royal treasury.

[11]Even the original landing site is not known for certain, but most scholars agree that it is probably San Salvador Island in the Bahamas. [12]After his voyage, Columbus sent his handwritten logs to Isabella. [13]The copy the queen had made is known as the Barcelona log. [14]The original handwritten one has disappeared, as has all but a fragment of the Barcelona log copied by a Dominican friar named Bartolome de las Casas.

30. Which of the following changes is needed?

    (A) Sentence 6: Change "Contrary to" to "Opposing."

    (B) Sentence 7: Delete the word "almost."

    (C) Sentence 9: Change "by" to "around."

    (D) Sentence 11: Change "probably" to "probable."

31. Which of the following sentences would best be added between Sentences 1 and 3?

    (A) Columbus was very adventurous.

    (B) However, many details about Columbus's life are unknown.

(C)  These logs provide many details of his journey to the Bahamas.

(D)  He is known by different names in different countries.

32. What change would best improve this passage?

(A)  Sentence 6: Delete the comma between "myth" and "most."

(B)  Sentence 8: Insert a comma between "sell" and "was."

(C)  Place Sentence 11 after Sentence 5.

(D)  Sentence 10: Change the semicolon to a comma.

33. What change would best improve Paragraph 2?

(A)  Sentence 6: Add an apostrophe to "1400s."

(B)  Sentence 7: Delete the word "almost."

(C)  Sentence 9: Delete the hyphen in "centuries-old."

(D)  Sentence 10: Delete the word "also."

## Settling a Dispute

¹The recent contretemps over the <u>proposed</u> hike in the student parking fee has provided a test for the new administration. ²After a proposed doubling of the current $40 per semester parking fee, students threatened a walkout and planned demonstrations. ³The fees were intended to cut down on the incidents of vandalism and potential assaults in campus parking lots. ⁴Faced with these threats, the director of student services, the provost, and several other administrators met with the president of the student body and heads of several student organizations. ⁵The increased fees, already approved by the board of regents, were to pay the salary of additional parking lot attendants. ⁶<u>Some</u> students viewed the rate increase as a means of subsidizing more campus minor bureaucrats and petty disciplinarians. ⁷Although our university has not had much trouble with vandalism in the past, and no reported incidents of assault, such incidents are rising in surrounding areas and are a growing problem in universities across the United States.

$^8$<u>After</u> the two groups met, complaints and fears were exchanged. $^9$The administration listened <u>attentively</u>. $^{10}$Rather than just paying "lip service" to the process of negotiation, the administration agreed to a compromise on the service fee in exchange for a well-organized student patrol which will be trained and monitored by the town's police force. $^{11}$It is hoped that the presence of these students, who will wear an identifying arm band, will deter potential criminal activity.

34. Which of the following makes the sequence of ideas clearer in the first paragraph?

    (A) Reverse the order of Sentences 1 and 2.

    (B) Delete Sentence 2.

    (C) Place Sentence 3 after Sentence 6.

    (D) Delete Sentence 7.

35. Which of the following, underlined in the passage, should be replaced by a more precise word?

    (A) proposed          (C) After

    (B) Some              (D) attentively

## DIRECTIONS FOR THE SHORT-ANSWER SECTION OF THE WRITING SUBTEST

There are seven questions in the short-answer section of the writing subtest. Each question is phrased in exactly the same way. You will be told that each text has two errors and that the proper names of people and places are correctly spelled. You will look for errors in construction, grammar, usage, spelling, capitalization, and punctuation. Then, you will rewrite each text so that it is correct. You may change the syntax but must keep the essential elements of the piece. Of course, you may not introduce any new errors.

## SHORT-ANSWER ASSIGNMENTS AND RESPONSE SHEET

36. The following sentence contains two errors (e.g., in construction, grammar, usage, spelling, capitalization, punctuation). Rewrite the text so that errors are addressed and the original meaning is maintained.

    The memories of when I last saw James and she are not ones I am proud of.

    _____

    _____

37. The following sentence contains two errors (e.g., in construction, grammar, usage, spelling, capitalization, punctuation). Rewrite the text so that errors are addressed and the original meaning is maintained.

    When the police stopped John and Dan, on the highway, he asked him for his license.

    _____

    _____

38. The following sentence contains two errors (e.g., in construction, grammar, usage, spelling, capitalization, punctuation). Rewrite the text so that errors are addressed and the original meaning is maintained.

    In order to qualify for the job, an applicant must be 21 or older have their own transportation, and pass a simple test.

    _____

    _____

39. The following sentence contains two errors (e.g., in construction, grammar, usage, spelling, capitalization, punctuation). Rewrite the text so that errors are addressed and the original meaning is maintained.

   "Not the same thing a bit!", said the Hatter. "Why, you might just as well say that 'I see what I eat' is the same thing as 'I eat what I see'!".

   _____

   _____

40. The following sentence contains two errors (e.g., in construction, grammar, usage, spelling, capitalization, punctuation). Rewrite the text so that errors are addressed and the original meaning is maintained.

   I enjoy different ethnic foods such as Greek Chinese and Italian.

   _____

   _____

41. The following sentence contains two errors (e.g., in construction, grammar, usage, spelling, capitalization, punctuation). Rewrite the text so that errors are addressed and the original meaning is maintained.

   Charles sent flowers, and wrote a long letter explaining why he had not been able, to attend.

   _____

   _____

42. The following sentence contains two errors (e.g., in construction, grammar, usage, spelling, capitalization, punctuation). Rewrite the text so that errors are addressed and the original meaning is maintained.

This is one of the best, if not the best colleges in the country.

---

## DIRECTIONS FOR THE WRITING SUMMARY EXERCISE

For this part of the test, you will read the passage on the next page and summarize it in your own words. Your summary should be approximately 150 to 250 words and effectively communicate the main idea and essential points of the passage. You are to identify the relevant information and communicate it clearly and concisely.

Your summary will be evaluated based on the following criteria:

- **FIDELITY:** Your accuracy and clarity in using your own words to convey and maintain focus on the main ideas of the passage

- **CONCISENESS:** Your appropriate use of length, depth, and specificity to convey the writer's main ideas

- **ORGANIZATION:** The clarity of your writing and your use of logical sequencing of ideas

- **SENTENCE STRUCTURE:** The effectiveness of your sentence structure and the extent to which those sentences are free of structural errors

- **USAGE:** Your care and precision in word choice and avoidance of usage errors

- **MECHANICAL CONVENTIONS:** Your use of conventional spelling and use of the conventions of punctuation and capitalization

The final version of your summary should conform to the conventions of edited American English, should be written legibly, and should be your own original work.

On the actual test you will be directed to write or print your summary on the pages provided in the test booklet.

## WRITING SUMMARY EXERCISE

*Directions:* Use the passage below to prepare a summary of 100–150 words.

[1]Students who are placed in residential programs for behavior or emotional problems or who are adjudicated into detention centers historically have not experienced success in school. [2]These students usually do not have a consistent record of school attendance; their absenteeism can be for more than an entire school year, as they often have been moved from different placements or institutions. [3]Residential treatment provides the longest period of secondary school attendance for many of the students. [4]As such, it provides an opportune setting for many of these students to experience some type of academic success both within the content area coursework and in their relationships with educators. [5]Students who are incarcerated have not experienced classroom involvement or positive teacher interaction prior to their detainment; this may be the only time they have ever been in a setting where they feel that the teacher recognizes them. [6]For some of them, their incarceration or admission to a residential treatment facility afford them opportunities to participate in appropriate relationships with teachers.

[7]Transitioning back to public schools, where they have not had success should be addressed by the school to which they are returning as well as the facility from which they are leaving. [8]This reintegration is essential in providing students with opportunities for success and a full measure of participation in the educational community; the students' success can be a measure of society's willingness to work with at-risk students.

[9]Academic achievement is related not only to delinquency; but also to recidivism. [10]The ability for students to quickly reintegrate into a public school promotes continued academic effort and better relationships within the school setting. [11]It may be possible in fact, to reduce recidivism by providing neces-

sary skills for academic achievement such as self-advocacy and self-determination, two skills used in developing transition plans for students.

## DIRECTIONS FOR THE COMPOSITION EXERCISE

For this part of the writing subtest you are asked to write a multiple-paragraph composition of approximately 300 to 600 words on an assigned topic. Your assignment will be to effectively communicate a complete message for the specified audience and purpose. The assessment of your composition will be based on your ability to express, organize, and support opinions and ideas. The position you take will not be part of the evaluation.

### Criteria for Evaluation:

- **Appropriateness:** Your attention to the topic and use of the language and style appropriate to the stated audience, purpose, and occasion

- **Mechanical Conventions:** Your use of standard spelling and use of the conventions of punctuation and capitalization

- **Usage:** Your care and precision in word choice and avoidance of usage errors

- **Sentence Structure:** The effectiveness of your sentence structure and the extent to which those sentences are free of structural errors

- **Focus and Unity:** Your clarity in stating and maintaining focus on your main idea or point of view

- **Organization:** The clarity of your writing and your use of logical sequencing of ideas

- **Development:** Your statements are of appropriate depth, specificity, and/or accuracy

Your final version needs to conform to the conventions of edited American English, be written legibly, and be your own original work.

On the actual test you will be directed to write or print your response on the pages provided in the test booklet.

## COMPOSITION EXERCISE

You are to write a composition, to be read by other teachers, in which you fully answer the questions asked with appropriate examples.

What specific characteristic do you think a person must possess in order to be an effective teacher? Fully explain each characteristic and show how the absence of each will reduce effectiveness in the classroom.

## PRACTICE TEST 2
## ANSWER KEY

### READING SUBTEST – MULTIPLE-CHOICE SECTION

| | | | |
|---|---|---|---|
| 1. (D) | 12. (D) | 23. (C) | 34. (C) |
| 2. (A) | 13. (D) | 24. (A) | 35. (C) |
| 3. (B) | 14. (C) | 25. (B) | 36. (B) |
| 4. (B) | 15. (B) | 26. (C) | 37. (C) |
| 5. (D) | 16. (A) | 27. (A) | 38. (C) |
| 6. (C) | 17. (A) | 28. (D) | 39. (D) |
| 7. (C) | 18. (B) | 29. (A) | 40. (C) |
| 8. (B) | 19. (D) | 30. (D) | 41. (B) |
| 9. (B) | 20. (A) | 31. (D) | 42. (D) |
| 10. (D) | 21. (D) | 32. (B) | |
| 11. (D) | 22. (B) | 33. (B) | |

### WRITING SUBTEST – MULTIPLE-CHOICE SECTION

| | | | |
|---|---|---|---|
| 1. (B) | 10. (B) | 19. (A) | 28. (B) |
| 2. (D) | 11. (B) | 20. (D) | 29. (A) |
| 3. (B) | 12. (C) | 21. (D) | 30. (B) |
| 4. (D) | 13. (C) | 22. (A) | 31. (B) |
| 5. (D) | 14. (A) | 23. (D) | 32. (C) |
| 6. (B) | 15. (C) | 24. (A) | 33. (D) |
| 7. (C) | 16. (C) | 25. (A) | 34. (C) |
| 8. (C) | 17. (D) | 26. (B) | 35. (C) |
| 9. (D) | 18. (A) | 27. (B) | |

# DETAILED EXPLANATIONS OF ANSWERS READING SUBTEST

## Multiple-Choice Section

1. **(D)** (D) is the best answer. The author is actually advising empires of the causes of revolutions and unrest. Even though the first sentence refers only to the wisdom of an ancient sage, more recent information is also imparted. Therefore, (A) is not the best answer. The advice is offered to rulers, not church ministers, so (B) should not be selected. Even though the first sentence states the passage is about how to make a little city into a great one, the second sentence clearly states the author is going to explain how to do the reverse. Therefore, (C) should not be chosen.

2. **(A)** The best answer is (A). The author compares an empire to a cake. (B) is incorrect because it is a minister, not the country, who is compared to a gingerbread baker. It has already been ascertained that it is a minister being compared to a gingerbread baker, so (C) is not the best answer. (D) is incorrect because it is not a religious minister who is compared to a gingerbread baker, but rather, a minister who has the "management of extensive dominions."

3. **(B)** The best answer is (B) because the article is tongue-in-cheek. Even though the suggestion is that Franklin is going to tell the reader how to make a little city of a great one, the author (who is not a simpleton) is actually giving advice. (A) is incorrect because Franklin addresses himself to ministers of "extensive" or large dominions rather than small countries. (C) is incorrect because the advice is being given to governmental ministers rather than being received from religious ministers. (D) is also incorrect because the word "fiddle" is used only as a vehicle for the satire of the passage and is not to be taken literally.

4. **(B)** In the last paragraph of the reading passage, the writer states that the General needs enough troops under his command. Therefore, (B) is the best choice. The writer is not suggesting that troops need to be kept in tow, so (A) should not be chosen. Even though the General should certainly be lucky to have troops endowed with skill under his control, there is no support in the passage for this answer; (C) should not be chosen. Because the clause has nothing to do with captured troops, (D) should not be chosen.

5. **(D)** (D) is the best choice because the article is written by Benjamin Franklin, who was a friend of the colonists and is writing to advise the mother country on how to behave.

Franklin is not writing to help rid the ministers of their troubles; therefore, (A) should not be selected. The writer is not hoping to help the ministers build their powers and increase their provinces, so (B) should not be chosen. Because the article was written by Benjamin Franklin, it could not have been written only a few years ago nor does it contain new ideas to help increase the provinces; (C) should not be chosen.

6. **(C)** The reader should note that the answer sought is the one which is *least* advisable. (C) is the answer which is least advisable because a minister should *not* treat the provinces as if he or she expects them to revolt and as if he or she supposes them to be always ready to revolt. To keep a large country intact, the General of the army should be limited to the constitutional powers, so (A) is *not* an answer which is *least* advisable. The provinces should be given the same rights as those in the mother country; thus, (B) is an advisable answer and should not be chosen. A mother country should not require taxation without representation, just as (D) says. Since (D) is true, it should not be selected. (A), (B), and (D) are incorrect because they are extremely advisable actions to take for keeping a large country intact and the question asks for the least advisable action.

7. **(C)** The item that the writer contends is *not* true is (C) because the first sentence of the reading passage uses the words "even when," implying that heat is no longer regarded as a substance. The other items (A), (B), and (D) are all items the writer states as being true in the first paragraph. None of them should be chosen.

8. **(B)** The best answer is (B) because the calorie and B.T.U. both relate to the amount of heat necessary to raise the temperature one degree. Because one unit relates to a kilogram (2.2 pounds) and one relates to a pound of water, (A) should not be chosen; it relates to one pound of water only. One unit relates to the customary system and one to the metric system, not both to the metric system. Thus, (C) cannot be chosen. Only the B.T.U. relates to a pound of iron, so (D) is also incorrect.

9. **(B)** The best answer is (B) because the melting of one pound of ice can cool a pound of hot water through a definite range of temperature and can cool two pounds of water through *half* as many degrees (C). (B) is therefore denied by the author. Neither (A) nor (D) can be the correct answer because they are stated, not denied, by the author in the first paragraph of the reading passage.

10. **(D)** The author states that the heat capacity of water or the B.T.U. per pound-degree is not constant, so (D) is the best answer. The author does not state that a water pound-degree is a constant; therefore, (A) should not be chosen. Because the temperature does make a

difference, (B) should not be chosen. (C) is exactly opposite of the correct answer (D) and should not be selected.

11. **(D)** The best choice is (D). The disagreement concerns how to limit and define the heat unit. Since the passage states without any indication of doubt or negation that the melting of a pound of ice will not cool the same weight of water from 200° Fahrenheit to 180° Fahrenheit as it will from 60° Fahrenheit to 40° Fahrenheit, (A) is not the best answer. As the opening sentence of the second and last paragraph states, there is general agreement that a water pound-degree is not quite constant; thus, (B) should not be chosen. There is no point of disagreement among scientists as to whether the equivalence of heat effects proved effects proportional to quantity. Consequently, (C) is not the correct answer.

12. **(D)** The best answer is (D). The author appears to suggest that there are good reasons for taking the freezing-point to the boiling-point as the range by including the words "which will probably become universal"—interesting, but not totally necessary, information that leads the reader to believe the author readily accepts this as a range. Both the metric and the customary systems are mentioned without preference for either system. Therefore, neither (A), which indicates a predilection for the metric system, nor (B), which indicates a predilection for the customary system, is the correct answer. Because the author precedes his mention of the mean calorie with the words "properly named," he is indicating his approval of, rather than his opposition to, the mean calorie; hence, (C) is another incorrect choice.

13. **(D)** The phrase "properly named" is applied to both the mean calorie and the mean British Thermal Unit in the last sentence of the reading passage and makes (D), which includes both mean calories and mean British Thermal Units, the correct choice. Neither (A) nor (B) is correct because each of these answers is only one-half of the correct answer. Because we already know that (D) is the correct answer, we can see that (C) is incorrect; there is no support for such opposition in the passage.

14. **(C)** The author predicts the universal acceptance of the mean B.T.U. and the mean calorie as mentioned toward the end of the reading passage; hence, (C) is the best answer. (A) should not be selected since it mentions the universal adoption of the B.T.U. alone. (B) mentions the universal adoption of the calorie alone and should not be accepted. Because the author predicts not the demise but the universal adoption of the calories, (D) is incorrect.

15. **(B)** The best answer is (B) because, in the first sentence, the author opposes the terms "Japanese" and "Occident." Later in the same paragraph, he opposes the terms "Oriental" and "Occidental," which effectively eliminates (D). Because there is no support for (A) in

the passage, the reader is able to infer that this is incorrect. Assuming the reader knows that both Japan and the Orient are part of the East, (C) is incorrect; the term "non-Western" implies "Eastern." By a process of elimination, the reader can determine that only (B) can be the correct choice.

16. **(A)** The best answer is (A); the author contrasts, or shows the differences between, the paintings of the Japanese and the Occident. The author discusses differences, rather than similarities (comparisons), between the two types of painting, so (B) is an incorrect answer. (C) and (D) are incorrect because the author writes about contrasts, rather than comparisons. In addition, (C) mentions only content whereas the author also mentions the stress—objective or subjective ideas—in the painting styles.

17. **(A)** The best answer is (A) because the main difference between Occidental and Japanese painting is the differing views concerning the primary object of art, as is explained toward the end of the second paragraph of the reading passage. While (B), (C), and (D) are mentioned, there is no in-depth analysis of any of these answers. The question asks for the *main* difference, so (B), (C), and (D) are all incorrect answers.

18. **(B)** Sei-ichi Taki refers to Oriental and Occidental art in general and to Japanese art in particular; therefore, (B) is the best answer. (A) is incorrect because the writer's area is not Occidental (Western) painting but Oriental painting, although he is able to make many comparisons between the two. The article does not cover the broad expanse of Oriental painting (C) or Asian painting (D), but concentrates on Japanese painting. Hence, (C) and (D) should not be selected.

19. **(D)** (D) is the best choice. The Japanese painter can be said to bring out the spirit of the object being portrayed, as stated by the author in the second paragraph. Because the correct answer (D) refers to the spirit of the object being portrayed, it is logical that neither the painter's own thoughts, ideas, or objective ideas can be the answer. Consequehtly, (A), (B), and (C) are incorrect choices.

20. **(A)** (A) is the best answer because the reader is asked to identify what the painters of Western art do. The author states near the beginning of the third paragraph that the painters of Western art give their foremost attention to the human figure. Because of this (B) should not be chosen; it is exactly the opposite of what the author states. The painters of Western art are not greatly concerned with the expression of the spirit but rather with the human figure; (C) should not be chosen. The painters in Western art are not always concerned with showing high esteem for God's creations, but rather with objective qualities; (D) should not be chosen.

21. **(D)** Item (D) in the first paragraph refers to this term with a correct definition: "those accumulations of religious notions and legends." (A) is incorrect; the first paragraph doesn't suggest that these "accretions" are anything but "incredible" and fiction. (B) is incorrect; the first paragraph maintains that Hostead's position rejects any soundness in such accretions. (C) is incorrect; again, "accretions," according to contextual clues, doesn't mean "implications," but rather "accumulations."

22. **(B)** Hostead's first assumption makes that statement about the essence of religion while the second sentence in paragraph two disputes it. (A) is incorrect; paragraph one defines Hostead's position, while the second paragraph addresses the first position, which doesn't deal with scientific validity of any belief in God. (C) is incorrect; these four ideologies are simply used to illustrate that immortality is not necessarily the essence of a religion, but the central idea of the passage is not the defense of these ideologies. (D) is incorrect; again the writer is not defending the validity of those ideologies, but using them to attack one of Hostead's points.

23. **(C)** The first two sentences of the second paragraph state this purpose exactly. (A) is incorrect; the writer only touches on one aspect of each of these beliefs to disprove Hostead's first point. (B) is incorrect; the writer touches only the first position, which does not deal with scientific credibility. (D) is incorrect; the writer disputes Hostead's definition of the essence of religion rather than provide his own definition.

24. **(A)** The fourth sentence of the selection states this. (B) is incorrect; the selection does not say that "spiritual superexistence" lives forever; the soul does. (C) is incorrect; the writer doesn't say man has "supreme" intelligence; he says that Aristotle felt the human soul had a superior intellect. (D) is incorrect; man has spiritual superexistence through his knowledge and love, but the writer doesn't say knowledge and love are the essence of spiritual superexistence.

25. **(B)** The first paragraph establishes man as a microcosm while the second paragraph attributes that condition to the human soul. (A) is incorrect; perhaps this is a statement with which the writer would agree, but it's only by inference that this statement would be considered true. (C) is incorrect; this true statement doesn't summarize the central idea of the passage; it only supports it. (D) is incorrect; this statement, which reflects the writer's opinion, doesn't constitute the main idea of the selection.

26. **(C)** This is not a factual statement; many would argue that man has no more will than any other creature. (A) is incorrect; while not all agree with this statement, it is a fact that Christians believe this. (B) is incorrect; this is the opposite of what the writer says. (D)

is incorrect; we can all agree that man is indeed subject to accidents, as the writer maintains; this is not an opinion.

27. **(A)** The writer says humans make their environment artificial and the result of their efforts is culture. (B) is incorrect; the writer does not suggest that culture in and of itself is a bad or destructive thing. (C) is incorrect; the writer doesn't allude to erudition or intelligence; even primitive, illiterate man had culture. (D) is incorrect; culture is an artificial element while nature's elements are not.

28. **(D)** Sentences 3 and 4 say this outright. (A) is incorrect; the writer introduces this term early in the passage before he even touches on man's relationship with nature. (B) is incorrect; the word "artificial" doesn't connote lack of sincerity; it suggests "not occurring in nature." (C) is incorrect; the passage does say man is inherently a part of nature, but this term is not used by the writer to describe that relationship.

29. **(A)** This is stated in the final sentence of the first paragraph. (B) is incorrect; the writer calls them primitive but not ignorant; in fact, the passage suggests enlightenment on their part. (C) is incorrect; the writer doesn't suggest that primitive man had no culture; their worship of nature didn't take the place of an artificial environment. (D) is incorrect; their concerns were not ecological but more theological; they may have acted in an "ecologically correct" fashion, but the writer doesn't emphasize any ecological concerns.

30. **(D)** The sentence that begins with this phrase in Paragraph 1 makes this statement. (A) is incorrect; while one may infer that organic cycles prompt plants and animals to act in clock-like fashion, the writer does not say that early humans used them as clocks. (B) is incorrect; these are qualities that the writer ascribes to nonhuman aspects of nature and animals. (C) is incorrect; the writer's reference to the spiritual being is not related to his discussion of primitive man's methods of telling time.

31. **(D)** As the passage presents information by various researchers on children's stories, the passage ends with an unanswered question that still needs to be addressed by reading researchers as provided in choice D.

32. **(B)** Although more information may be needed about story content and story structure as indicated in choices A, C, and D, the main question that remains to be answered is choice B.

33. **(B)** Each choice provides partially correct information about story content and story structure; choice B provides the most complete response.

34. **(C)** Each choice is a possible definition. However, choice C is most appropriate as there was an increased interest by researchers in these and other areas even though it has been an ongoing concern of some researchers.

35. **(C)** The question asks for the "message" conveyed in the passage. Choice C is the correct answer, as it gives a warning. In choice A, pesticides cannot necessarily be dangerous to all living things—some are good for the protection of plants, for example; in B, water can be contaminated by something other than pesticides; the statement in choice D may be true, but it is certainly not the best answer.

36. **(B)** The train is definitely a cargo train, hence, B is the correct answer. In A, if it were a passenger train, hundreds would have been killed; in C, according to the clues, the choices here don't apply; and in D the answer used "special train" but could have appropriately used "cargo train" instead.

37. **(C)** The question here asks for the most "serious problem" that could have come about; so, of all the choices, C provides the most serious problem resulting from the pesticide spill for Californians. Choices A, B, and D are not life-threatening as is C.

38. **(C)** C is the most logical and straightforward answer. C prioritizes which action should be first taken, and is therefore the correct answer. While the choices in A, B, and D are sound answers, they don't list the most urgent thing to do.

39. **(D)** All the choices in this question are possible answers; however, since the question asks what lead poisoning, if not detected early, "can lead to," it calls for the ultimate consequence. Hence, D is the correct answer inasmuch as the passage states "life-threatening disorders" as among the possible consequences.

40. **(C)** The correct answer to this question is choice C—it gives the complete and precise category. Other choices are incomplete—A left out the age group and the Medi-Cal eligibility; B is narrowed down and all inclusive of "children with learning disabilities" and choice D is incorrect.

41. **(B)** As indicated by figures in the passage, the correct answer is B. Other choices A, C, and D are obviously incorrect. This is an example of a question in which the incorrect choices are not possible answers. The correct answer is derived from the figures provided in the passage.

42. **(D)** The implications provided in choices A through D are correct. However, each of the implications for A through C is narrowed down to only one specific category of

children—not any one is inclusive of all that needs to be addressed. Hence, D is the best and appropriate answer because it addresses the thousands who will not be screened, which include those in choices A through C.

# WRITING SUBTEST

## Multiple-Choice Section

1. **(B)** The word "theorists" should not be capitalized.

2. **(D)** The correct spelling is "lose."

3. **(B)** There should be a comma after the word "language."

4. **(D)** The word "loose" is incorrect in this context. The correct spelling "lose."

5. **(D)** The word "ones" should be "one's."

6. **(B)** The correct spelling is "therefore."

7. **(C)** There should be a comma after the word "moreover."

8. **(C)** The word "Nakazema" is a proper name and should be capitalized.

9. **(D)** The correct spelling is "utterance."

10. **(B)** This sentence needs a comma after the word "adult."

11. **(B)** The apostrophe is incorrectly placed twice. It should be "children's stories." "Characters" does not need an apostrophe.

12. **(C)** The correct spelling is "grammar."

13. **(C)** The word "models" should not be capitalized.

14. **(A)** The comma after the word "seldom" is not needed.

15. **(C)** The word "post" should not be capitalized in the phrase "post-Sputnik."

16. **(C)** The correct spelling is "currents."

17. **(D)** The word "American" should be capitalized.

18. **(A)** The correct spelling in this context is "device."

19. **(A)** There should be a comma after the word "however."

20. **(D)** The end of this sentence would be correctly punctuated with a period.

21. **(D)** The comma after the phrase "political regime" should appear inside the quotation mark.

22. **(A)** Choice (A) is correct because any time one item is being compared or contrasted with other items in the same category or group, it is necessary to include the words "other" or "else." Choice (B) creates an awkward construction, "applying of." Choice (C) creates some awkward wording and does not improve the sentence. In choice (D), the word "off" is necessary to the meaning of Sentence 9.

23. **(D)** Choice (D) has unnecessary repetition of the phrase "protect us." Choices (A), (B), and (C) are tightly worded sentences.

24. **(A)** Choice (A) shows correct use of present tense. Choices (B) and (D) incorrectly use past tense. Choice (C) is the incorrect use of present progressive.

25. **(A)** Choice (A) places Sentence 5 before Sentence 9. This creates a logical flow of ideas because Sentence 9 is the explanation of the drawback of the refinancing fee mentioned in Sentence 5. Choice (B) is incorrect because a sentence beginning with "However," needs to follow a contrasting idea. Choice (C) is incorrect because Sentence 7 is a sentence concluding the advantages and train of thought presented in Sentences 4 and 6. Choice (D) would delete a vital piece of information.

26. **(B)** Choice (B) is missing a clear subject, a person paying the money. It is obvious that a home cannot pay a loan. Choices (A), (C), and (D) are clear sentences.

27. **(B)** Choice (B) is correct because "such as" is used to introduce an example; "like" signals unequal comparisons. Choice (A) changes the meaning of the sentence; pearls are not the most valuable gems. In choice (C) the change would omit the correct transition "until" which shows time sequence. Choice (D) would create an incoherent sentence.

28. **(B)** Choice (B) combined the fragment in Sentence 13 with the complete sentence in Sentence 12. Choice (A) is not a necessary addition. Choice (C) would delete a neces-

sary sentence, one which provides the lead into the idea of grinding down imperfections. Choice (D) is unnecessary because examples of defects ("lumps and stains") have already been listed in Sentence 14.

29. **(A)** The plural noun "crystals" needs the verb "reflect." Choices (B) and (C) are correct as they are. Choice (D) would not make an appreciable difference.

30. **(B)** Choice (B) would delete the unnecessary adverb "almost." Choice (A) creates a poorly worded transition. Choice (C) creates a sentence that is self-contradictory, making the traders appear to avoid the route they actually took. Choice (D) changes the correct adverb "probably," meant to modify the verb "is," to the incorrect adjective "probable."

31. **(B)** Choice (B) provides a smooth transition from Sentence 1 to Sentence 3. Choice (C) continues the subject of Sentence 1 but does not mention that of Sentence 3. Choice (D) does not provide a smooth transition between the two sentences and does not allow for the other inconsistencies such as Columbus's country of birth. Choice (A) begins a new topic and should not be chosen.

32. **(C)** Sentence 11 continues the topic of the uncertain details of Columbus's life and voyage. Choices (A), (B), and (D) are all incorrect answers and should not be chosen.

33. **(D)** In Sentence 10, the words "also" and "another" are redundant. They both imply that a new example will follow. Choices (A), (B), and (C) are incorrect answers; the sentences are correct in the passage.

34. **(C)** Choice (C) would move the sentence that discusses the reason for the fees to the end of the paragraph. Sentence 5 introduces the use for the fees, and Sentence 6 presents student objections to the attendants. Sentence 3 should be placed before Sentence 7, which further explains the problem of vandalism and assaults. Choice (A) would move Sentence 2, introducing the idea of threatened demonstrations and walkouts, away from Sentence 4, which contains reference to "these threats." Choice (B) would eliminate the crucial cost of the fees. Choice (D) would eliminate the overriding reason for the fee hike.

35. **(C)** In choice (C) the incorrect word "After" should be replaced with the correct word "When." It is unlikely that fears and complaints were not exchanged until after the meeting between administration and students. Choice (A) is shown with concrete details in Sentence 2. Choice (B) is not necessary; inclusion of the protestors' names would be irrelevant and counterproductive to the conciliatory tone of the article. Choice (D) needs no elaboration because the administration has shown its responsiveness with a compromise.

## Short-Answer Section Sample Responses

36. The memories of when I last saw James and she are not ones I am proud of.

    ***Errors:***    1.   incorrect use of nominative case (she)

                    2.   dangling preposition

    ***Sample Correct Response:***

    *The memories I have of my last meeting with James and her are not ones of which I am proud.*

37. When the police stopped John and Dan, on the highway, he asked him for his license.

    ***Errors:***    1.   vague use of pronoun (which him?)

                    2.   no comma needed after the word "Dan"

    ***Sample Correct Response:***

    *The police asked John for his license when they stopped Dan and him on the highway.*

38. In order to qualify for the job, an applicant must be 21 or older have their own transportation, and pass a simple test.

    ***Errors:***    1.   missing comma between clauses

                    2.   noun and pronoun agreement: an applicant/ their own transportation

    ***Sample Correct Response:***

    *In order to qualify for the job, applicants must be 21 or older, have their own transportation, and pass a simple test.*

39. "Not the same thing a bit!", said the Hatter. "Why, you might just as well say that 'I see what I eat' is the same thing as 'I eat what I see'!".

    ***Errors:***    1.   incorrect placement of comma – should be inside quotation marks

2. Because of the preceding exclamation point, there shouldn't be a period at the end.

***Sample Correct Response:***

*"Not the same thing a bit!" said the Hatter. "Why, you might just as well say that 'I see what I eat' is the same thing as 'I eat what I see'!"*

40. I enjoy different ethnic foods such as: Greek Chinese and Italian**.**

***Errors:*** 1. Colon not to be used after a preposition.

2. Commas need to be used in a list.

***Sample Correct Response:***

*I enjoy different ethnic foods such as Greek, Chinese, and Italian.*

41. Charles sent flowers, and wrote a long letter explaining why he had not been able, to attend.

***Errors:*** 1. Subject is the same for both verbs—no comma needed

2. Second comma has no usefulness.

***Sample Correct Response:***

*Charles sent flowers and wrote a long letter explaining why he had not been able to attend.*

42. This is one of the best, if not the best colleges in the country.

***Errors:*** 1. Do not omit the first category of a comparison.

2. "One of the best" requires the plural word "colleges."

***Sample Correct Response:***

*This is one of the best colleges in the country, if not the best.*

## SCORING RUBRIC FOR THE WRITTEN SUMMARY EXERCISE

### Scoring Scale:

### Score of 4:  A well-formed written response

- You have accurately conveyed the main ideas of the passage, maintaining focus and unity, while using your own words.

- Your response is concise, but you have provided sufficient depth and specificity to convey the main points of the passage.

- Your response shows control and organization.

- You have used correct and effective sentence structure.

- Your usage and choice of words are careful and precise.

- You have shown a mastery of mechanical conventions (i.e., spelling, punctuation, and capitalization).

### Score of 3:  An adequately formed written response

- Generally using your own words, you have accurately conveyed most of the writer's main ideas and in most cases maintained focus and unity.

- Your response may have been too long or too short, but you generally provided sufficient depth and specificity to convey most of the main points of the passage.

- Your organization of ideas might be ambiguous, incomplete, or partially ineffective.

- You use adequate sentence structure, but minor errors may be present.

- Your usage and choice of words display minor errors.

- You have made some errors in the use of mechanical conventions (i.e., spelling, punctuation, and capitalization).

## Score of 2: A partially formed written response

- You have conveyed only some of the main ideas of the passage and/or did not keep focus on the topic. You relied heavily on the writer's words.

- Your response is too long or too short and/or did not included sufficient depth to effectively develop your response.

- You made a generally unsuccessful attempt to organize and sequence ideas.

- Your sentence structure contains significant errors.

- You are imprecise in usage and word choice.

- You have made frequent errors in the use of mechanical conventions (i.e., spelling, punctuation, and capitalization).

## Score of 1: An inadequately formed written response

- You have not identified the main ideas of the passage.

- You have failed to effectively develop your the response.

- You have very little organization and what is there is not sequential.

- Your sentence structure is poor and most sentences contain errors.

- Your usage is imprecise and your word choices are ill-advised.

- You have made serious and numerous errors in the use of mechanical conventions (i.e., spelling, punctuation, and capitalization).

## Score of U

The response is unrelated to the assigned topic, illegible, primarily in a language other than English, not of sufficient length to score, or merely a repetition of the assignment.

## Score of B

There is no response to the assignment.

## SCORING RUBRIC FOR THE WRITTEN COMPOSITION EXERCISE

### Scoring Scale:

### Score of 4:  A well-formed written response

- You have addressed the assignment fully and used appropriate language and style.

- You have shown a mastery of mechanical conventions (e.g., spelling, punctuation, and capitalization).

- Your usage and choice of words are careful and precise.

- Your sentence structure is effective and free of errors.

- You have clearly stated a main idea and/or point of view, and maintained focus and unity throughout your composition.

- You have shown excellent organizational skills.

- You have fully developed your composition, providing ample and appropriate depth, specificity, and accuracy.

### Score of 3:  An adequately formed written response

- You have addressed the assignment adequately and have generally used appropriate language and/or style.

- You have some errors in the use of mechanical conventions (e.g., spelling, punctuation, and capitalization).

- You have some minor errors in usage and word choice.

- Your sentence structure is adequate, but there are some minor errors in your writing.

- The presentation of your main idea and/or point of view is generally clear and focused and you generally maintain unity.

- Your organization of ideas is a bit ambiguous, incomplete, or partially ineffective.

- You have provided sufficient depth, specificity, and accuracy to adequately develop the response.

## Score of 2: A partially formed written response

- You have only partially addressed the assignment and may have used inappropriate language and/or style.

- You have made frequent errors in the use of mechanical conventions (e.g., spelling, punctuation, and capitalization).

- You have been imprecise in your usage and word choice.

- Your sentence structure is poor with a number of errors.

- Your main idea and/or point of view is inconsistently treated and/or you have not maintained the focus and unity of your discussion.

- You have made an effort to organize and sequence ideas, but your organization is largely unclear.

- Your response includes very few ideas that aid in its development.

## Score of 1: An inadequately formed written response

- You have attempted to address the assignment, but your language and style are generally inappropriate for the given audience, purpose, and/or occasion.

- You have made many serious errors in the use of mechanical conventions (e.g., spelling, punctuation, and capitalization).

- You have been imprecise in usage and word choice.

- Your sentence structure is ineffective and error ridden.

- You have not identified your main idea and/or point of view.

- Your limited organization fails to follow a logical sequence of ideas.

- You have failed to include ideas that would aide in the development of your response.

## Score of U

The response is unrelated to the assigned topic, illegible, primarily in a language other than English, not of sufficient length to score, or merely a repetition of the assignment.

## Score of B

There is no response to the assignment.

## The following is a strong response to the Composition exercise.

*When I think of what specific characteristics a person must possess in order to be an effective teacher I think of these characteristics: upstanding values, compassion, and a thorough knowledge of their subject matter.*

*First, a person who becomes a teacher must keep in mind that they are a role model to the children in their midst. Their private and professional life must be beyond reproach. A teacher is responsible for setting values as well as teaching values. A teacher has a big influence on a child's life; therefore, a teacher must be careful about the kinds of signals he sends out to the children in his environment. Today, it is hard to tell teachers from students because they dress alike, wear their hair alike, associate together, and act the same. A teacher should set himself apart if he is to be a positive influence on the students he comes in contact with. Once a teacher loses his credibility and/or self-respect, he is no longer effective in the classroom.*

*Compassion is a quality that allows a teacher to have a sense of humor, get to know students' qualities, and be supportive of students' efforts. A teacher must be able to laugh with his students. This creates a relationship between learner and teacher, and shows the students that the teacher has a human side, and tells the students that the teacher is approachable. A good teacher will get to know each of his student's learning abilities and styles. This will allow the teacher to get the most from each student. Compassion allows the teacher to empathize with the students who are having problems in school or at home by being supportive and by providing a positive direction. Students can be turned off if they perceive that a teacher does not care.*

*Finally, if a person is going to be an effective teacher, he must have a thorough knowledge of his discipline. This gives the teacher a sense of confidence and allows the teacher to be well organized. An effective teacher knows and likes what he teaches, and the enthusiasm will show and will become a part of the students. Without a good mastery of the subject matter, a teacher is unable to make well-informed decisions about objectives to be covered.*

*In conclusion, by possessing and demonstrating upstanding values, showing compassion, and exhibiting a thorough knowledge of his subject area, the right person can make a good teacher. If students are to learn, they must be influenced by persons who have all three of these characteristics.*

## Analysis

This essay, even though it contains minor errors in punctuation and pronoun-antecedent agreement, is well written, as evidenced by the clarity, organization, and mature language.

The opening sentence is a complex sentence. Therefore, a comma should have been used to separate the dependent clause ("When I think of what specific characteristics a person must possess in order to be an effective teacher,") from the rest of the sentence (the independent clause). Also, in the first sentence, the pronoun *their* (plural) is used to refer to a *person* (singular). This a pronoun-antecedent disagreement. The pronoun *his* or *her* should have been used. This problem disappears later, suggesting that the writer may have been careless. Always save enough time to proof your essay. When writing hurriedly, it's very easy to make careless mistakes: their for there, a for an, no for know.

The writer adequately introduces the topic "Characteristics of an Effective Teacher" by outlining the three characteristics to be discussed. Each of the three paragraphs of the body contains a characteristic as the main idea and details to explain and/or support it. The conclusion is a summary of the essay and an explanation of why these characteristics are important. The reader should have no difficulty understanding the message the writer is conveying.

## The following is a weak response to the Composition essay assignment.

*If you pick up a newspaper, turn on your radio, you will hear, see, and read about the declining of education. Discipline is a problem, test scores are down, and the teacher is being slained. Society has asked the perplexing question: What makes an effective classroom teacher?*

*First, to become an effective classroom teacher, there has to be an internal love within self, along with external love of the art of teaching. Secondly, devotion, dedication, and discipline among self and the environment in which you are entering will demonstrate the first procedure of effectiveness in the classroom and set up the essential elements involved in teaching. Thirdly, carrying the three "P's" in your heart will produce an effective classroom teacher, being "Proud" of what you are, being "Patient" with whom you are teaching, and being "Persistent" in what you are teaching. Finally, living beyond the classroom, I think, is the most effective in an effective classroom teacher, staying beyond your paid time, getting emotionally involved with your students after your paid time and setting up the ability to cope with the stress of the educational process before your paid time. In order to endure effectiveness, there is long-suffering, perservance, and understanding any situation at any given moment to entitle all children to a worthwhile education of an effective classroom teacher.*

## Analysis

The writer of this essay partially addresses the topic, but the essay itself is totally unacceptable. The initial paragraph, which should have outlined the characteristics to be discussed, leads one to believe that the essay will address "declining of education," "test scores," and "slained teachers." To identify problems that demand effective teachers is an acceptable way to introduce the topic, but the writer of this essay does it very poorly. Additionally, the past participle of *slay* is *slain,* not *slained.*

The writer does present the characteristics of an effective teacher, but these characteristics are all contained in one paragraph, and they are very unclear due to poor word choice, ambiguous expressions (awkward), and poor sentence structure. Three paragraphs should have been used, one for each characteristic, and each should have contained details to explain and support the characteristic.

This essay is filled with awkward expressions that suggest an inability to effectively use the language: "declining of education," "internal love within self," "external love of the art of teaching," "demonstrate the first procedure of effectiveness in the classroom," "set up the essential elements," "Finally, living beyond the classroom, I think, is the most effective in an effective classroom teacher," "staying beyond your paid time," and others.

The writer excessively uses "you" and "your"—second person. Essays should be written in the third person—"he," "she," or "they." For example, the noun *teacher* or *teachers* should have been used as well.

# MTEL Communication and Literacy Skills

## ANSWER SHEETS

## PRACTICE TEST 1
## ANSWER SHEET

### READING SUBTEST
### MULTIPLE-CHOICE SECTION

| | | | |
|---|---|---|---|
| 1. Ⓐ Ⓑ Ⓒ Ⓓ | 15. Ⓐ Ⓑ Ⓒ Ⓓ | 29. Ⓐ Ⓑ Ⓒ Ⓓ | |
| 2. Ⓐ Ⓑ Ⓒ Ⓓ | 16. Ⓐ Ⓑ Ⓒ Ⓓ | 30. Ⓐ Ⓑ Ⓒ Ⓓ | |
| 3. Ⓐ Ⓑ Ⓒ Ⓓ | 17. Ⓐ Ⓑ Ⓒ Ⓓ | 31. Ⓐ Ⓑ Ⓒ Ⓓ | |
| 4. Ⓐ Ⓑ Ⓒ Ⓓ | 18. Ⓐ Ⓑ Ⓒ Ⓓ | 32. Ⓐ Ⓑ Ⓒ Ⓓ | |
| 5. Ⓐ Ⓑ Ⓒ Ⓓ | 19. Ⓐ Ⓑ Ⓒ Ⓓ | 33. Ⓐ Ⓑ Ⓒ Ⓓ | |
| 6. Ⓐ Ⓑ Ⓒ Ⓓ | 20. Ⓐ Ⓑ Ⓒ Ⓓ | 34. Ⓐ Ⓑ Ⓒ Ⓓ | |
| 7. Ⓐ Ⓑ Ⓒ Ⓓ | 21. Ⓐ Ⓑ Ⓒ Ⓓ | 35. Ⓐ Ⓑ Ⓒ Ⓓ | |
| 8. Ⓐ Ⓑ Ⓒ Ⓓ | 22. Ⓐ Ⓑ Ⓒ Ⓓ | 36. Ⓐ Ⓑ Ⓒ Ⓓ | |
| 9. Ⓐ Ⓑ Ⓒ Ⓓ | 23. Ⓐ Ⓑ Ⓒ Ⓓ | 37. Ⓐ Ⓑ Ⓒ Ⓓ | |
| 10. Ⓐ Ⓑ Ⓒ Ⓓ | 24. Ⓐ Ⓑ Ⓒ Ⓓ | 38. Ⓐ Ⓑ Ⓒ Ⓓ | |
| 11. Ⓐ Ⓑ Ⓒ Ⓓ | 25. Ⓐ Ⓑ Ⓒ Ⓓ | 39. Ⓐ Ⓑ Ⓒ Ⓓ | |
| 12. Ⓐ Ⓑ Ⓒ Ⓓ | 26. Ⓐ Ⓑ Ⓒ Ⓓ | 40. Ⓐ Ⓑ Ⓒ Ⓓ | |
| 13. Ⓐ Ⓑ Ⓒ Ⓓ | 27. Ⓐ Ⓑ Ⓒ Ⓓ | 41. Ⓐ Ⓑ Ⓒ Ⓓ | |
| 14. Ⓐ Ⓑ Ⓒ Ⓓ | 28. Ⓐ Ⓑ Ⓒ Ⓓ | 42. Ⓐ Ⓑ Ⓒ Ⓓ | |

### WRITING SUBTEST

| | | |
|---|---|---|
| 1. Ⓐ Ⓑ Ⓒ Ⓓ | 13. Ⓐ Ⓑ Ⓒ Ⓓ | 25. Ⓐ Ⓑ Ⓒ Ⓓ |
| 2. Ⓐ Ⓑ Ⓒ Ⓓ | 14. Ⓐ Ⓑ Ⓒ Ⓓ | 26. Ⓐ Ⓑ Ⓒ Ⓓ |
| 3. Ⓐ Ⓑ Ⓒ Ⓓ | 15. Ⓐ Ⓑ Ⓒ Ⓓ | 27. Ⓐ Ⓑ Ⓒ Ⓓ |
| 4. Ⓐ Ⓑ Ⓒ Ⓓ | 16. Ⓐ Ⓑ Ⓒ Ⓓ | 28. Ⓐ Ⓑ Ⓒ Ⓓ |
| 5. Ⓐ Ⓑ Ⓒ Ⓓ | 17. Ⓐ Ⓑ Ⓒ Ⓓ | 29. Ⓐ Ⓑ Ⓒ Ⓓ |
| 6. Ⓐ Ⓑ Ⓒ Ⓓ | 18. Ⓐ Ⓑ Ⓒ Ⓓ | 30. Ⓐ Ⓑ Ⓒ Ⓓ |
| 7. Ⓐ Ⓑ Ⓒ Ⓓ | 19. Ⓐ Ⓑ Ⓒ Ⓓ | 31. Ⓐ Ⓑ Ⓒ Ⓓ |
| 8. Ⓐ Ⓑ Ⓒ Ⓓ | 20. Ⓐ Ⓑ Ⓒ Ⓓ | 32. Ⓐ Ⓑ Ⓒ Ⓓ |
| 9. Ⓐ Ⓑ Ⓒ Ⓓ | 21. Ⓐ Ⓑ Ⓒ Ⓓ | 33. Ⓐ Ⓑ Ⓒ Ⓓ |
| 10. Ⓐ Ⓑ Ⓒ Ⓓ | 22. Ⓐ Ⓑ Ⓒ Ⓓ | 34. Ⓐ Ⓑ Ⓒ Ⓓ |
| 11. Ⓐ Ⓑ Ⓒ Ⓓ | 23. Ⓐ Ⓑ Ⓒ Ⓓ | 35. Ⓐ Ⓑ Ⓒ Ⓓ |
| 12. Ⓐ Ⓑ Ⓒ Ⓓ | 24. Ⓐ Ⓑ Ⓒ Ⓓ | |

# PRACTICE TEST 2
# ANSWER SHEET

## READING SUBTEST
## MULTIPLE-CHOICE SECTION

1. Ⓐ Ⓑ Ⓒ Ⓓ
2. Ⓐ Ⓑ Ⓒ Ⓓ
3. Ⓐ Ⓑ Ⓒ Ⓓ
4. Ⓐ Ⓑ Ⓒ Ⓓ
5. Ⓐ Ⓑ Ⓒ Ⓓ
6. Ⓐ Ⓑ Ⓒ Ⓓ
7. Ⓐ Ⓑ Ⓒ Ⓓ
8. Ⓐ Ⓑ Ⓒ Ⓓ
9. Ⓐ Ⓑ Ⓒ Ⓓ
10. Ⓐ Ⓑ Ⓒ Ⓓ
11. Ⓐ Ⓑ Ⓒ Ⓓ
12. Ⓐ Ⓑ Ⓒ Ⓓ
13. Ⓐ Ⓑ Ⓒ Ⓓ
14. Ⓐ Ⓑ Ⓒ Ⓓ

15. Ⓐ Ⓑ Ⓒ Ⓓ
16. Ⓐ Ⓑ Ⓒ Ⓓ
17. Ⓐ Ⓑ Ⓒ Ⓓ
18. Ⓐ Ⓑ Ⓒ Ⓓ
19. Ⓐ Ⓑ Ⓒ Ⓓ
20. Ⓐ Ⓑ Ⓒ Ⓓ
21. Ⓐ Ⓑ Ⓒ Ⓓ
22. Ⓐ Ⓑ Ⓒ Ⓓ
23. Ⓐ Ⓑ Ⓒ Ⓓ
24. Ⓐ Ⓑ Ⓒ Ⓓ
25. Ⓐ Ⓑ Ⓒ Ⓓ
26. Ⓐ Ⓑ Ⓒ Ⓓ
27. Ⓐ Ⓑ Ⓒ Ⓓ
28. Ⓐ Ⓑ Ⓒ Ⓓ

29. Ⓐ Ⓑ Ⓒ Ⓓ
30. Ⓐ Ⓑ Ⓒ Ⓓ
31. Ⓐ Ⓑ Ⓒ Ⓓ
32. Ⓐ Ⓑ Ⓒ Ⓓ
33. Ⓐ Ⓑ Ⓒ Ⓓ
34. Ⓐ Ⓑ Ⓒ Ⓓ
35. Ⓐ Ⓑ Ⓒ Ⓓ
36. Ⓐ Ⓑ Ⓒ Ⓓ
37. Ⓐ Ⓑ Ⓒ Ⓓ
38. Ⓐ Ⓑ Ⓒ Ⓓ
39. Ⓐ Ⓑ Ⓒ Ⓓ
40. Ⓐ Ⓑ Ⓒ Ⓓ
41. Ⓐ Ⓑ Ⓒ Ⓓ
42. Ⓐ Ⓑ Ⓒ Ⓓ

## WRITING SUBTEST

1. Ⓐ Ⓑ Ⓒ Ⓓ
2. Ⓐ Ⓑ Ⓒ Ⓓ
3. Ⓐ Ⓑ Ⓒ Ⓓ
4. Ⓐ Ⓑ Ⓒ Ⓓ
5. Ⓐ Ⓑ Ⓒ Ⓓ
6. Ⓐ Ⓑ Ⓒ Ⓓ
7. Ⓐ Ⓑ Ⓒ Ⓓ
8. Ⓐ Ⓑ Ⓒ Ⓓ
9. Ⓐ Ⓑ Ⓒ Ⓓ
10. Ⓐ Ⓑ Ⓒ Ⓓ
11. Ⓐ Ⓑ Ⓒ Ⓓ
12. Ⓐ Ⓑ Ⓒ Ⓓ

13. Ⓐ Ⓑ Ⓒ Ⓓ
14. Ⓐ Ⓑ Ⓒ Ⓓ
15. Ⓐ Ⓑ Ⓒ Ⓓ
16. Ⓐ Ⓑ Ⓒ Ⓓ
17. Ⓐ Ⓑ Ⓒ Ⓓ
18. Ⓐ Ⓑ Ⓒ Ⓓ
19. Ⓐ Ⓑ Ⓒ Ⓓ
20. Ⓐ Ⓑ Ⓒ Ⓓ
21. Ⓐ Ⓑ Ⓒ Ⓓ
22. Ⓐ Ⓑ Ⓒ Ⓓ
23. Ⓐ Ⓑ Ⓒ Ⓓ
24. Ⓐ Ⓑ Ⓒ Ⓓ

25. Ⓐ Ⓑ Ⓒ Ⓓ
26. Ⓐ Ⓑ Ⓒ Ⓓ
27. Ⓐ Ⓑ Ⓒ Ⓓ
28. Ⓐ Ⓑ Ⓒ Ⓓ
29. Ⓐ Ⓑ Ⓒ Ⓓ
30. Ⓐ Ⓑ Ⓒ Ⓓ
31. Ⓐ Ⓑ Ⓒ Ⓓ
32. Ⓐ Ⓑ Ⓒ Ⓓ
33. Ⓐ Ⓑ Ⓒ Ⓓ
34. Ⓐ Ⓑ Ⓒ Ⓓ
35. Ⓐ Ⓑ Ⓒ Ⓓ

## READING SUBTEST
## MULTIPLE-CHOICE SECTION

1. Ⓐ Ⓑ Ⓒ Ⓓ
2. Ⓐ Ⓑ Ⓒ Ⓓ
3. Ⓐ Ⓑ Ⓒ Ⓓ
4. Ⓐ Ⓑ Ⓒ Ⓓ
5. Ⓐ Ⓑ Ⓒ Ⓓ
6. Ⓐ Ⓑ Ⓒ Ⓓ
7. Ⓐ Ⓑ Ⓒ Ⓓ
8. Ⓐ Ⓑ Ⓒ Ⓓ
9. Ⓐ Ⓑ Ⓒ Ⓓ
10. Ⓐ Ⓑ Ⓒ Ⓓ
11. Ⓐ Ⓑ Ⓒ Ⓓ
12. Ⓐ Ⓑ Ⓒ Ⓓ
13. Ⓐ Ⓑ Ⓒ Ⓓ
14. Ⓐ Ⓑ Ⓒ Ⓓ

15. Ⓐ Ⓑ Ⓒ Ⓓ
16. Ⓐ Ⓑ Ⓒ Ⓓ
17. Ⓐ Ⓑ Ⓒ Ⓓ
18. Ⓐ Ⓑ Ⓒ Ⓓ
19. Ⓐ Ⓑ Ⓒ Ⓓ
20. Ⓐ Ⓑ Ⓒ Ⓓ
21. Ⓐ Ⓑ Ⓒ Ⓓ
22. Ⓐ Ⓑ Ⓒ Ⓓ
23. Ⓐ Ⓑ Ⓒ Ⓓ
24. Ⓐ Ⓑ Ⓒ Ⓓ
25. Ⓐ Ⓑ Ⓒ Ⓓ
26. Ⓐ Ⓑ Ⓒ Ⓓ
27. Ⓐ Ⓑ Ⓒ Ⓓ
28. Ⓐ Ⓑ Ⓒ Ⓓ

29. Ⓐ Ⓑ Ⓒ Ⓓ
30. Ⓐ Ⓑ Ⓒ Ⓓ
31. Ⓐ Ⓑ Ⓒ Ⓓ
32. Ⓐ Ⓑ Ⓒ Ⓓ
33. Ⓐ Ⓑ Ⓒ Ⓓ
34. Ⓐ Ⓑ Ⓒ Ⓓ
35. Ⓐ Ⓑ Ⓒ Ⓓ
36. Ⓐ Ⓑ Ⓒ Ⓓ
37. Ⓐ Ⓑ Ⓒ Ⓓ
38. Ⓐ Ⓑ Ⓒ Ⓓ
39. Ⓐ Ⓑ Ⓒ Ⓓ
40. Ⓐ Ⓑ Ⓒ Ⓓ
41. Ⓐ Ⓑ Ⓒ Ⓓ
42. Ⓐ Ⓑ Ⓒ Ⓓ

## WRITING SUBTEST

1. Ⓐ Ⓑ Ⓒ Ⓓ
2. Ⓐ Ⓑ Ⓒ Ⓓ
3. Ⓐ Ⓑ Ⓒ Ⓓ
4. Ⓐ Ⓑ Ⓒ Ⓓ
5. Ⓐ Ⓑ Ⓒ Ⓓ
6. Ⓐ Ⓑ Ⓒ Ⓓ
7. Ⓐ Ⓑ Ⓒ Ⓓ
8. Ⓐ Ⓑ Ⓒ Ⓓ
9. Ⓐ Ⓑ Ⓒ Ⓓ
10. Ⓐ Ⓑ Ⓒ Ⓓ
11. Ⓐ Ⓑ Ⓒ Ⓓ
12. Ⓐ Ⓑ Ⓒ Ⓓ

13. Ⓐ Ⓑ Ⓒ Ⓓ
14. Ⓐ Ⓑ Ⓒ Ⓓ
15. Ⓐ Ⓑ Ⓒ Ⓓ
16. Ⓐ Ⓑ Ⓒ Ⓓ
17. Ⓐ Ⓑ Ⓒ Ⓓ
18. Ⓐ Ⓑ Ⓒ Ⓓ
19. Ⓐ Ⓑ Ⓒ Ⓓ
20. Ⓐ Ⓑ Ⓒ Ⓓ
21. Ⓐ Ⓑ Ⓒ Ⓓ
22. Ⓐ Ⓑ Ⓒ Ⓓ
23. Ⓐ Ⓑ Ⓒ Ⓓ
24. Ⓐ Ⓑ Ⓒ Ⓓ

25. Ⓐ Ⓑ Ⓒ Ⓓ
26. Ⓐ Ⓑ Ⓒ Ⓓ
27. Ⓐ Ⓑ Ⓒ Ⓓ
28. Ⓐ Ⓑ Ⓒ Ⓓ
29. Ⓐ Ⓑ Ⓒ Ⓓ
30. Ⓐ Ⓑ Ⓒ Ⓓ
31. Ⓐ Ⓑ Ⓒ Ⓓ
32. Ⓐ Ⓑ Ⓒ Ⓓ
33. Ⓐ Ⓑ Ⓒ Ⓓ
34. Ⓐ Ⓑ Ⓒ Ⓓ
35. Ⓐ Ⓑ Ⓒ Ⓓ

# MTEL Communication and Literacy Skills

## INDEX

# Index

**H**

**I**

**K**

**L**

**M**

## S

# NOTES

# NOTES

## NOTES